MINNESOTA'S MIRACLE

**Also of Interest Published by
the University of Minnesota Press**

Region: Planning the Future of the Twin Cities
Myron Orfield and Thomas F. Luce Jr.

Doorstep Democracy: Face-to-Face Politics in the Heartland
James H. Read

*This Is Not Florida: How Al Franken Won the Minnesota
Senate Recount*
Jay Weiner

*Making Minnesota Liberal: Civil Rights and the Transformation
of the Democratic Party*
Jennifer A. Delton

*Reforming Welfare by Rewarding Work: One State's
Successful Experiment*
Dave Hage

The Conscience of a Liberal: Reclaiming the Compassionate Agenda
Senator Paul Wellstone

How the Rural Poor Got Power: Narrative of a Grass-Roots Organizer
Paul Wellstone
Forewords by Robert Coles and Frances Fox Piven

Powerline: The First Battle of America's Energy War
Paul Wellstone and Barry M. Casper
Foreword by Senator Tom Harkin

*Professor Wellstone Goes to Washington: The Inside Story
of a Grassroots U.S. Senate Campaign*
Dennis J. McGrath and Dane Smith

Crossing the Barriers: The Autobiography of Allan H. Spear
Foreword by Barney Frank
Afterword by John Milton

Inside the Ropes with Jesse Ventura
Tom Hauser

Minnesota's
Miracle

LEARNING FROM THE GOVERNMENT THAT WORKED

Tom Berg

 University of Minnesota Press
Minneapolis
London

Published by the University of Minnesota Press
111 Third Avenue South, Suite 290
Minneapolis, MN 55401-2520
http://www.upress.umn.edu

Library of Congress Cataloging-in-Publication Data
Berg, Tom.
  Minnesota's miracle : learning from the government that worked /
Tom Berg.
  Includes bibliographical references and index.
  ISBN 978-0-8166-8053-5 (pb : alk. paper)
1. Minnesota—Politics and government since 1951. I. Title.
  JK6141.B47   2012
  320.9776—dc23

                                                    2012018077

Printed in the United States of America on acid-free paper

The University of Minnesota is an equal-opportunity educator and employer.

19 18 17 16 15 14 13 12   10 9 8 7 6 5 4 3 2 1

To Margit, who willingly and ably helped with my political life twice: once when I lived it and again when I wrote about it. Both times involved many long days away from home and family. Our wonderful sons, Erik and Jeff, daughter-in-law, Jill, and grandchildren, Althea and Maceo, are the best proof of your devotion, skills, and good humor. I am forever grateful.

Contents

Preface

I had the privilege of being a state legislator from 1971 to 1978. This was an especially turbulent time in America. Among other things, the war in Vietnam was lost, social unrest that had begun in the 1960s continued, and Presidents Nixon, Ford, and Carter all spent time in the White House. This turbulence spilled over to my state of Minnesota as well. Controversies over property taxes, school funding, closed government meetings, and environmental concerns served as catalysts for a historic election in 1972. In that year the Democratic (DFL) Party took control of both branches of the legislature, and for the first time in the state's 114-year history controlled both the legislative branch and the executive branch of government.[1] It was an exciting time to be a young legislator.

This book describes some of the actual experiences of deal cutting, arm twisting, and hard work—often frustrating and sometimes satisfying—that led to a better-functioning state. Part of the excitement for me was the meeting, arguing, and working with many talented people from both major political parties—people who cared about their state and their country, and who were willing to take personal and political risks to help both. These people included four governors (two Republicans and two Democrats), dozens of state representatives and senators, and some very bright legislative staff people. All played a key role in bringing about the major changes that took place then in Minnesota, as the state and the country worked at solving the major social and economic issues they faced.

In particular, I met and worked with seven people who have added significantly to this book. They are people who were in the majority DFL Party from 1972 to 1978 whom I came to know and highly respect as legislators and legislative staff. To provide a broader view of how things actually worked, I wrote the book with their assistance. The eight of us are not professional historians or political scientists, but we are people with a strong interest in history and politics and with a commitment to having our system of governments function at a high level. We are Martin Sabo, who became Speaker of the Minnesota House of Representatives, president of the National Conference of State Legislators, and a fourteen-term member of the U.S. Congress; four legislators from Minnesota's DFL Party first elected in 1970, myself, Joe Graba, Bill Kelly, and Ray Faricy; two key legislative staff members, Eileen Baumgartner and Ed Dirkswager; and Jim Pederson, an important member of the executive branch, who worked for Democratic Governor Wendell Anderson. We eight are all Democrats and all held important legislative positions during our time in state government service.

We were uniquely fortunate to meet, and on occasion work with, a number of the national leaders intimately involved with the war and the changes in the country: Senator Gene McCarthy and Vice Presidents Hubert Humphrey and Walter Mondale, all leaders in the federal legislative branch and all presidential candidates. We also got to know a number of leaders in local governments from Minnesota and around the country, as well as legislators and legislative staff from other states. Face-to-face discussions with these people helped clarify our own thinking as to the proper role of state, local, and federal governments in America and added a marvelous perspective to our personal and political lives.

The eight of us started out to complete a "history project," simply trying to preserve some of the history of the period. We soon found that placing this history in a broader context was critical to our goal of creating a project that was relevant, entertaining, and educational. We also found that our efforts generated significant interest from many others of various personal and political backgrounds. We consulted with historians, political scientists, and elected officials of all political stripes, and with their encouragement, the "history project" grew into this book.

As we moved forward with numerous and lengthy interviews with the Republicans and Democrats who made the changes happen, and dug through boxes of clippings, reports, correspondence, and memorandums, we realized that many of the ideas and beliefs we encountered transcended specific issues, political parties, and time frames. For example, the most fundamental motivation that led legislators and staff members to initially get involved in the rough and tumble of politics was remarkably similar. At its simplest level, it was old-fashioned patriotism. Some wore patriotism on their sleeves (or their lapels) more than others, and some were more politically ambitious than others, but all held a common belief in the importance of the United States and its constitutionally mandated Union of state and federal governments known as federalism. To put it in the words of the founding documents of the country, all expressed a strong interest in assisting in forming a more perfect Union and in helping the citizenry in their pursuit of happiness.

We also found that as we selected specific issues to discuss, they were, to a remarkable degree, the same issues facing the Congress, state legislatures, and local governments today. These often hotly contested issues and the strategies employed by the various interest groups, caucuses, and political parties form the backdrop for the interaction among the personalities, programs, and policies described in these pages. To provide perspective and relevance to the current political world, the book places the changes made into the broader context of America's evolving federalism.

The look at state government and politics begins with a quick view of the mid-1960s and then begins a closer analysis of the decade from 1968 to 1978. This decade began under the conservatively controlled legislature and Republican Governor Harold LeVander.[2] In the 1970 election, when many of us in the book were first elected, the DFL came close to gaining control of the legislature. This momentum continued after a reapportionment of Minnesota's legislative districts in 1971, and the DFL gained control in the historic election of 1972.

From 1972 through 1978, the group of DFLers then ensconced in elective and staff positions in the state legislature and executive branch of government, working well with the state's prominent Democratic leaders in Washington, dominated the state's politics. The Democrats were then trounced in a surprising 1978 election. As explained in these pages, the politics of 1978 and the election results not only significantly changed the lives of the eight of us, they were a harbinger of several national and state elections, starting with the election of Ronald Reagan in 1980.

Since this book reflects not just my point of view, I have written it in the third person. All eight of us involved in the book (as well as many others from across the political spectrum) have reviewed it carefully. This brought significant private, public, and not-for-profit sector perspectives to the process. We argued and talked about the text, the sources, the illustrations, and our individual experiences at length. I asked that the group make particular efforts to verify and cross-check facts and opinions that refer to me. I can assure the reader that these people, while all friends, are not bashful about such things. All eight of us had our respective egos bruised at some point in the process. The book is better because of it. This having been said, I alone am responsible for all the written words and any errors that may exist.

Breaking Out of the Holding Pattern

When a freeway bridge in Minneapolis carrying rush hour traffic falls into the Mississippi River, killing thirteen, when an airliner cannot land in the nation's capitol because the flight controllers are sleeping, or when an entire state government shuts down for three weeks because of failure of elected officials to compromise, one can understand why citizens grumble about dysfunctional and inept governments. And when you add in the legislative chaos that almost caused the federal government in 2011 to default on its financial obligations, and the undertone of political hostility that seems to be a part of almost every news report and conversation about government, the reasons for the general disgust with politics and concern about the country become apparent. The list of problems in cities, states, and Washington makes even the most Pollyannaish among us a bit cynical about the ability of our governments to break out of the morass in which we seem to be stuck. While there have always been mistakes by governments and harsh political talk, history shows us they do not have to lead to gridlock and near universal cynicism. The country has done better, and we can do so again.

Our Constitution was created during a time that also involved hard-hitting politics. But out of that period came compromise and a remarkable document that begins by calling for a more perfect Union—a union of people, states, and a federal government. This "more perfect Union" was to turn the hopes and dreams of the representatives of the people in thirteen states into reality. Over the intervening 220-plus years, the Union has at times functioned well, at times poorly, and once not at all, as a bloody civil war was fought. A careful look at a period when the Union functioned well and the application of the lessons learned by people who were then in the governmental trenches will help us understand how we can again get back to making our Union more perfect.

This book takes a look at one such period, the decade from approximately 1968 to 1978, in one state that worked. The book is not a public policy book but a book about people in and around a state legislature and how and why they acted as they did. The book tells the stories behind changes made in legislative policies and programs in Minnesota during that decade. It describes many of the key players, their emotions, the politics they employed, their electoral wins and losses, the impact of national politics when Walter Mondale was elected vice president, and the role of important court decisions.

Major changes were made, but contrary to some popular thinking in the state, this was not some kind of "golden era" in state politics. Things were far from perfect in that decade. Much like in the nation as a whole, there were heavy doses of partisanship, argumentative people, and high emotions, as protests abounded over the Vietnam War, abortion, taxes, and environmental issues. There were tough political fights over levels of spending, gun control, pollution, education, health care, and the proper role of labor unions. Women's rights and related issues were in the forefront of activity, and gays were beginning a fight for basic civil rights. The delivery of health care, the role of money and lobbyists in the legislative process, reapportionment issues, building expensive sports stadiums, regulating or not regulating handguns, and designing transit systems are more examples of issues for which legislation was developed. Interestingly, they are also issues that are again front and center on today's legislative agendas.

What makes the period unique is that despite the complexity of the problems and the partisan politics, the Minnesota Legislature was able to make meaningful changes—often with bipartisan support. Transparency in state and local governments was strengthened, budgets were balanced, school funding was made more fair, and the legislative leaders who were selected by their party caucuses talked respectfully to each other. The majority party changed the legislative rules so as to treat the minority party fairly. During this same general period, several other states were also taking steps to make their operations more professional, technically competent, and responsive to current problems.

As a result of many of these far-reaching changes in Minnesota, the leading news magazine in the country in 1973 put Minnesota's governor on its cover and said Minnesota was "A State That Works." At about the same time, a national bipartisan commission declared an important piece of legislation that passed the Minnesota

Legislature a "miracle" and a "model for other states." Today, few would use these words to describe Minnesota state government or any other state government—or for that matter, the federal government. The populace has turned sour on its sovereign governments, and evidence showing the resulting lack of support or consensus for any major governmental action may be found in nearly every media story about government or politics.

To understand how all this fits into the workings of the federal system, the book briefly looks at the reasons for the adoption of the Constitution and the Tenth Amendment in the Bill of Rights. For perspective, the questionable record of performance of all the states in the more than 220 intervening years since the Constitution went into effect is noted, and the dramatically increased role of the federal government starting in the 1930s and continuing to today is discussed.

One of the "happy incidents" of our unique and complex system of federal and state governments was famously described by Supreme Court Justice Louis Brandeis in 1932 as allowing the states to serve as laboratories of democracy. In 2009, a distinguished political science professor from Rutgers, Alan Rosenthal, used another metaphor to describe the role of state legislatures; he called them "Engines of Democracy."[1] Both metaphors accurately make the point that the states, and in particular their legislatures, have a vital role in making the machinery of federalism work. As many examples throughout this book show, the problems of modern society have proven to be so complicated, rapidly changing, and intertwined with international factors that neither the states nor the federal government individually can solve all of them.

On the national scene during the 1968 to 1978 decade, several issues similar to those faced today were addressed. Gas and fuel oil shortages caused by an OPEC embargo led to high prices and lines at gas stations, and states and cities faced tough fiscal decisions, such as when New York City came within hours of filing for bankruptcy.[2] The war in Vietnam ground on. Congress realized it could not do everything itself and began a creative partnership with the states and local governments. A system of revenue sharing was implemented, and coordination of state, local, and federal programs was required. The Union continued to improve.

Today we again need a creative and well-functioning partnership.

The state legislative laboratories and their legislative engines need to produce the ideas, provide appropriate financial resources, and combine those with the savvy of local governments and federal government assistance to achieve common aims. Without all three levels of government working more or less in harmony toward the common goals set out in the Constitution, the Union does not work.

Unfortunately, over the past several decades, the anti-this-and-that forces (anti, for example, government, science, immigration, taxes, compromise, etc.) have been effective in making their anti-this-and-that points. These forces have successfully used the 24/7 news cycle, talk radio, newspapers, books, magazines, TV, blogs, social media, and well-staged protests to virtually take over the domestic political agenda. The pro-this-and-that forces have been on the defensive. The result of all this adversarial effort is a politics that is unable to develop and pass thoughtful approaches to modern problems. It is a politics that relies too much on name-calling and simplistic slogans. While some of the name-calling and slogan making is entertaining, little, if any, sheds light on how the country can get out of the current holding pattern. This frustrating problem applies at all levels of government.

The book's last chapter describes three key lessons learned (some the hard way) from the Minnesota experience. Specific changes based on these lessons are proposed. These changes should be promptly considered by all states and modified and supplemented by them as appropriate to their circumstances. The chapter also calls upon the federal government to look at its own legislative procedures and analyze carefully the role it sees for itself, the states, and local governments in our diverse society. These proposed actions will improve the complex union of federal, state, and local governments that make up American federalism as it is practiced today. Without such analysis and thoughtful change, our governments will be plagued at every level by more gridlock, excess partisanship, incompetence, unethical conduct, and, worst of all, increasing voter cynicism.

We can do better.

CHAPTER 1

Forming a More Perfect Union

It is ours to write about, it is ours to read about. But there was in the life of each of these [people] something that is difficult for the printed page to capture—and yet something that has reached the homes and enriched the heritage of every citizen.

▪ John F. Kennedy, *Profiles in Courage*

With enough candles, silver foil, and dim light, even a National Hockey League arena can look posh. The sheet of ice at the home of the Minnesota North Stars gave way to candlelit tables and catered food as Minnesota's Democrats enjoyed the fanciest inauguration ever held in the state. Rented tuxedos and cocktail dresses mixed with corduroy pants and jean jackets, while one of the country's most popular folk singers entertained with his guitar and melodic voice. "Leaving on a Jet Plane" gave way to a patriotic "America the Beautiful" as John Denver led eight thousand guests in a heartfelt celebration of the major change that was under way in Minnesota's politics.

It was January 6, 1971, and America's thirty-second state had just sworn in a photogenic thirty-seven-year-old Democrat and state senator as governor, an attorney general who had been the chair of the Democratic Party, a lieutenant governor from Minnesota's liberal Iron Range region, and forty-eight new liberal legislators in the house and senate, many in their early thirties. On the national scene, the state had just sent Hubert H. Humphrey back to the U.S. Senate to join its other senator, Walter Mondale, had elected a new Democratic congressman, and had reelected three others from the state's eight-person congressional delegation.[1] The victorious Democratic Party (Democratic-Farmer-Labor Party, or DFL, as the party is known in Minnesota) was in a mood to celebrate its big election victory.[2]

But the significant Democratic win was not complete. Representative Martin Sabo, a five-term member of the Minnesota House of Representatives and its youngest minority leader, circulated among the partygoers. His sixty-five-member caucus was still three short of the sixty-eight needed to gain control of the house. State senate minority leader Nicholas Coleman and several newly elected state senators also basked in the candlelit glow despite being unsure if their group would control the senate.

Once elected, legislators joined forces in groups known as caucuses. The majority caucuses in the house and senate were known as "Conservatives" (most all of whom believed in the Republican philosophy), while the smaller (minority) caucuses, led by Sabo and Coleman, were the "Liberals" (most all of whom believed in the Democratic or DFL philosophy).[3] In the senate, the election had resulted in a thirty-three to thirty-three tie between the Liberals and the Conservatives, and one senator-elect, Richard Palmer, who had campaigned as an "Independent." He also had said he would caucus with the majority caucus. After the election, Palmer was wooed by both caucuses until he finally announced that he would caucus with the Conservatives. However, Palmer's Liberal opponent had filed an election contest against Palmer, and the Liberal senators refused to vote to seat him. After much political and legal maneuvering, some of it involving issues similar to the Norm Coleman versus Al Franken U.S. Senate recount battles in Minnesota in 2008 and 2009 concerning the authority of a legislative body to determine the qualification of its own members, the Minnesota Supreme Court sided with Palmer.[4] Thus, while the influence of the Conservative Caucus old guard had been reduced by the 1970 election, particularly by the defeat of two longtime powerful state senators, Gordon Rosenmeier and Donald O. Wright, the Conservatives nevertheless continued to control the Minnesota legislative process.[5]

In the 1960s and early 1970s, the Minnesota Legislature did not apply the standard party labels of Republicans and Democrats to its members. The legislature was officially "nonpartisan," and the ballot for the legislature did not state which party the candidate belonged to. In political shorthand, there was "no party designation." In reality, however, partisanship was very much present, as both major political parties endorsed candidates and typically campaigned for their respective choices. As we will see, this caused confusion among voters.[6] The confusion was finally clarified in 1973 when Minnesota adopted party designation for its legislative candidates.

The Conservative legislative leaders had vowed to keep the new ideas of the younger generation of leaders such as Governor-elect Wendell Anderson, Lieutenant Governor Rudy Perpich, Attorney General Warren Spannaus, and the newly elected legislators bottled up in the legislature. Nevertheless, the partying on that very cold January night at the hockey arena proceeded with great enthusiasm and with a spirit of change in the air. There was a palpable sense of historic opportunity ahead for the somewhat naive but very inspired DFLers.

To understand what happened and the far-reaching impact of the flood of laws and legislative process changes that this group of people helped bring about during the 1970s, we need to step back and review the prescribed role of state government under America's federal system. We need to look at how state government has performed in practice over the years and consider the profound impact of the federal and state courts on the workings of our federal system and the legislative process. Finally, we need to bear in mind the social and cultural changes that occurred in America during the 1960s and 1970s and consider the importance of individual leadership.

American Federalism: A Unique and Evolving Method of Governing

It became clear shortly after the Revolutionary War that the system of government of thirteen sovereign states working together in a loose confederation as described in the Articles of Confederation simply did not work. The Founding Fathers realized that a revised form of government with additional powers for a national government was required. A constitutional convention was called. The delegates were selected from and by the states and sent to the convention. In 1787 after much argument and compromise, the delegates proposed and sent to the states for ratification a unique federal system of government involving thirteen separate states and one federal government. The proposed constitution was quite short. It begins with a one-sentence preamble—a sentence that should be reread often as the country's voters, legislators, judges and justices, governors, and presidents struggle to think through the proper role of their governments and apply the profound 1787 words to complex twenty-first-century problems. The preamble states:

We the people of the United States, in order to form a more perfect Union, establish justice, insure domestic tranquility, provide for the common defense, promote the general welfare, and secure the blessings of liberty to ourselves and our posterity, do ordain and establish this Constitution for the United States of America.

The body of the Constitution is also quite short. It contains just seven articles, which spell out general powers for three branches of a federal government. While there are only limited references to the role of the states, it is clear that the federal government is to be limited in its powers. The experience with the British was not readily forgotten. But even with this general understanding, extensive and heated discussions took place as to how strong the federal government should be, and what was to be the proper role of the states. James Madison and Patrick Henry were two leaders on opposite sides of the debate as the Federalists (who generally favored a strong role for the national government) and the Antifederalists (who favored a stronger role for the states) argued back and forth.

The result was a system that has often been called "dual federalism." In the words of historian Joseph Ellis, it was "a new and wholly unprecedented version of federalism." This was a form of government in which sovereignty could reside in more than one place, that is, in both the federal government and in the state governments.[7] Samuel Elliot Morrison describes this federalism as a

work of genius, since it set up what every other political scientist had thought impossible, a sovereign union of sovereign states. This reconciling of unity with diversity, this practical application of the federal principle, is . . . the most original contribution of the United States to the history and technique of human liberty.[8]

As ratification of the Constitution proceeded through the states, a Bill of Rights containing twelve amendments was proposed in 1789, and ten were ratified by 1791 to make even more clear the importance of the states and the limited nature of the federal government. The Tenth Amendment explicitly reserves unspecified governmental powers to the states or the people. It simply says, "The powers not delegated to the United States by the Constitution, nor prohibited by it to the States, are reserved to the States respectively, or to the people." The Civil War seventy years later made it clear that while both the states and the federal government are sovereign, there is but one nation.

While all these words and political theory sound fine in a constitutional convention, a classroom, or a book, in practice they often result in a political and even a constitutional mess. However, after 220-plus years of dealing with this unique system, at least two things are clear: the American concept of federalism is still evolving, and for this unique form of government to work, both the federal government and the states must perform ably. If either fails, the citizenry suffers, and the nation does not keep its place of leadership in the rapidly changing world.[9]

Throughout our history, the U.S. Supreme Court has attempted to sort out the powers of the federal government and the states in disputes involving a variety of facts and a variety of articles of the Constitution. This process continues; for example, recent court rulings on the authority of states and local governments to regulate guns and immigration have been issued, and key lawsuits over the authority of the federal government to require citizens to obtain health insurance over the objections of their sovereign states were brought by various states' attorneys general and decided by the court in 2012 (see chapter 7).

In defining the appropriate role of the states, the court has been reluctant to delve into certain matters the court thought were "political questions." These types of questions, the court said, were best solved by the legislative and executive branches of government. Deciding where the lines should be drawn for the districts of the members of Congress, or "reapportionment" or "redistricting" decisions, as they are called in political circles, was found to be not only a political question; it was, in the words of Justice Felix Frankfurter, a "political thicket" that the court should not enter. The same held true for reapportionment of state legislative districts.[10] Thus, as population patterns changed in America over the years, the politically important reapportionment decisions were left in the hands of state legislators.

In the 1930s, the federal government pushed its powers to the constitutional limits, and in some cases beyond, to get the country out of the Depression.[11] The onset of World War II followed with even more concentration of power in Washington. The Korean War and the cold war continued to focus the American public's attention on the federal government during the post–World War II period. Meanwhile, the country's state legislatures languished. They did not reapportion themselves to reflect changing population patterns and provide fair representation to all. They usually did not even meet every year. And when they did meet, it was for only a few weeks per year. At the same time, the living patterns and expectations of the country's citizens had changed dramatically, as had the social issues associated with the more urban America.

The result was a broken system of federalism. Numerous articles, studies, and editorials have recognized and analyzed the problem. For example, a review of an American Political Science Association 1954 committee report noted that

> with the exception of those problems created by the cold war, perhaps the most serious difficulties facing the nation today lie in the areas which our federal system allocates to the states. It is no coincidence that these—education, housing, crime prevention and roads, to name only four— have been so grossly mishandled over a long period of years that the national government may well be obligated to step in.[12]

A few years later, *The Nation* in a 1963 editorial said:

> Our state legislatures are the least competent and most cor- rupt of all our constituted political bodies. Their members are as a general rule the pettiest, the most readily bribed of all public officials....
>
> The states ... have rarely been able to carry through ad- ministrative jobs more complicated than mailing of license plates....
>
> In many aspects ... state government is dead, and ripe for burying.[13]

The Vietnam War, the assassinations of Robert Kennedy and Martin Luther King, and shifting cultural forces began to change America's focus in the late 1960s. President Lyndon Johnson realized the weaknesses of state government and discussed what he called "Creative Federalism" as a means for state and local governments to bring out new ideas. The concept of federal revenue sharing with the states gained credence during this period as a way to help solve America's growing governance problems. A University of Minnesota economist, Walter Heller, who had been appointed chair of the Council of Economic Advisers by President John Kennedy, noting that the federal government in peace time was "generating revenues faster than they generate new demands on the federal purse," proposed that a portion of federal income tax revenues be distributed to the states on a per capita basis with "next to no strings attached."[14] Other revenue-sharing proposals did attach strings, strings that would force the states and local governments to modernize if they wished to share in federal revenues.[15]

In 1969, in an interesting mixture of politics and policy, two political warriors weighed in on the importance of federalism and the need for tax revenues to solve governmental problems. Both President Richard Nixon and former vice president Hubert Humphrey identified the need to improve the workings of federalism as then practiced, and called for more federal tax revenues to do it. Nixon followed Heller's concept and proposed that "federal revenues be returned annually to the States to be used as the States and their local governments see fit without Federal strings." He proposed starting revenue sharing with $500 million in 1971 and increasing this amount to $5 billion annually by 1975.[16] Humphrey, remembering his experiences as a former mayor, senator, and vice president and writing in a foreword to Congressman Henry S. Reuss's book calling for revenue sharing with strings attached, said, "I know from first hand experience that our federal structure is a relic from the horse-and-buggy past—a structure fundamentally intractable to successful grappling with today's complex social and economic issues."[17]

Senator Walter Mondale recalled that some senators likened the revenue sharing proposals to a Depression-era practice involving assistance to people having trouble making ends meet. In a tacit agreement that more or less kept everyone's dignity intact during that tough period, some out-of-work individuals would anonymously perform chores such as chopping firewood or doing yard work for people who had a job, in hopes of getting some compensation for performing the chore. The person receiving the benefit of the labor would discover that work had been done, and quietly place food or money on a nearby stump for the worker. The worker would later return to pick up whatever had been left as compensation. Mondale said several senators referred to revenue-sharing funds as "stump money." As they described it, "The Feds put it on the stump, and the states would come and take it away."[18]

The final result of all the Washington deliberations was the State and Local Fiscal Assistance Act of 1972, with a minimum of strings and $30.2 billion of "stump money" flowing from the federal government to the states over a five-year period.[19] Also during this period, the federal government passed and implemented sweeping planning legislation that forced the states and local units of government to coordinate their various programs and projects. Statutes with such descriptive titles as the Demonstration Cities and Metropolitan Development Act of 1966 and the Intergovernmental Cooperation Act of 1968 led to a sometimes painful and public analysis of the role of the states and local government in delivering, or failing to deliver, services. This emphasis on intergovernmental coordination was a bipartisan effort, and both Presidents Johnson and Nixon were supportive. For example, under President Nixon, the Office of Management and Budget (OMB) issued a key planning document known in bureaucratic circles as OMB Circular A-95. This document explained the role of the federal government under these new statutes and also acted as "an instrument for facilitating the needed coordination without encroaching on the constitutional domain of the States or the statutory responsibilities of Federal program administrators." Simply put, the A-95 Circular required the various units of state and local government involved in programs receiving federal assistance to plan and talk to the federal government and to each other before implementing the programs.[20]

All of these factors and the books, articles, conferences, and editorials they inspired provided an opportunity for the state legislatures to reassert their proper role in the federal system. But there were powerful groups and businesses that were doing quite well under the weak state legislative system. Their role and impact on society were not being seriously analyzed by any level of state or local government. These groups had amassed significant political and economic power and did not look kindly on any change increasing the visibility or capability of state legislatures. The status quo, they thought, was just fine.

The Supreme Court Sows Seeds of Change

In Minnesota, a group of strong patriarchal Conservatives had controlled the Minnesota legislative process for much of the state's history. The Conservatives had controlled the state senate continuously since 1930. During the twenty legislative sessions between 1930 and 1970 (the legislature then met only every other year), the Conservatives also controlled the house for all but six of those sessions. Rural interests were strongly represented in Minnesota during this period even though the population had increased faster in the metropolitan areas of the state.[21]

The Minnesota Legislature finally passed reapportionment legislation in 1959 based on 1950 census data. This was the first reapportionment since 1913. It created significantly more representation from the Minneapolis–St. Paul metropolitan area. The first election under these new legislative districts was in 1962, and it resulted in significant new blood coming into the legislature.[22] However, the new legislative districts lasted for only the 1962 and 1964 elections. Then the impact of a momentous series of cases decided by the U.S. Supreme Court made itself felt and forever changed Minnesota and the nation.

In 1962, the Supreme Court, in *Baker v. Carr,* a case involving the Tennessee legislature where some districts had ten times as many people as others, issued a ruling saying that reapportionment was now a "justiciable question," and thus federal courts could get involved in reapportionment issues. The court decided to enter the political thicket over the strong dissent of Justice Frankfurter. Subsequent decisions ruled that the equal protection clause of the Constitution mandated "one person, one vote" in all legislative districts and in congressional districts.[23] This ended the practice of allowing districts with far different population sizes—such as the one represented by Dick Parish in metropolitan Minnesota in the late 1960s, which had over a hundred thousand people, and the one represented by Cliff Graba (the father of one of the new legislators partying in the hockey arena in 1971) in rural Minnesota, which had only approximately twelve thousand people—to each have one vote in the legislature.[24]

In 1964, in a suit brought by a Republican congressman, Clark MacGregor, (representing metropolitan suburbs) and others, the federal court in Minnesota ruled that the Minnesota legislative districts established in 1959 did not meet the new equal protection standards required by the Constitution.[25] This decision was part of the nationwide battle being fought in courts and legislatures over how to reapportion legislative districts. The net result was a significant increase in state legislators from densely populated districts in metropolitan areas and fewer legislators from large but sparsely populated legislative districts in rural areas of the state. The one person, one vote requirement would prove to have a profound effect on state legislatures throughout the country and on America's renewed interest in making federalism work.

CHAPTER 2

The Pendulum Begins to Swing

The wave of the future is coming and there is no
stopping it.

■ Anne Morrow Lindbergh, *The Wave of the Future*

During the decades of Conservative Caucus dominance of the
Minnesota Legislature, key industries, such as railroads, insurance, liquor, and mining, had gained a strong influence over the
process of passing state laws. The legislature only met a few months
every other year, and these industries made sure they were well represented both with receptive legislators and effective lobbyists during those few months. As redistricting in the late 1960s resulted in
new faces in the legislature and gave more legal clout to urban and
suburban populations, those industries found it more difficult to per-
petuate their political power.

New legislators from both major political parties were gaining
knowledge about how the legislature worked in actual practice, and
about the impact of state policies on their constituents. These legislators were not always pleased with what they learned, and they began
to challenge long-standing practices and personalities. Some of the
challenges were merely of the garden variety, based on personality or
generational factors. But other challenges were less superficial and
were based on sound principles, such as the need to adjust government programs and policies to fairly reflect the needs of previously
underrepresented constituents in urban and suburban areas, and the
importance of providing critical information and analysis to all legislators, not just a few caucus leaders. The practice of making legislative decisions based only on the word of a lobbyist or a legislative
leader, who usually had an ax to grind, was beginning to come under
close scrutiny.

In 1962, the Republican Party in Minnesota named Lyall Schwarz-kopf the chair of its "Young Republicans." Schwarzkopf was a dedicated and a talented tactician who in high school had decided that he wanted to be a U.S. senator. Up until this time, the Republican Party had not been heavily involved in state legislative races. Schwarzkopf, working together with several other young Republicans, set out to elect candidates who identified themselves as Republicans, as opposed to the older Conservative Caucus legislators, who were often not involved in Republican Party activities. The goal was to elect enough Republicans to take over the Conservative Caucus and control the legislature. Schwarzkopf and his group put together an effective campaign manual that provided candidates with valuable information on fund-raising and the nuts and bolts of how to win a seat in the legislature. They also recruited a talented group of candidates for the newly established legislative districts. The campaign efforts were very successful, and many new young Republican legislators, including Schwarzkopf, were elected that fall. But the success was not sufficient to allow the newly identified Republican legislators to gain control of the long-established Conservative Caucus, so the new Republicans joined the Conservative Caucus and used their influence within that caucus to try and change government policy. This allowed the Conservatives to take back control of the house in 1962 from the Liberals, while continuing the long-standing Conservative dominance in the senate.[1]

The new, primarily urban and suburban legislators recruited by Schwarzkopf came to be known in Republican Party circles as the "Young Turks." The Young Turks generally aligned themselves with the more moderate of the Conservative Caucus legislators and quickly began to make waves within that caucus and in the legislature. Most of the Young Turks were reelected in 1964 and began to analyze the structure and capabilities of the legislature and local governments in Minnesota. They also began working on progressive legislation concerning such topics as human rights and mental health. In 1965, Schwarzkopf became the full-time chair of the Republican Party in Hennepin County, the most populous county in Minnesota.

In the 1967 and 1969 sessions, the legislature, with a strong push from a number of the Young Turks and Republican Governor Harold LeVander, passed several pieces of progressive legislation. These included increased spending on education, expansion of the authority of the Pollution Control Agency, and the establishment of a number of new regional governmental units called Regional Development Commissions (RDCs). These were established throughout the state.[2]

The most well known of the regional governments was the Metropolitan Council, an appointed agency of fifteen members that was to help plan key governmental services for the seven-county Twin Cities metropolitan region. A region-wide agency to plan and deliver transit services throughout the region and a board to oversee sewer construction in an attempt to control costs and shape development in the metropolitan area were also established. Martin Sabo and many of his Liberal Caucus colleagues joined forces with the Young Turks and supported much of this legislation.[3] This metropolitan-wide approach and these agencies began to draw favorable national attention as issues such as urban sprawl and transportation came to the fore in America.[4]

The legislation establishing the RDCs did not cause much of a stir, but Governor LeVander's speech proposing them certainly did. It also illustrated the dangers of youthful political help. A twenty-four-year-old speech writer in the governor's office wrote the speech, and in discussing local governments she included the line, "Some towns are going to die, should die, it should be as natural for towns to die as it is for them to be born." The speechwriter knew the governor had glanced at the speech late one night, and she assumed he had given it his OK. As is often done with important speeches, advance copies of the speech were given to the media to help ensure extensive coverage.

In the car on his way to a rural part of the state to announce the RDC proposal, the governor was reviewing his speech when he heard a radio report about his upcoming RDC announcement. It made him feel good about the RDC initiative and about the speech. Then he heard the "some towns should die" line. His political antenna immediately kicked in, and he grabbed a pen and blotted out the offending line. When he delivered the speech and came to the deletion, he ad-libbed for several minutes about such things as how he loved to visit small towns, the virtues of small-town living, the importance of small towns, and so on, in an effort to limit the political damage he was sure the statewide news report would generate. He did not succeed.[5]

Hundreds of protest letters poured into the governor's office during the next few days, and the governor's executive secretary, Dave Durenberger, investigated how the "some towns should die" line could possibly have gotten into the speech in the first place.[6] He discovered that the young speechwriter was miffed at a small town she thought had recently snubbed the governor's offer to help the town solve a problem. He also discovered that the speechwriter was none other than the governor's daughter, Jean. Durenberger decided this was a teaching moment, and he made Ms. LeVander write the first draft of each of the eight-hundred-plus response letters to the citizens from rural Minnesota that had protested her "some should die" speech. Recalling the incident many years later, Jean LeVander King laughingly said her dad never once mentioned the incident to her, but that Durenberger sure had—at least eight hundred times.[7] As discussed in chapter 8, the infamous speech line, which was never actually spoken by the governor, lived on and caused more political headaches a decade later.

Along with this new approach to governmental structure, the legislature began to deal with several seemingly mundane issues that had an impact on legislators' ability to do the jobs they were elected to do: office space, the handling and copying of the bills, amendments and committee reports to be voted on, and research assistance. Until then, in the words of Ed Burdick, one of a handful of house employees in the 1950s and its distinguished chief clerk from 1967 to 2005, legislative operations were an "old fashioned, horse-and-buggy operation." Burdick noted these problems were not unique to Minnesota's legislature but extended nationwide.[8]

Except for the Speaker and majority and minority leaders, legislators had no place to work except for their small desks in the very public and ornate House Chamber on the second floor of Minnesota's state capitol. Even when office space was finally provided in 1969, it was only a small, open "bull-pen" area in the basement of the capitol. And the secretarial help to keep constituents informed, arrange meetings, and so on was limited to sharing a small stenographic pool.

Prior to the late 1960s, legislators usually did not even have copies of the bills or amendments they were voting on. They had to rely on what they were told was in the legislation by persons with a clear conflict of interest—the author or the committee chair. Bills were often literally cut and pasted together to reflect amendments that had been adopted. The Chief Clerk's Office, which is the legislative office in charge of keeping track of bills as they are introduced and amended, of keeping track of the progress of the bills through committees, and of preparing the final laws for the governor's signature and publication, had a limited staff. Modern word-processing and copy machines finally began to be used more extensively in the late 1960s.[9] This helped individual legislators see and decide for themselves what was in a bill or committee report.

Research assistance was another problem. It did not even exist for most of the 135 legislators until 1967. Before that time, the House Appropriations Committee had limited research staff for its four divisions, and there was a small legislative drafting office to help put ideas into proper legislative form.[10] The research assistance that was finally established in 1967 consisted of one attorney, who had been hired at the request of the then majority leader. A small Legislative Reference Library began in 1968.[11] The changes in space, technology, and staff were very limited and were not part of any comprehensive plan to improve or reform the legislative branch. The changes merely "evolved" and "just happened."[12]

Despite these small changes in legislative support, it was clear that the legislative branch of state government in 1971 was still a weak link in the governmental chain. The federal government, the executive branch of state government, the various special-interest groups, and even some of the large local units of government with their lobbyists and fiscal analysts all had the upper hand in analyzing proposed legislation and its impact on the citizenry. A strong and independent state legislature simply did not exist in Minnesota. Even within the legislative branch, a handful of Conservative Caucus leaders still largely controlled what happened.

Schwarzkopf and the Young Turks had developed a good working relationship with the leaders of the Republican Party, but they were not as close as the elders of the Conservatives Caucus were to a powerful independent group of business interests called the "Good Government Committee." The chair of that committee, Warren Gahloon, had for years worked closely with the Conservative Speaker of the House Lloyd Duxbury and had recruited candidates for the Conservative Caucus. Gahloon, while being paid by the committee, even functioned as the public relations person for the Conservative Caucus and acted as a fund-raiser for its members. The committee made financial contributions to candidates and generally made itself known as a major player in legislative circles. The strong influence of this committee and the role of other business interests and their lobbyists with the controlling Conservatives would provide the Liberals with key campaign issues in 1972.

Two Conservative Caucus leaders who played key roles in dealing with the Conservative Caucus conflict and the role of special interests in the legislative branch in 1971 were Aubrey Dirlam, a farmer from Redwood Falls, a farming community in southwestern Minnesota, and Ernie Lindstrom, a lawyer and certified public accountant from Richfield, a growing suburb next to Minneapolis. Dirlam had been the majority leader of the Conservative Caucus since 1963 and was a polite and cautious legislator. Within the Conservative Caucus, Dirlam was not in the inner circle of people who worked with longtime and very powerful Speaker of the House Duxbury. Dirlam was not as closely tied to the powerful special business interests as Duxbury was. Nevertheless, when Duxbury resigned his house seat in 1970 to become a lobbyist for the National Railroad Association, the Conservative Caucus elected Dirlam as Speaker.

Lindstrom was a successful political leader who had learned to deal with the unexpected. He counted his votes carefully in his bid to succeed Dirlam and become the first majority leader of the Conservative Caucus from the Twin Cities metropolitan area. He had not, however, counted on a harsh Minnesota snowstorm on the eve of the meeting of the Conservative Caucus to elect its majority leader. At about ten o'clock that night, Lindstrom received a call from one of his newly elected supporters from southeastern Minnesota, Leonard Myhra. Myhra, a former Navy fighter pilot and a farmer, was used to dealing with bad weather, but he reported to Lindstrom that as a result of the howling snowstorm then under way, there was no way he could get out of his farm home to make it to the important Conservative Caucus meeting the next morning in St. Paul. Lindstrom thought for a moment and then called the Minnesota Highway Patrol, which by law has certain public safety responsibilities for legislators, to see if anything could be done.[13] The Highway Patrol promptly sent a rotary plow to Myhra's farm, dug him out, and got him to the caucus meeting just as it began. Lindstrom defeated Tom Newcome, another suburban lawyer first elected in 1964, by just one vote. Both Myhra and the Minnesota Highway Patrol had made a good friend in a high place.

Lindstrom was not a folksy guy. He was a serious, tend-to-business CPA and lawyer who had grown up in a small North Dakota town. When asked why he ran for the legislature, he described serving in elected office as being a "volunteer for democracy."[14] One of his Conservative Caucus colleagues described Lindstrom as "the most stubborn guy I've ever seen." Another described him as "riding a white horse" and "not as flexible as he should have been."[15] As would become clear in the upcoming 1971 session, Lindstrom was not only stubborn, he was not afraid of an argument with the newly elected DFL governor, the newly elected minority legislators, members of his own caucus, or state senators of either caucus. The clashes between Lindstrom and Governor Wendell Anderson, Sabo, and others were at times harsh and at times lighthearted. But they were frequent and interesting and made good copy for the media.

Newcome worked well with Speaker Duxbury and with Dirlam but was not close to Lindstrom. Newcome had been recruited to run for the legislature by Gahloon and his Good Government Committee as well as by a well-known railroad lobbyist, Gordon Forbes. Lindstrom was not close to either Gahloon or Forbes, nor was he one of the Young Turks recruited by Schwarzkopf. Thus Lindstrom was without close ties to several key groups that historically had a strong influence on his Conservative Caucus and the legislative process. This independence of Lindstrom and his supporters would lead to controversial actions within the Conservative Caucus and begin the downfall of the powerful Good Government Committee.[16] After the loss to Lindstrom, Newcome joined forces with Lindstrom as an assistant majority leader.

Sabo had the Liberal Caucus organized and ready to do political battle with the Conservatives. Governor Anderson was also eager to implement the changes he had argued for on the campaign trail. The next few months would test the resolve of individual legislators, both the Liberal and the Conservative Caucus leaders, and the DFL governor. These months would prove to be a learning experience for all and would illustrate the importance of leadership, friendship, and compromise in overcoming stubborn partisanship and making a government function for the betterment of the people of the state.

CHAPTER 3

Life in the Minority Caucus

The times, they are a'changin'.

- Bob Dylan

Most people around the farm community where Minority Leader Martin Sabo was born used his full name, Martin Olav Sabo, when referring to the young son of Bjorn and Klara Sabo, both Norwegian immigrants who homesteaded a 160-acre plot near Alkabo, a small town in the northwest corner of North Dakota. Bjorn was a farmer, and Klara was a homemaker and part-time school lunch cook in the local three-room school that Martin attended for twelve years. His middle name eventually faded from use as he went on to become the valedictorian of his senior class—a class, as was frequently mentioned by his colleagues when teasing the minority leader, that consisted of three students. While the schoolhouse and its classes were small, the topics discussed were not, and the three teachers were very good. Sabo credits his senior high teacher, Mr. Baglien, for teaching him to think clearly and critically: "Mr. Baglien was always pushing us and trying to get us to disagree with him."[1]

At age seventeen Sabo left the prairies of North Dakota and its heritage of Norwegian farmers and Nonpartisan League politics to attend Augsburg College in Minneapolis. Augsburg is a small liberal arts college with ties to the Lutheran Church. He graduated cum laude from Augsburg four years later with a degree in political science and history. He started work as an orderly in a hospital and was planning to go back to graduate school. He never made it.[2]

Instead he became active in local Democratic politics with a friend, Jim Pederson, whom he met at Augsburg. Pederson worked on the staff of the DFL Party and was working for Ray Hemenway, DFL Party chair. At a meeting at state senator Don Fraser's home in 1960, Hemenway said he wanted to find a candidate to run against

· 19 ·

an incumbent member of the Minnesota House who many felt was vulnerable. Hemenway told Pederson that his job was to find a candidate to run. Pederson mentioned his roommate, Sabo. Hemenway replied, "Sabo, is he even old enough to vote for himself?" Pederson assured Hemenway: "Yes, Sabo was old enough." Pederson then went home and told Sabo that he had to run. Sabo, already a person of few words, thought for a moment and said, "Are you crazy?" Pederson said, "No, and I will get you the party endorsement at the local ward club."[3] Pederson delivered on his promise, and Sabo became a candidate. He knocked on doors and passed out thousands of leaflets to the approximately thirty thousand people in his district during the fall of 1960 and was elected from South Minneapolis at the age of twenty-two. Sabo at the time was the youngest person ever elected to the Minnesota Legislature.[4] To this day, door knocking and leaflet distribution are techniques key to winning a legislative seat in Minnesota, where a legislative district now has approximately forty thousand people.[5]

Sabo was a quiet, serious, and down-to-earth young man, befitting his heritage and his predominantly Scandinavian district. But he proved to be a bit naive about politics. He almost lost his bid for reelection two years later to a candidate who barely campaigned but was named Johnson.[6] Sabo, a quick learner of the craft of politics, then started using his full name, Martin Olav Sabo, on his campaign materials and on the ballot. He never had another close call.

While working at the hospital, Sabo met a young nursing student, Sylvia Lee. She too was from the prairies of North Dakota and also from Scandinavian heritage. They fell in love, and in the summer of 1963 were married at St. John's Lutheran Church in Sioux Falls, South Dakota, where Sylvia's father was the minister. Martin began selling insurance and legislating, and Sylvia practiced nursing. They had two girls, Karin and Julie, and raised their family in South Minneapolis as Martin continued his legislative career.[7]

During his early years as a legislator, Sabo primarily watched and learned. He met and served one term with a state representative from St. Paul, Wendell Anderson, who would later become a state senator, a governor, and a U.S. senator and play a big part in Sabo's legislative life. He learned that speaking on the house floor during a debate can be intimidating, as one's comments are often strongly challenged by others. Sabo's seat in the House Chamber was immediately in front of

Bob Latz, an affable Liberal legislator from North Minneapolis. Sabo rarely participated in the floor debate but would often lean back and suggest to his good friend Latz what should be said. One day Latz decided it was time for Sabo to get over his reticence about speaking out on the house floor. When Sabo made his next suggestion, Latz smiled and replied, "Why the hell don't you say it yourself?"[8] Sabo, a bit stunned, realized he was getting good advice, and began to participate more in the give-and-take of floor debates.

Sabo also observed the Conservative Speaker of the House Lloyd Duxbury work the levers of power and control the flow of legislation by the quick use of his gavel. Sabo thought "Dux" was quick but fair. Sabo was reelected every two years and became minority leader in 1968. He was reelected as minority leader in 1970 with the support of many veteran rural legislators and a large number of the newly elected legislators he had met and helped on the campaign trail. He began to think about how to build a team that could ultimately win control of the house, and what changes needed to be made in the legislature's procedures.

Rookie Legislative Life

New legislators such as Joe Graba, from Wadena, a town of 4,640 people in rural north-central Minnesota, and the son of a farmer who had been a legislator and a mother who was a teacher, came to St. Paul in January 1971 with some idea of what it was like to be a legislator. Bill Kelly, on the other hand, a new legislator from East Grand Forks, also in the northern part of the state, had no family or political connection to the legislature. Kelly's dad worked for a beer distributor, and his mother was a homemaker. Both Kelly and Graba were high school teachers; both had a good sense of humor and were passionately interested in making changes in how Minnesota was governed. Kelly had served a stint in the Peace Corps in Ethiopia before becoming a teacher. This was Graba's first try for a legislative seat, and Kelly's second. Kelly's committee assignments included Education and Government Operations, and Graba's included Education and Natural Resources. These committees were important, and the knowledge gained there would serve them well in coming sessions. They listened, learned, became good friends, and developed a close working relationship with Sabo.

Two other rookies, Ray Faricy and Tom Berg, were practicing attorneys from the Twin Cities. Berg had migrated to Minneapolis from Willmar in west-central Minnesota, where his dad had worked in the post office and his mother had worked as a telephone operator. Berg's district was in Minneapolis, where he practiced law with a small law firm. Faricy was a native of St. Paul, where his dad was a realtor and his mother a nurse and homemaker. Faricy's legislative district was in St. Paul, where he also worked in a small law firm. His grandfather had been in the legislature. The 1970 election was the first try for elective office for both. The two attorneys began to study legislative and parliamentary procedures in some detail. Faricy was appointed to the Appropriations Committee, a choice committee assignment for a freshmen. Berg and Faricy became good bull-pen friends and worked well with Sabo.

Since desk space was so limited, seniority was used to select desks, both "on the floor," that is, in the House Chamber, and in the bull pen. In their first day on the job, Kelly, with a somewhat awkward look on his face, walked over to where Berg was sitting, introduced himself, and promptly bumped Berg from his desk. Kelly had drawn a lower number than Berg in the drawing used to assign desks, and Kelly held up the number for Berg to see. Berg responded with a quizzical look, picked up his papers, and headed off to a less desirable spot from which to begin his legislative career. This game of musical chairs continued until all the rookies had a chair and a desk. Regardless of location, basic office equipment such as copying machines and calculators were in short supply for everyone.

In the early days of the session, Sabo and Assistant Minority Leader L. J. Lee met frequently with their new caucus colleagues to teach them about legislative procedure and decorum and to preach patience. The rookies and the veterans sized each other up, and, as in most any group working together with deadlines and in close quarters, friendships developed, and some relationships grew strained. The relationship between Kelly and Berg survived the desk bumping, and soon the two joined Faricy and Graba and other freshman in bonding together to exchange stories about the process of legislating. All began to get to know Governor Anderson's very active staff, including Sabo's Augsburg friend Jim Pederson and the governor's executive secretary, Tom Kelm. In the process, one thing became clear to all: this session of the legislature would not be business as usual. The new governor and the newly elected legislators did not feel bound by tradition.[9]

The newcomers also got to know the only woman in the 135-member house, Helen McMillan. McMillan was a veteran legislator from Austin, a strong labor town in the prime agricultural area of southern Minnesota. (There were no women in the state senate at the time.) McMillan was highly regarded by all. She had been active in community matters in the Austin area for many years before becoming a legislator. McMillan retired from the legislature in 1974 after serving five terms.[10] As we will see, the role of women in the legislative process grew rapidly in the 1970s, starting with the 1972 election. "A woman's place is in the House" was soon to become far more than a powerful political slogan.

The group of enthusiastic new legislators liked to continue their discussions after the formal legislative meetings were completed. In addition to gossiping about the various committee chairs and their styles of running a meeting, they discussed the governor's staff and how best to deal with their colleagues in the senate. They also began to discuss more abstract concepts of governing, such as what it meant to be the controlling party in the legislative branch, and what they would like to do should the day come when they might be in that position.

Beer was the usual beverage of choice for the after-hours discussions. It fit both the tastes and the budgets of the young legislators, who were paid $4,800 per year. Legislators also received a per diem allowance for each day of their legislative work. The per diem was set for metropolitan area legislators like Faricy and Berg (who could go home at night) at $16, and at $24 for rural legislators like Kelly and Graba, who needed to rent an apartment in or near St. Paul during the legislative session.[11]

The amount of the per diem was set by the legislators by rule for each session. Per diem was a controversial topic, as some thought it nothing but a backdoor pay raise. Certain legislators (who were usually wealthy) argued that no additional money was needed, that serving in the legislature was a public service and that was pay enough. Others pointed out it was not wise to have the legislative branch of government consist only of wealthy people or those with a strong sense of noblesse oblige. Those legislators (who were usually not wealthy) listed the sacrifices both financial and personal made necessary by the legislative session. As with most discussions of legislative pay, whether in a city council, a legislature, or the U.S. Congress, there was more than a little bit of grandstanding and hypocrisy. The TV stations got into the per diem showmanship game by showing pictures of cash registers ringing up the thousands of dollars per day it cost taxpayers to have their elected representatives doing their jobs. In those reports, the earnest-looking TV reporters never mentioned the complex and difficult decisions that these legislators were making.

Various special interest groups sponsored dinners and receptions almost every evening for the legislators, and sometimes their spouses, during the first two months of the legislative session. The sponsoring groups included governmental units, nonprofits, labor unions, corporations, and industry-wide groups. Such diverse groups as the Minnesota Association of Commerce and Industry (MACI), the Minnesota Historical Society, and the Corn Growers Association all sponsored events. There were often two and three such events in a day. Some were for the entire legislature, and some for just the members of certain committees. The events were an opportunity for the legislators to get to know each other on an informal basis with little or no partisanship involved. These dinners were viewed by some legislators as a way to help hold down their personal food expenses.

For new legislators, these events provided an opportunity to take each other's measure and see what alliances could be formed. The contacts and friendships could prove helpful as the session continued and time for thoughtful discussions grew shorter. But for the most part, the events were understood to be what they were in fact, opportunities for lobbyists and interest groups of all stripes to tell their side of a legislative story and to curry favor with legislators. This unique access for the sponsoring special interests began to cause a number of the new legislators to have an uneasy feeling that this was not always just about friendly socializing. Kelly and Berg were two who worried about this, and they began to discuss ways to limit and provide more public disclosure of such activities without eliminating the benefits of social interaction among legislators across party lines.

Spouses played a key role in legislative family life during the intense legislative session, as the hours at the capitol were long. One legislator told about his young son asking his mother near the end of a session when the father had been putting in fourteen-hour days, "Is

Dad dead?"[12] Absence did not always make the heart grow fonder, and a number of marriages grew strained, and some came apart. The families of a number of the legislators from outside of the metropolitan area moved to St. Paul, while others remained in their home districts. For legislators like Graba, with young children, it was particularly difficult, as the legislative session came right in the middle of the school year. Moving a family for five months in the middle of winter was not an easy task.

Graba, Kelly, Berg, and Faricy spent long hours in the early months of 1971 with their freshman colleagues in the bull pen and in committee hearings learning the legislative ropes. They found that sessions of the entire legislature are rare and short in the beginning of a legislative session, as no legislation has yet worked its way through the all-important committee process. They also developed a solid understanding of the committee process as well as of the power of the Speaker of the house, committee chairs, and the Rules and Legislative Administration Committee over proposed legislation. After a few months this group and their newly found friends developed into a cadre of able newcomers who liked and trusted each other. This cadre had varying interests and abilities but a common willingness to work hard. They shared a common belief that politics in general and state legislation in particular were vehicles that could bring meaningful and positive change to the lives of the people they represented. In this regard, many of this group had beliefs not dissimilar from those described by Ernie Lindstrom's phrase "volunteer for democracy," or from what had motivated Lyall Schwarzkopf and his colleagues to recruit and elect the Young Turks. However, as was becoming more clear every day, the political philosophy over the proper role of government and the specific ideas that the minority caucus freshmen sought to adopt to help people reach their full potential, such as a progressive tax policy, funding for education, and environmental protections, clashed sharply with the political philosophy and ideas of Lindstrom and his Conservative Caucus colleagues, including many of the Young Turks.

Rules Matter

One of the first items of business for both the house and the senate in every legislative session is to adopt their respective rules. These rules

define the process used to appoint legislators to standing committees, such as Taxes, Appropriations, Judiciary, and so on, and to conference committees. Conference committees attempt to reconcile
differences between different versions of similar legislation that is
passed by both the house and the senate. These rules also cover other
important topics and are crucial not only to the day-to-day functioning of a legislative body but to the passage or failure of legislation.
The contentious discussions in 2010 at the federal level concerning
the rules used to adopt national health care legislation illustrate that
the impact of procedural rules can be far greater than most people,
including most legislators, realize.

Minority Leader Sabo was one of those who understood that importance. Sabo had spent a good share of his ten-year legislative career chafing under unfair legislative rules and was soon to apply his
Norwegian determination to the process of changing them. He also
realized that votes taken in January 1971 on the proposed rules could
be a significant tool in an election campaign two years later.

On the third day of the session in 1971, Sabo and other minority caucus leaders, with the united support of their caucus, offered
amendments to the proposed Permanent Rules of the House as they
were being proposed by Majority Leader Lindstrom and his Conservative Caucus. Sabo had strongly advised his caucus to limit the
number of amendments so that the media coverage would be focused and readily understood by the public. He also said the caucus
must be prepared to live with the changes proposed in the event the
caucus were ever to gain control of the house. The caucus agreed,
and the amendments were limited to requiring more of the legislative process to be open to the public, requiring a statement of financial interests of legislators and their immediate family to allow voters
to evaluate any potential or real conflicts of interest, holding more
recorded votes so the public could follow who was doing what, and
providing fairer treatment of minority caucus legislators. Specifi-
cally, the amendments required that all house committee hearings
be open to the public "except in such cases as in [the Committee's]
opinion may require secrecy" (thus forcing legislators to publicly
vote to close a hearing), that legislators file a report listing their economic interests (in broad categories, not specific dollar amounts),
that all committees have "proportionate representation" of minority
(caucus) members, and that debate be recorded during the house

sessions and a copy of the recordings be placed in the Legislative Reference Library for public access.[13]

The practice for years had been to have a very powerful committee, Rules and Legislative Administration ("Rules"), control which legislation gets to the house floor and when it gets there. Timing can be a life-or-death decision for a piece of legislation, particularly near the end of a session, with a constitutional deadline for adjournment. The majority caucus held 100 percent of the members of that committee. The rules proposed by Lindstrom anticipated continuing that practice, while Sabo and colleagues with their "proportionate representation" amendment wanted the practice changed.

The chief clerk of the Minnesota House, Ed Burdick, standing at his desk just in front of the Speaker's rostrum in the House Chamber, dutifully reported each of the proposed amendments in his loud voice to Speaker Dirlam and the entire 1971 session of the Minnesota House of Representatives. The Speaker, standing at the rostrum above the chief clerk's desk and in front of a large portrait of Abraham Lincoln, would recognize Minority Leader Sabo or one of his colleagues, who would rise from his seat on the left side of the House Chamber facing Dirlam and explain what each of the proposed changes would do. Sabo or another veteran minority caucus member would make an argument why the amendment was fair and should be adopted. Dirlam would then recognize Majority Leader Lindstrom, who would rise from his chair on the right side of the chamber and argue there was no need for the change, or that it was worded poorly or was somehow unfair or unworkable. An example of the Conservative Caucus's arguments is found in a statement by Speaker Dirlam: "Tape recording of debates is primarily for political purposes so you can have your speeches ready for the next campaign." All of the amendments were voted down, generally following Liberal-Conservative caucus line voting.[14] To most of the observers in the gallery of the House Chamber that day, the failure of the Liberals to get their amendments adopted was a foregone conclusion, and the debate and voting process were just political theater. But, as would be become clear in the election of 1972 and beyond, it was theater with profound meaning and long-lasting effect.

According to the rules that were adopted that January 7, 1971, all legislators, including the thirty-one new legislators in the Liberal Caucus, were to be assigned to committees by Speaker Dirlam.

Committee assignments are near and dear to a legislator and may often play a significant role in the legislator's political career. Individual legislators from the minority caucus gave Sabo a list of their committee preferences, and Sabo in turn submitted a list of proposed committee assignments of minority members to Dirlam. Sabo won some and lost some as Dirlam made assignments for the Liberals to all committees—except Rules, which remained 100 percent in control of the majority Conservative Caucus.

A War's Influence

To understand what was happening in the state legislatures across America in the 1970s, it is necessary to have a sense of the social and political turmoil that had started to build in the 1960s as the war in Southeast Asia ground on. Few, if any, institutions or parts of the country were exempt from the war's impact. While the focus for the freshmen legislators was on state taxes, government operations, and the like, they were well aware of the growing turmoil and social change that continued to evolve in their country, their state, and their legislative districts.

This turmoil led to a meeting early in the legislative session between Majority Leader Lindstrom and two representatives from the federal government in Washington. The federal officials were analyzing the physical security in and around state capitols in view of the potentially violent protests that were taking place across America. Lindstrom, who had quietly rescheduled some sessions of the legislature to avoid potential confrontations with protestors, was very aware of the abortion, tax, and war controversies taking place at the state capitol. He listened to the suggestions, which included placing bullet-proof glass in the visitors gallery and in front of the Speaker's rostrum. In addition, special security personnel were recommended for the legislative session. Lindstrom thought about it and rejected the suggestions. He viewed these as "abnormal times that will pass." He also had confidence in his friends at the State Highway Patrol, who had the public safety responsibility for the capitol, the governor, and the legislature.[15]

The turmoil also directly affected the freshman legislators early in their first term. In March 1971, a bill was introduced giving the state attorney general authority to bring a lawsuit to contest the legality of the war. In a hearing before the Judiciary Committee, an amendment was added to modify the preamble of the bill to state, "if constitutional questions about the United States' . . . involvement do exist . . . the state, without passing judgment on the merits, can aid in raising said issues before the federal courts of this nation."[16] The amendment passed, but the bill ultimately did not. However, the constitutional issue concerning the role of the states in making and implementing war policy did not go away. Nor did the antiwar protests.

Over a year later, on May 13, 1972, after the legislature had adjourned, an antiwar rally was held at the capitol in St. Paul. The rally was at the end of a march that "capped five days of sometimes violent protests that shook the University of Minnesota." To deal with the ongoing violence, Governor Anderson activated three units of the Minnesota National Guard, at the request of Minneapolis mayor Charles Stenvig.

On the day of the rally, about forty State Highway patrolman with helmets and batons guarded the doors of the capitol. Berg and a number of legislators were present. Earlier in the week the governor had said he would be willing to call a special session if "it seems the legislature would act positively on it." As a result, a bipartisan list of legislators requesting a special session to consider an antiwar resolution was released to the public at the rally. During the noisy two-hour demonstration, a constituent and neighbor of Berg's, Sharon Walsh, spoke to the several thousand people in attendance. Her husband was a lieutenant colonel who was being held as a prisoner of war in North Vietnam, and her testimony was thoughtful and emotional. At about five o'clock, the rally ended peacefully, and no special session to deal with the war issue was ever called.[17] But that week in May 1972 vividly illustrated to the freshman legislators that issues of federalism were still very much alive. The extent of the federal government's war powers and the role of the states and control of their National Guards, which had concerned the nation's founders in the 1780s, were still important two hundred years later to legislators' discussions and votes on how federalism should work.

CHAPTER 4

Legislating a Miracle

You are in the legislative branch . . . anything is possible.

▪ Rahm Emanuel, *New York Times,* February 11, 2009

The 1971 session of the Minnesota Legislature at one level was more of the same: abortion, money, and politics. At another level, the session was an impressive development and application of sophisticated and sensible public policy to complex problems facing the people of Minnesota. Under either analysis, it took the constitutionally permitted 120-day session of the legislature, the actions and vetoes of a strong governor, compromise, bipartisan support, personal friendships, and the longest special session of the legislature in the state's history to complete a historic change in Minnesota's fiscal policy. A change that served Minnesota and its schoolchildren well for years. A change that also came to be viewed as a "miracle" and helped put the governor on the cover of *Time* magazine.[1]

At the same time, it took the involvement of the judicial branch of the federal government to complete the political map drawing necessitated by the constitutionally required reapportionment of the legislature, as the partisan politics of the reapportionment process proved to be too strong for the legislature and the governor to surmount.

Taxes and Revenue Distribution

The genesis for the fiscal policy change began years earlier with increasingly loud protests from thousands of taxpayers that their property taxes were too high, in some cases becoming confiscatory. The 1967 legislature under Conservative Caucus control had passed permanent and significant property tax relief for businesses and had instituted a general sales tax for the first time in Minnesota.

The legislature had also passed property tax relief for homeowners, but this relief was not mandated to be permanent.[2] And as had been predicted, property taxes on homeowners and farmers soon started going back up.[3] Complaints and protests mounted throughout the state. By the time the 1970 gubernatorial campaign got under way, homeowner property taxes had become a significant issue for the candidates.

State senator Wendell Anderson, the DFL candidate, talked constantly about the permanent property tax relief for businesses and only temporary relief for homeowners. He pointed out that this had been passed by the Republican-controlled 1967 legislature. He said he would provide relief for the homeowners. Doug Head, the state attorney general and Republican candidate for governor, was more vague; he talked about crime and violence, reduced reliance on real estate taxes, and "better balanced economic growth."[4]

During the summer and fall of 1970, a group of citizens had begun a detailed study of Minnesota's complex system of distributing state revenue. This group was part of the Citizens League, a well-respected eighteen-year-old nonpartisan organization devoted to studying and recommending policies to solve various state and local problems. The league issued reports on their findings and their proposed solutions. The league did not endorse candidates, but it did actively advocate for the implementation of proposed solutions. The league was open to all, although it consisted largely of corporate and business folks, a few labor people, and a good number of students and policy wonks.

The rather boring-looking and boring-sounding report from the league titled *New Formulas for Revenue Sharing in Minnesota* was to become a key catalyst in deciding who would be Minnesota's next governor, and in the development of a dramatic change in the state's fiscal policy. The chair of the committee that produced the report was Bill Hempel, who had earlier worked closely with Republican gubernatorial candidate Head, as the number two person in Attorney General Head's office. The report focused on how the state distributed revenue raised by various units of government in Minnesota. The report noted that federal revenue sharing was about to begin and that Minnesota had its own version of revenue sharing with local units of government, even though the term *revenue sharing* was not used at the state level.[5]

In Minnesota, as in many states, local officials such as county commissioners, city council members, and school board members set local property taxes. These taxes generally fund such things as public schools, local roads, bridges, parks, and libraries. State legislators generally deal with the statewide income and sales taxes, certain licenses and fees, such as those on motor vehicles, and limited personal property taxes on businesses. The state then distributes state tax revenues back to cities, towns, counties, and school districts. In government and policy language, this distribution is referred to as school aids and municipal or local government aids (LGA). Complicated formulas are used by the state to determine the specific amount going to the various local government units. Since the raising and distribution of funds within the state can be dreadfully boring to all but the most dedicated policy wonks, most legislators do not understand the detailed workings of the formulas. In the 1970 campaign, however, this topic became anything but boring, and legislators were forced to study, learn, and take a position on revenue distribution and property tax issues or risk the voters' wrath.

On September 1, 1970, the Citizens League's board approved its report. The report said that a "broad look" at state policy for the fiscal affairs of local government was "urgently needed." It noted that "political resistance to higher taxation is rising" and that the state legislature should play a "central role" in determining which levels of local government should levy taxes and what limits should be placed on these local units of government. The report then called for a reduction in local property taxes and a replacement of most of the local property taxes with state-collected taxes. The state was asked to "give priority attention" to aids to municipalities and to schools.[6] The report's recommendations for more state action raised eyebrows in tax, local government, and political circles.

On October 1, the Citizens League held its annual dinner. After some negotiating, the two major party candidates for governor agreed to attend and answer questions from a panel of league members. Both candidates knew that one of the questions at the dinner would relate to the report and its proposals to change the state's fiscal policy. When the question came, DFL candidate Anderson expressed his support for the ideas in the league's proposal and explained why. Republican candidate Head said he had "misgivings about the League's proposals."[7] The Republicans thought that

Anderson's support for the ideas in the proposal was a mistake and that it gave them a strong issue against Anderson. The next day Head's "misgivings" gave way to a sharp attack on Anderson and his support for the proposal. Head and the Republicans claimed the ideas would significantly raise taxes and erode "local control."[8]

Forty years later, when asked about the position he took at that dinner, Anderson said he "feels good" about his support for the controversial report but is highly critical of the league's conduct during the campaign. He noted that neither the league nor its leaders came to his defense, nor provided any help during the intense battle over the league's proposal. "Worthless" and "an example of political cowardice" are phrases Anderson used to describe the league's actions during the fall of 1970.[9]

As the campaign progressed, the news media continued to cover the issue extensively, and more and more people began to realize that the legislature's actions could have a significant impact on their property taxes. People also realized that the method of distribution of state money was critical to their local municipality and school district. More people began to pay attention to such arcane terms as *mill levies* and *assessed valuations*. With less than a month to go, a headline in the *Minneapolis Tribune* raised the issue to the top of the political pile: "School-Tax Proposal May Decide Governor's Race." During the last four weeks of the campaign, Anderson fueled the fire over too-high property taxes and kept talking about the need for a more fair system of aids for school districts and municipalities.[10]

Finally, on November 3, the voters decided, and Anderson won with 54 percent of the vote.[11] The Anderson administration quickly realized that the Republican escalation of what had started out as just an idea in Anderson's mind gave the new administration a politically acceptable vehicle to make sweeping changes in the state's tax and revenue distribution policies. Anderson claimed the election victory gave his administration a "mandate" to do something about the "fiscal mess" left by the previous Republican administration and the Conservative-controlled legislature.[12] While Republicans had talked about Anderson's "plan," in fact, no plan existed. There was merely a concept to reduce property taxes and to implement a revenue distribution system that was thought by the governor to treat school districts and local governments more fairly.[13]

Fulfilling the mandate and developing a plan were easier said than done. First, the general campaign proposals had to be put into proper legislative language. Second, supporting explanatory material needed to be prepared using language and examples of aid distribution so that it could be understood by people in all of Minnesota's different school districts, counties, and municipalities. Third, and by far the most difficult, a majority of the legislative branch of government, controlled by the Conservatives, who had virtually controlled the distribution of state aid funds for many years, had to be convinced to vote for it.

The governor's office, led by its chief fiscal advisor, John Haynes, a bright twenty-six-year-old who had worked on the governor's campaign staff, took the lead in producing the legislation, working with the Office of the Revisor of Statutes. Since personnel in the Department of Education had worked closely with Conservatives who had controlled the legislature for many years, the newly elected Anderson administration was not initially comfortable working with this department on the major changes being planned for education funding. This changed over time, but at the outset staff people from Minnesota's State Planning Agency, which was headed by Anderson appointee Jerry Christenson, were brought in to help with the difficult and technical task of putting the campaign rhetoric into actual legislative language. Christenson, at age forty-one, was the elder statesman of the group bringing together the details. A few years earlier he had written his Ph.D. thesis on the disparities in Minnesota's school-aid distribution formula. Governor Anderson joked that "this was the only Ph.D. thesis in history ever to be used as a practical matter for anything useful."[14]

Eileen Baumgartner, a smart twenty-eight-year-old who worked for Christenson on this project, described the scene when they were trying to figure out if the Citizen's League proposal could even be done in one legislative session: "We had pieces of big, brown paper on the wall, scribbling notes in magic marker to come up with the numbers. . . . [When] we got done . . . John said, 'We can do it.' And Jerry said, 'Well, let's take this up to the governor right now.' "[15] Baumgartner said, "We were so excited we brought the big sheets of scribbled-on paper directly to the governor. He told us to take the next steps."[16]

This involved developing detailed distribution formulas for the eighty-seven counties, 434 school districts, and eight hundred some municipalities. Baumgartner, with a degree in chemistry from the College of St. Catherine in St. Paul and a master's degree in public policy from the University of Minnesota, was very comfortable with mathematics and developed an algebraic formula to determine the amount of money that would go to school districts and other local units of government. "I did them all on a hand calculator because we didn't have PCs and spreadsheet technology in those days," she said. The algebra was actually in the legislation along with the words describing the algebraic formulas, but legislators, not so adept at mathematics, became worried they might be passing something they did not understand, and forced the staff to remove the algebra from the bill.[17]

Haynes said, "Eileen started tutoring me about what it was we were supposed to be doing. I really kind of learned on the job. It's nothing that I picked up ahead of time." As the plan was being developed, Governor Anderson, Minority Leader Sabo, Haynes, and Christenson all realized that one possible way to implement the equalization of taxation and spending talked about in the campaign was to abolish the local property tax and put in its place a state-mandated property tax and a state distribution system for the revenue raised by the new state property tax. Sabo argued against this and played a significant role in convincing the governor and the drafting team that the existing local property tax system could be adjusted to achieve the goals discussed in the campaign. All knew changing the existing structure would be politically preferable to starting an entirely new state-run tax system.[18]

The final plan developed by the drafting team and approved by Anderson called for an eye-popping $762,000,000 increase in state taxes, a 37 percent increase. Importantly, it also reduced the taxing and spending disparity between school districts and mandated the reduction of school property taxes by over 18 percent.[19] The governor unveiled this "Fair School Finance Plan" in January.

The plan also put the clamps on school districts so they could not, as had happened after the 1967 legislation, get the new state money and then turn around and raise property taxes right back to previous levels. The mechanisms to control these local property taxes were called "levy limits." These limits effectively limited the amount of real estate taxes school officials could raise from their district. This measure too would prove to be controversial, as a number of legislators thought levy limits violated the concept of local control that Republican candidate Head had talked about.

The legislators' instincts told them something needed to be done during the legislative session. They could not agree, however, on just what that something was. At one point in the session, there were six separate bills dealing with school aids and related taxes, and all were active simultaneously. One of those bills in the house was authored by Harvey Sathre, a longtime member of the House Education Committee. He did not like the governor's approach, and his bill had only modest alterations to the existing school funding program. Sathre had been a key player for years, and he accurately felt that he was being pushed aside.[20]

In the senate, one of the Republican Young Turks, Wayne Popham, agreed to carry a bill closely tracking the Citizens League proposal. The league had an active presence at the legislature during the session to support its proposal. The governor's complicated proposal, which covered more than the Citizens League plan, was formally introduced in the senate by Senator Gene Mamenga, a professor at Bemidji State College. When it came time to present the controversial Fair School Financing Plan to the Senate Tax Committee in a jam-packed hearing room, Mamenga, to the surprise of Haynes, simply turned to the young Haynes and said, "John, please explain the bill to the committee." Forty years later Haynes said, "I can still remember how nervous I was as I walked to the podium. As I began to speak, I felt my knees shaking inside my trousers."[21]

Opposition to the governor's proposed legislation was swift. It was led by the Conservative Caucus in the house and its majority leader, Ernie Lindstrom. As the governor traveled the state touting his proposal, Lindstrom followed as a one-man "truth squad" and called the governor's proposed statewide tax increases "reckless." He said they would "devastate Minnesota's economy." He said the projected tax relief was a fraud and that the "real dollar saved is the one not spent." Speaker Aubrey Dirlam also weighed in as a sharp critic of the governor's proposal.[22]

The governor kept pounding away at the need to reduce local property taxes and to reduce the disparity in taxation and spending between school districts and municipalities that have a high property tax base because of such things as significant commercial property and valuable homes, and "poorer" districts or municipalities with primarily low-value residential property. He claimed that his proposal was a fair and fiscally sound mechanism to do this. Media coverage on these issues continued to be extensive, and editorialists from across the state weighed in on the discussion.

As the legislative session ground on and Anderson and Lindstrom traveled the state, thousands of homeowners and farmers in Minnesota continued to protest their property taxes. In April 1971, many of these taxpayers came to the capitol to make their voices heard and to attend a rare joint hearing of the House and Senate Tax Committees. There were so many people involved that the hearing had to be moved from the capitol to the state armory.[23]

Anderson and DFL proponents of the proposal such as Minority Leaders Sabo and Nick Coleman knew that Conservative Caucus votes were needed to pass the legislation. They tried hard to get at least some bipartisan support for the legislation. At the same time, they had their hands full trying to keep most of the Liberal Caucus members on board. The caucuses had not made this bold fiscal policy change a strict "party-line" or "caucus issue," and thus legislators did not have extensive organized internal political pressure to vote for the bill. But there was plenty of other pressure from all sides. Many legislators were nervous about the major change in relationships between the state and school districts and local governments and were not sure how to vote.

Stanley Holmquist was the majority leader of the senate's Conservative Caucus. Holmquist had a tough job as he had only a one-vote margin to work with on partisan issues. He was also a businessman, a former teacher, school principal, and school superintendent. He held a deep philosophical belief in the importance of education and knew that it takes money to run a good school district. Holmquist had served in the senate with Wendell Anderson for eight years, and they were friends.[24] At the large and boisterous April hearing in the state armory, Holmquist made the argument to the protesters that the legislature does not set the local property taxes. He was booed and hissed. Sabo described the crowd's reaction: "The folks were not going to be fooled. They knew that the legislature and the governor did have impact on property taxes." Holmquist continued to think about the governor's proposal.[25]

All the while the governor used what has become known in political circles as the "bully pulpit," the inherent ability of a governor to get public attention just because he or she is a governor. Anderson used every chance he could to convince and cajole everyone who would listen to support his plan. Lindstrom and his Conservative Caucus supporters tried to create their own bully pulpit to match the governor's. However, in a contest between a governor and a legislator, even a legislator as important as a majority leader or a Speaker, the governor usually gets more media attention. The executive branch of government almost always has the biggest pulpit. And at least in this situation, size matters. The photogenic and aggressive Anderson did all he could to take advantage of his position. He also had a more extensive staff than the house Conservatives, and in this case, the staff were very savvy. Tom Kelm, the governor's executive secretary, and David Lebedoff, the governor's campaign chair and then a speechwriter and advisor, were very good at plotting strategy and getting favorable media attention for the proposal.

A good example of these skills occurred when Anderson requested to speak to a joint session of the legislature to discuss his proposal. The governor asked for only fifteen minutes in late April. The controlling Conservatives, through Speaker Dirlam, refused his request. Anderson then called a press conference in the ornate and large reception room that is part of his office area to explain his position. He also invited all legislators to attend the May 4 press conference. The house Conservatives, led by Lindstrom, tried to upstage the governor by releasing their tax and revenue proposals on the morning of the same day. The result of all this posturing was significant help for the governor. First, his press conference got the headlines and more media coverage than Lindstrom's did. Second, and more important, Senator Holmquist came to the governor's press conference and sat in the front row. He became a public supporter and played a key role in rounding up Conservative votes in the senate.[26]

Ultimately the house passed the Sathre bill, which reflected his unchanging philosophy. The senate passed the Popham bill, but no agreement was reached between the house and senate on the significant differences between the two bills. The normal appropriation bills were passed so that the government could keep on running, but the major proposed changes in taxes and school and municipal aids were still an open question. The legislature's 120 days expired without any agreement on this controversy.[27]

Governor Anderson immediately called the legislature back to St. Paul for a special session to keep working on his Fair School Finance Plan.[28] During the special session, Minority Leaders Sabo and Coleman played as strong a supporting role for the governor as they could, but the Conservatives had control, and they were making full use of it. They were not agreeing to much of anything with the DFL governor or Liberal Caucus members.

The state constitution requires that the legislature convene at least once every three days during a session unless both the house and senate agree to a different schedule. They did not agree, so even though there was almost nothing for the 180-plus legislators not on the tax negotiating teams to do, they were expected to check in at the capitol every three days.[29] As a result, the frustration level of the legislators grew and grew. Gary Flakne, one of the Young Turks, said he was never consulted at all by Lindstrom and was "fed up" by the process.[30] Berg was so frustrated he talked with personnel in the Office of the Revisor of Statutes about the procedure to resign from the legislature. Faricy helped out rural legislators by letting Joe Graba and a number of others sleep at his house when they had to drive to St. Paul from their rural homes to attend one of the short and inconsequential required sessions. In one of the more entertaining expressions of frustration, Senator Florian Chmielewski, a polka band leader from northern Minnesota, staged a "polka protest" at the capitol, criticizing the house majority leader for not being willing to compromise, and playing "Please Release Me" on his accordion for most of the day.[31]

Finally, in late July, the house and senate managed to pass a comprehensive bill relating to taxes and school and municipal aids. The bill raised taxes by $599.9 million and increased state and municipal aid. The majority caucus leaders were able to muster only the bare minimum number of votes necessary to pass the bill: sixty-seven Conservatives in the house and thirty-four Conservatives in the senate. Only one Liberal in the house and one in the senate voted for the bill.[32] The house and the senate then adjourned to October 12, which stopped the needless every-three-day sessions, and the legislators went home.[33] Anderson let speculation build for a few days as to whether he would sign the controversial legislation. On August 4 he vetoed the bill.

In his veto message, Anderson castigated the Conservatives for passing a bill under which "the less you make, the harder you are hit. The more you make the better this bill takes care of you . . . the mining companies [and the] liquor interests are pleased with this bill." He went on to explain his veto as:

> vetoing an approach . . . vetoing the idea that special interests are entitled to write the people's laws . . . the idea that those with the most power and wealth should get the most tax relief . . . the assumption that a legislature can be out of touch with the people it was elected to serve.[34]

Then the governor changed his strategy. He did not ask that the legislature go back into special session. Instead he requested that a ten-person committee be appointed by the legislative caucuses: six Conservatives and four Liberals. He also suggested that this committee meet at the governor's residence, not at the capitol. Anderson and others believe this change in environment played a significant role in ultimately getting an acceptable bill through the legislature that the governor would sign. There were fewer distractions outside of the capitol, and as various ideas were floated in the politically charged meetings, it was easier for the negotiators to avoid discussing them with the press and lobbyists.[35]

The legislative branch was then, in reality, only the ten leaders the caucuses had named to work with the governor's office.[36] The discussions ground on day after day. Sabo and Coleman showed up at the governor's residence each day and did what they could. Lindstrom rarely showed up, and when he did, "he was not a happy camper."[37] The governor seldom attended, instead leaving the negotiations and drafting to his staff. The meetings at times were extremely tense, and Kelm would try and position Sabo and Haynes on each side of him, as he felt they "were capable of going berserk, and he wanted to hold them down."[38] But during the tedious negotiations, significant compromises were slowly being reached as all sides made concessions. The governor, Sabo, Coleman, and the Liberals agreed to the Conservatives' request for a one-cent increase in the sales tax. In addition, the governor and the Liberals slightly dropped the amount of proposed new income taxes. They also agreed to place a limit on the amount of property taxes that could be raised by municipalities and counties (a "levy limit"), and this concession helped gain the support of an important house Conservative, Salisbury Adams. Changes in the distribution formulas were also made, and these helped gain the support of another key house Conservative, Charlie Weaver. Weaver represented Anoka, a community that generally had low property valuations. Sabo and Coleman (who represented districts in Minneapolis and St. Paul) successfully pushed for changes in the municipal aid formula to reflect the large amount of municipal services required in the central cities. This helped secure Liberal support from legislators representing these cities.[39]

Majority Leader Holmquist chaired the meetings and never called for any votes on specific issues. Instead, he would simply say, "We are close to agreement on that, and the staff can work it out." He would then move the group to another topic, never to return to the point that the staff then "worked out." No minutes were kept.[40]

While these discussions were under way, a California court issued a decision declaring certain parts of the California system for funding education unconstitutional. The case found that the "substantial disparities among individual school districts in amount of revenue available per pupil for the districts' educational grants invidiously discriminates against the poor and violates the equal protection clause of the Fourteenth Amendment."[41] In Minnesota there were also suits filed claiming that the disparity in different districts made the existing system of financing education unconstitutional. A colorful and former DFL attorney general, Miles Lord, was the federal judge hearing those cases. He issued a memorandum refusing to dismiss the cases. In the memorandum he noted the similarities between the Minnesota financing system and the unconstitutional California system. While the Lord memorandum did not come out until October 12 and the California case was not directly applicable, the threat of judicial intervention added another argument for the governor's proposal to make state aid and spending more equal for the 434 school districts.[42]

Finally an agreement was reached. The legislative compromises, the staff work on the detailed fiscal impact of various options, the long negotiating sessions, and the guiding hand of the Liberal governor and his Conservative Caucus friend, Senator Holmquist, had worked.[43] On October 27 a bill was brought to the full legislature. The bill's negotiators had reached an agreement that they would fight off all amendments to the bill. The Liberal leaders were to oppose any amendments brought by Liberal legislators, and Conservative leaders would oppose any amendments brought by Conservative legislators. Few amendments were offered, and the bill passed without any amendments being adopted. It was signed by the governor on October 30, and the legislature adjourned.[44] The ten-month ordeal was over.

The final product was known in legislative circles as the Omnibus Tax Act, and it raised state taxes by $580 million. The rate in every income tax bracket was increased, the sales tax was increased a penny, and taxes were raised on beer and cigarettes. Other taxes were raised in various amounts. Total state revenues went up 23 percent. But property taxes went down throughout Minnesota as the new state revenue was distributed back to school districts and municipalities. The state aid to school districts went up from 43 percent of operating costs to 65 percent.[45] This increase in aids to school districts not only reduced property taxes on farms and homes, its distribution formula dramatically reduced the educational spending disparity between the wealthy districts and poor districts. The end result moved the state much closer to meeting the state constitution's mandate of "a general and uniform system of public schools."[46]

In the house, forty-seven Liberals, or 72 percent of the Liberal Caucus, supported the bill, and only thirty Conservatives, or 43 percent of the Conservative Caucus, supported it. A similar pattern occurred in the senate, where twenty-nine Liberal senators, or 88 percent of the Liberal Caucus, voted for the bill, and only twelve Conservatives, or 35 percent, voted for the bill.[47] When Minority Leader Sabo saw the strong support from his caucus, he said he knew that the young Liberals had matured and were ready to make the tough political decisions necessary to govern.[48]

Jerry Christenson reported on the governor's description of the signing ceremonies for the school aid bill that distributed the new money to the school districts, and the tax bill that paid for it: "Wendy still kids about all the people who crowded the capitol for the signing of the school aids bill (which distributed millions of dollars to school districts throughout the state), while only Martin Sabo showed up for the signing of the tax bill to pay for it." This story illustrates what people who worked with Sabo knew well: he not only talked a good game about balanced budgets, he practiced what he preached. This belief in balanced budgets served Sabo well, as he would go on to the U.S. House of Representatives and be appointed to the Appropriations Committee and then be selected by his peers to chair the Budget Committee of the House of Representatives.[49]

The national Advisory Commission on Intergovernmental Relations dubbed the passage of the legislation a "Minnesota Miracle," and said the Minnesota legislators "made Minnesota a model for other states to follow." This name stuck, and the legislation is to this day used as a case study of creative state policy development.[50]

One other significant and far-reaching piece of legislation relating to taxes that passed in the 1971 session, which is sometimes included in the definition of Minnesota's Miracle, is known as the Fiscal Disparities Act. That legislation, authored by Conservative Charlie Weaver, dealt with disparities in the values of real estate tax bases that existed in local units of government in the Minneapolis and St. Paul metropolitan area. The purpose of the legislation was to help even out the tax base between the districts that had significant high-value property within their borders and those that did not. A goal of the legislation was to reduce destructive economic competition between municipalities. It was another idea developed in part by the Citizens League. Like the Minnesota Miracle legislation, it employed complex formulas to achieve its goal. It passed with strong bipartisan support and continues to help ameliorate the differences in tax base between the so-called have and have-not municipalities in the Twin Cities area. It is still an example of sound planning and coordination throughout a large metropolitan area.[51]

Abortion

While the money issues were being debated and protested, another hot-button issue was being dealt with in a basement hearing room of the capitol. Like many states, Minnesota law prohibited abortions except to save the life of the mother. Criminal penalties were imposed for persons participating in the process.[52] Bills were introduced in both the house and the senate to liberalize the process. This was not a partisan political issue. House members Robert Bell, a Conservative, and Helen McMillan, a Liberal, introduced a bill to repeal the existing abortion law, thus allowing physicians to perform abortions.[53] A physician legislator and Liberal, Vern Sommerdorf, introduced a bill to provide that an abortion may be performed under the supervision of a licensed physician after counseling during the first thirteen weeks of pregnancy. After that period the approval of a three-person panel appointed by the Minnesota Board of Medical Examiners would be required.[54] A third bill, authored by Conservative Robert Johnson, provided that no doctor, nurse, or hospital would be liable for refusing to assist in or perform an abortion.[55] A fourth bill, authored by Conservative Warren Chamberlain, would make any abortion referrals a crime.[56] Speaker Dirlam sent all the bills to the Health, Welfare, and Corrections Committee, chaired by Gary Flakne.

No one was sure what would happen to these very controversial bills. A committee chair has significant power, and many are not afraid to use it. Sometimes a bill sent to a committee remains in the chair's desk drawer and never has a public hearing, because either the chair does not like it or, for political reasons, the chair does not think it wise to proceed with the bill. On rare occasions this is done with a wink and nod from the author of the legislation. The author can then tell his or her constituents that a strong effort was made, a bill was drafted and introduced, but the stubborn committee chair from another part of the state refused to give the bill a hearing. However, on most matters hearings do eventually get held, due either to a committee chair who thinks fairness requires a hearing or to pressure from the bill's authors or the interested public. In this case, Flakne promptly agreed that a hearing should be held. He appointed a special subcommittee to hear the bills. Tom Berg was one of the members of that eleven-member subcommittee.[57]

Monday evening hearings were held to make it easier for citizens to attend. Major portions of the hearings were broadcast live from the capitol by WCCO, then the state's most powerful and listened-to radio station. The hearings were lengthy, and emotions ran high as the pro-life and pro-choice factions presented hour after hour of testimony to the subcommittee. Citizens with picket signs jammed the hearing room, causing security concerns and at times making it almost impossible for the legislators to even get to their seats at the committee table. Ethics charges were filed, and an attorney general's investigation was requested as some of the protagonists argued back and forth in very heated and, at times, vitriolic exchanges.[58]

After hours and hours of emotional testimony, thousands of letters to legislators, and extensive media coverage, the committee rejected all bills except one, which said there was no liability for medical providers refusing to participate in performing an abortion.[59] This bill ultimately passed and was signed into law.[60] Thus Minnesota was left in the rather curious statutory situation where abortions were illegal and medical providers were explicitly not liable for refusing to participate in the illegal act. It was clear that there would be no abortion law reform in the 1971 session.[61] Some cheered and some cried, but all knew the fight over the issue of abortion was far from over.

Approximately eighteen months later, in a stunning example of the importance of the judicial branch of government in American society, the U.S. Supreme Court decided *Roe v. Wade,* and in a majority opinion written by Justice Harry Blackmun decided that women have a constitutional right to an abortion. State laws, such as the one in Minnesota that the subcommittee had failed to repeal, were invalid.[62] Again, there were cheers and tears. And again, it was clear to all that the fight over this issue was far from over. The issuance of an executive order relating to federal funding for abortions by President Barack Obama thirty-seven years later, as a part of the deal making to pass the national health care bill, well illustrates the staying power of this complex and emotional issue.[63]

Political Control and Money

In addition to the contentious tax and abortion issues, which were being covered extensively by the media, a simmering controversy from the previous fall involving the Conservative Caucus burst into public view. In April, Majority Leader Lindstrom attempted to "destroy an informal political financing system through which the loosely knit business lobby has penetrated the Minnesota House Conservative Caucus."[64] Lindstrom wrote a letter to his caucus colleagues stating that the "real issue facing our caucus" is: "[w]ho is in control of the funds raised for caucus campaign purposes—the members of the caucus or lobbyists pulling strings from the outside." Lindstrom sought an accounting of the $35,000 proceeds from a fund-raising dinner organized by lobbyists the previous fall.[65]

The lobbyists he was referring to were those working with members of the Good Government Committee headed by Warren Gahloon. There was a dispute over whether a large portion of the funds should be used to pay Gahloon a salary for political operations outside of the scrutiny of the caucus. Speaker Dirlam and Assistant Majority Leader Tom Newcome opposed Lindstrom's efforts. The "highest councils" of the Republican Party were brought in to deal with the messy internal fight.[66] Gahloon resigned shortly after Lindstrom raised his allegations, and Newcome defended the handling of the money saying, "this is an above board operation. . . . There has been no hanky-panky."[67] Finally, after several days of media coverage and a four-hour closed session, the Conservative Caucus sided with Dirlam and against Lindstrom by a forty-five to twenty vote. The caucus waived any claims to the funds raised at the fall dinner but named a committee to "develop guidelines for the raising and distribution of future funds." At a press conference after the meeting, Dirlam sought "harmony," and Lindstrom was "subdued." Dirlam said he hoped that in the next session the Conservatives would be "less divided than they were today."[68] The Liberals took notes and filed them for possible future use.

Housing

The foundations for many homes as well as for an agency that would become a major player in Minnesota's housing policy were built in the 1971 session. The convergence of federal legislation, an innovative governor, legislators who were willing to listen and learn, excellent staff work, and strong citizen input led to legislation that became the cornerstone for decades of sound policy on housing.

Jim Solem, a talented bureaucrat and a political science professor at the University of Missouri in St. Louis in the 1960s, had served in a variety of governmental policy development positions in Washington, D.C. He also knew Dave Durenberger, then executive secretary to Minnesota's governor Harold LeVander.[69] While in St. Paul working on a program-budgeting training session, Solem stopped in to see Durenberger. Durenberger suggested that Solem consider joining Minnesota's fledgling State Planning Agency. Solem did, and by March 1970, he was putting his knowledge to work for the people of Minnesota.[70]

As a result of the 1970 election, in January 1971 Solem found himself working for the new head of the State Planning Agency, Jerry

Christenson, and a new governor. Solem liked both, and he was directed to pursue establishing a statewide building code and a Housing Finance Agency (HFA) for Minnesota.[71]

Governor Anderson made special mention in his inaugural address of the need for a better housing program in Minnesota.[72] Then, in a special message to the legislature in March—which Solem helped write—the governor detailed his housing proposals and described his views concerning the proper relationship between the federal and state governments in housing policy. In a partial role reversal of the criticisms of state government over many decades, the governor pointed out that "federal programs and private industry are failing to deal effectively with the demand" and called for a "working partnership with the federal government and its housing assistance programs." The governor also discussed the role of the state and of local units of government such as municipalities and the need for a new "regional approach" to provide decent affordable housing for citizens of the state.[73]

This message and the implementation work that followed were not just academic exercises in intergovernmental powers that excite political science professors, they were an example of a state applying political science principles to real problems facing thousands of its citizens. They also were of high interest to people who for a wide variety of nonacademic or governmental reasons were concerned about Minnesota's housing stock. A coalition of builders, developers, community activists, lenders, and union members worked with Solem to make sure that foundations of concrete would actually be built on the existing but shaky foundation of laws, regulations, and policy statements then in existence.

This coalition studied the existing federal laws and regulations, such as Section 701 of the Federal Housing Act of 1954. The coalition then drafted state legislation and got bills introduced for the HFA and the statewide building code. Both Liberals and Conservatives were supportive, and in a rare instance of minority caucus legislators carrying major legislation, the chief authors of the legislation in both the house and the senate were Liberals: Representative Fred Norton and freshman Senator Bob Tennessen.[74] On May 24, the HFA bill passed including $150 million of housing bonding authority.[75] Minnesota thus became one of the first states in the nation to have a state agency solely devoted to housing. The statewide building code also passed.[76] Minnesota now had the tools to properly work with the federal government and begin to build housing that would be well built and affordable.

Electing a Regent

Legislators do many things during a legislative session besides proposing and voting on laws. In Minnesota, one of the most important of these ancillary functions is the election of the Board of Regents of the state's largest higher education institution, the University of Minnesota. Of great importance to the state, this land-grant college, established in 1851, has its main campus in Minneapolis–St. Paul and four coordinate campuses throughout the state. It consistently educates tens of thousands of students and brings hundreds of millions of dollars of research money into the state.

In 1971 there were three open at-large seats on the twelve-member Board of Regents. The legislative election procedures called for the Higher Education Committees of the both the house and the senate to get together and nominate a slate of candidates. The election then takes place in a "joint convention" of the house and senate, in which all members of both bodies crowd into the House Chamber in the capitol. The committees nominated the three incumbents, a woman and two men. All had ties to Conservative Caucus members.

The majority caucuses had not carefully orchestrated this election process, and some of their members were supporting the owner of a local savings and loan, Harold (Hal) Greenwood, instead of one of the candidates on the slate. Greenwood had a connection with Hubert Humphrey and thus had some Liberal support as well. The governor was recommending an African American woman, Josie Johnson, an instructor at the University of Minnesota. The Liberal legislators were strongly supportive of Johnson.

The cumbersome voting procedure specified a roll call vote, during which the clerk of the house called out the names of all 202 legislators, who would then respond orally with their three choices. The top three candidates would win. Votes could be changed as long as the voting process remained open.

A loosely structured "deal" was proposed by a Conservative Caucus senator, Glen McCarty, who wanted to dump one of the incumbents and replace him with Greenwood. The Liberals agreed as long as some of the Conservatives would vote for Johnson. As soon as the slate was proposed, McCarty moved to amend it by dropping one of the incumbents and adding Greenwood. The Liberal legislators voted in support of that motion, and the slate was amended by a vote of 111 to 90.[77] Greenwood was in the house gallery watching the proceedings.

Then the roll call vote started. As the process went on, it became clear that the Conservatives were not delivering their votes to Johnson. The Liberals sensed there was a chance to elect Johnson if enough Liberals switched from Greenwood to Johnson. The word was passed, and the Liberals then started standing up to be recognized by the Speaker and switching their votes from Greenwood to a variety of other candidates but always keeping one vote for Johnson. By the end of this several-hour process, twenty-eight different candidates had received at least one vote, but Johnson kept moving up in the ever-changing tally.[78] Greenwood remained in the gallery watching his presumed victory unravel.

In the confusion, no one was sure who had enough votes to win, except that Minority Leader Sabo had kept a running tally on a scratch pad at his desk. When Sabo's hash marks showed that Johnson was in the top three, Sabo and the Liberals agreed to support a motion to close off the voting and move on to other business. That motion passed, and the clerk tallied the official votes and announced who had won: two incumbents and Johnson. In addition to ninety-seven Liberal votes, three Conservative legislators had ended up voting for Johnson. Greenwood was in fourth place and had lost.[79]

A few minutes later the phone rang in the Johnson household. Regent-elect Johnson was just coming home from watching her daughter act in a school play. The call was from the governor's office telling her she had just been elected to the Board of Regents. For several minutes Johnson refused to believe the news. Once the reality sunk in that she was the first African American to serve as a regent, she was elated and proud.[80]

In reporting on the lengthy and unusual session, the news media described it as "acrimonious," and the Liberal maneuvering as "crafty" and using "effective parliamentary ploys."[81] Sabo, a sports fan, downplayed the political skill involved and simply said, "I'm glad I developed the habit of keeping a running score of basketball games I attend."[82]

Johnson served successfully for two years on the Board of Regents before her husband was transferred to Denver. She went on to receive her doctorate degree, came back to Minnesota, and had a distinguished career as an educator. The University of Minnesota established the Josie R. Johnson Human Rights and Social Justice Award in recognition of her "lifelong contributions to human rights and social justice." It is awarded annually.[83]

It is interesting to note how concerns over conflicts of interest have changed in the intervening forty years since Johnson, who was working as an instructor at the university, became a regent without any question as to real or potential conflicts of interest. In 2011, Steve Sviggum, a former Republican Speaker of the Minnesota House, a teacher, "a legislative fellow" at the university's Humphrey Institute of Public Affairs, and a newly elected regent at the university, was required to choose between being an unpaid regent or a paid "fellow," due to concerns about potential conflicts of interest between the two positions. Sviggum elected to remain a regent and resigned from his paid position at the university.[84]

About eight months later, Regent Sviggum again walked into the conflicts of interest morass. He accepted a well-paid job as an assistant and communications director for the Republican Party Caucus in the Minnesota Senate. Sviggum initially tried to keep both positions but eventually resigned as a regent after legal opinions said the caucus job created an "unreasonable systematic clash of duties."[85]

The Legislative Process

This 1971 session with all its complexities showed that more than four months every other year was needed for the legislative branch to get its job done—at least to get it done in a thoughtful manner and in a way that allowed for significant input from citizens around the state. As a result, the legislature passed an amendment to the state's constitution specifying that the legislature could define by statute what was a "legislative day." This allowed the 120-day constitutional limit on legislative days to remain but would allow the days to be spread out over the two-year term of house members. Thus the legislature could meet annually, instead of every other year as was then the case. In addition, the period between the officially defined "legislative days" could be used for legislative hearings, research, study, and discussion without counting against the limit. If used properly, this procedure could significantly enhance the power of the legislative branch vis-à-vis the executive branch, special interest groups, and all entities with a full-time professional staff. The change would mean more long trips back and forth from their homes for legislators like Kelly, Graba, and their non–metropolitan area colleagues. It also would cut into everyone's nonlegislative work time.

Amending Minnesota's constitution is not easy. The legislature must first approve the change and the exact wording of the ballot question, which then must be put on the general election ballot for the voters of the state. To make it even harder, a majority of voters voting in the election, not just those voting on the ballot question, must approve the change. Thus, if a voter skips the amendment, it effectively counts as a no vote. Despite a historical reluctance of voters to change the machinery of Minnesota's government, the legislature thought it critical to use its two years in a more productive manner to adequately deal with the complex issues arising from a changing society.[86] Accordingly, the legislature sent the following question to the voters to answer in November 1972:

> Shall the Minnesota constitution be amended to alter the manner of determining the length of legislative sessions permitting variations in the times for meetings of the legislature?[87]

The Minnesota voters approved this "flexible session" amendment, and Minnesota's relatively weak legislative branch was given the opportunity to change.[88] How to take advantage of this opportunity would be up to the 1973 session of the legislature.

Reapportionment

The makeup of a new legislative district is one of the most analyzed things in politics. It is carefully studied by incumbent legislators, potential political candidates, lobbyists, political party interests, university political scientists, media analysts, and, since the *Baker v. Carr* decision in 1962, legal scholars. The demographics of a proposed district are reviewed for age, income, ethnicity, percentage of renters, homeowners, small businesses, and anything else the analyzers can think of that might somehow be used to predict a voting pattern. Past voting statistics are usually the number one predictor, and these statistics are sliced and diced in every way imaginable.

Voting for the president or a governor brings out a larger turnout of voters. The political parties have determined that these every-four-years voters are typically less party oriented than the reliable every-two-years voter. The parties have used this fact (and others they think will provide a good reading of how a district is likely to vote) to develop indexes to analyze proposed districts to see if their candidates have a good chance of winning. In the 1970s, this "DFL index" or "Republican index" was usually a simple combination of voters for the party's attorney general and lieutenant governor candidates in previous elections. For example, if the voters had voted in the past two elections for Republican attorney general and lieutenant governor candidates by 55 to 45 percent, the district would commonly be said to have a "55 percent Republican index" or a "45 percent Democratic index." Not precise science but also not just guesswork.

A hard-fought campaign is tough on the participants. Emotions run high, and the time commitments are huge. Strains are put on family relationships, and money is always an issue. As a result, candidates like districts that fit their political philosophy and their style. In political terms, they want a "safe district."

Many political analysts and editorial writers, on the other hand, argue that competitive, or "swing districts," are best for the voters and for good government. They argue that competition results in better candidates and better government. They point to the situation in Massachusetts where, as the *Boston Globe* lamented, "last year [2008], just 17 percent of house races were contested, the lowest rate in the nation." The author explored several reasons for this, including pay and time commitment, and compared the situation to

> the political culture in Minnesota which has the highest rate of contested elections in the nation at a perfect 100 percent.
>
> In some ways Minnesota is a lot like Massachusetts, with a highly educated populace and a history of progressive policies. But people run for office there in a way they do not here, in part because voters have put in place structures to foster competition.[89]

With these arguments and interests very much in play, the 1971 Minnesota Legislature attempted to reapportion itself and Minnesota's eight congressional districts in accordance with the constitutional requirement for one person, one vote, and the just-released 1970 census data. The congressional reapportionment went reasonably well and was signed into law on May 24, 1971.[90] The state legislative reapportionment was another matter.

Minority Leader Sabo described the process as being "as close to bare-knuckle politics as it gets." The process began with Sabo meeting with Schwarzkopf to try and reapportion districts in the city of Minneapolis. Sabo and Schwarzkopf started with District 34 in South Minneapolis. They got absolutely nowhere.[91] The Conservatives controlled the legislature, and they decided to take over the process. On the Liberal side, Governor Anderson and Minority Leaders Sabo and Coleman all privately agreed among themselves that if any one of the three did not like the plan that was proposed, they would all oppose it.[92]

At the end of October, in special session, the legislature passed a legislative reapportionment plan. The media reported that Sabo was "the key to whether a legislative redistricting compromise will be approved this session."[93] Very few house Liberals voted for the plan. Sabo, who "had been a tough bargainer on partisan and tax issues all session," decided he did not like the legislative plan.[94] He and his caucus decided it was worth the gamble to have the legislature try again or toss the legislative reapportionment plan to the courts.[95] In accordance with the earlier agreement with the governor and at the request of Sabo and DFL Party chair, Dick Moe, Anderson vetoed the plan.[96] Anderson said Sabo's request played " a very, very strong role" in his decision to veto the bill.[97] What followed was judicial involvement and the associated inevitable delay and uncertainty.

A reapportionment lawsuit had previously been filed in federal court, and after the veto, activity in the case picked up. A three-judge panel had been appointed to deal with the case. Eighth Circuit Court Judge Gerald Heaney from Duluth, a former Democratic national committeeman, headed the panel. District Judge Earl Larson, a former law partner to former Minnesota Democratic governor Orville Freeman, was on the panel, along with District Judge Edward Devitt, a former Republican member of Congress. On December 3, 1971, the panel surprisingly said it would not only redistrict the legislature, it would sharply reduce the size of the legislature. Under this court order, the senate was to be reduced from 67 to 35 members, and the house reduced from 135 to 105.[98] This caused political chaos and angst to many, particularly in the state senate. Ten days later the senate appealed the ruling to the U.S. Supreme Court.

Four months later, in a very rare Saturday session, the U.S. Supreme Court, paying attention to America's unique federal system, made it crystal clear that federal courts must be very careful in dealing with the states and reapportionment. The court reversed the three-judge panel and said, "We know of no federal constitutional principle or requirement that authorizes a federal reapportionment court to by-pass the State's formal judgment as to the proper size of its legislative bodies." The court concluded:

> the action of the three-judge court in so drastically changing the number of legislative districts and the size of the respective houses of the Minnesota legislature is not required by the Federal constitution and is not justified as an exercise of federal judicial power.

The case was sent back to the three-judge panel for "further proceedings."[99]

During the four months the case was pending at the Supreme Court and during the time the "further proceedings" were taking place before the three-judge panel, politics in Minnesota was chaotic. Incumbent legislators and potential candidates had no idea what the final legislative districts would look like or against whom they might be running. The lines changed so often under the various plans that one legislator joked he was thinking about getting a mobile home "and moving it around until I find out where the lines are going to be."[100] DFL Party chair Moe said that "the elections are going to suffer . . . we can't make preparations to get good candidates or put on a good campaign."[101] On June 2 the three-judge panel redrew the district lines for a legislature with 67 senators and 134 house members. This order was not appealed. Thus, new districts were in place, and both major parties began to gear up for a very contentious 1972 election.[102]

It was not at all clear if Sabo and his caucus had won their gamble in letting the court do the reapportionment. In the northern part of the state, where districts cover a lot of territory, Graba was very disheartened. Under the vetoed plan he had been placed in a district that would likely have been favorable to him. Under the court plan, he retained only a small portion of his 1970 district. The new rural territory included in the court plan held many Republican farmers. The DFL index was a very low 41.2 percent. Graba began to seriously consider not running for reelection.

Both the vetoed plan and the final court plan placed various incumbents in the same district, usually ensuring a tough contest for all. Berg was one of those incumbents, and he was worried. He had been placed in a district with two strong Republican incumbent legislators. One was a four-term incumbent named Humphrey, and one a fellow freshman, Arne Carlson. The district had only a 46.4 percent DFL index.

Ray Faricy had a tough district for a Democrat in 1970 and won by only forty-six votes. The new district looked every bit as tough and had only a 46.2 percent DFL index. Bill Kelly's new district was actually slightly more favorable to him than the district under the vetoed plan, with a 54.5 percent DFL index. Sabo was very comfortable with his new 63 percent DFL index district.[103]

But for better or worse, the playing field was now established. According to a news report analyzing the court plan, "observers said Conservatives should win in 59 to 64 house races and the DFLers in 52 to 54, with 16 to 23 races rated as toss-ups." Republican Party chair David Krogseng was concerned: "it's not as favorable to us as the original plan. There's a tough campaign ahead." DFL Party chair Moe said, "it's our best opportunity in many years to win control of the Legislature."[104] The chaos of reapportionment was over, and the chaos of campaigning was about to begin.

The 1971 session had proven to be a critical and productive one for the Liberal Caucuses and the DFL. Its legislators had been through the longest special session in history. The many new members had learned the legislative ropes well. Sabo and Coleman had honed their skills as leaders of large caucuses. Members had witnessed public policy made and adopted with bipartisan support in the Minnesota Miracle and housing legislation. They had experienced partisan politics in the reapportionment battle and had seen firsthand the angry voters protesting taxes and the emotional issue of abortion. All had learned the importance of a popular governor who had learned how to use the powers of his office effectively. These players wanted very much to gain control of the legislative branch and implement the many changes they thought were necessary to better the legislative process and make Minnesota a better state.

For the Conservative Caucuses and the Republican Party, the session had produced sound legislation, and they had shown some bipartisanship. They could campaign on a record of moving the state forward. But there was clearly a split in the house, where Lindstrom's inflexibility had caused resentment to build. The blatant influence of the business community in the legislature and in the Conservative Caucus in the house had also been publicly exposed. In addition, the Republican Party had no well-known statewide leaders to help, as their top tier lost in the 1970 election.

And America was changing: social mores were becoming more liberal, and the country continued to be split and angry about an increasingly unpopular war. The stage was set for the 1972 election, and the DFL sensed a big opportunity.

CHAPTER 5

A Truly Historic Election

Who are those guys?

▪ *Butch Cassidy and the Sundance Kid*

Taking control of the legislative branch of government from an entrenched party is an extremely difficult task. Ten years after the Young Turks almost succeeded in doing it in Minnesota in 1962, and twenty-two years before Congressman Newt Gingrich and colleagues with their "Contract with America" pulled it off in the U.S. Congress in 1994, the DFL Party set out to make it happen in Minnesota.[1]

To achieve such an elusive goal, many complex moving parts spread across the state have to work. Issues need to be identified and framed, able candidates identified and recruited, a core of campaign workers motivated to give up big chunks of free time over several months, significant money raised and spent wisely, and a common theme developed that will appeal to voters across 201 legislative districts. In addition, a strong "get out the vote" effort for loyal supporters during the days just before election day is necessary. The DFL thought it had all this in place by the fall of 1972, when both the house and the senate were up for election.

Leadership was crucial, and the DFL had a strong leadership team. Minnesota had two popular U.S. senators, Walter Mondale and Hubert Humphrey, who could help. Mondale was up for reelection in 1972, so he was already out working the state hard and could easily put in a word for the legislative candidates. Humphrey had a group of experienced and talented people from his failed presidential campaign who wanted a victory. The governor, in midterm, was willing to work very hard to achieve a majority of friendly legislators to implement his agenda. Attorney General Warren Spannaus was well liked in party circles from his days as party chair, and Lieutenant

Governor Rudy Perpich was a leader on northern Minnesota's liberal Iron Range. The caucus leaders, Martin Sabo and Nick Coleman, were experienced and aggressive, and the caucus had a solid cadre of candidates ready to go.

But there were also problems. There was a big split in the party. Senator George McGovern had defeated Humphrey for the presidential nomination, and hard feelings remained. There was a definite and public split between the liberal and moderate wings of the party. As the fall wore on, it was clear that the McGovern–Shriver ticket was not doing very well in Minnesota or nationally against Nixon–Agnew.[2]

The DFL Party chair, Dick Moe, had his hands full trying to heal the party split while at the same time coordinating the many moving parts in the effort to gain control of the legislature and help the presidential campaign. In the Fifth Congressional District (Minneapolis), there was an active group that called itself the DFL Gay Rights Caucus. This group attacked Humphrey, Mondale, Congressman Donald Fraser, and Tom Berg, calling them "sexual bigots" and claiming they had not done enough publicly to support gay rights.[3] At the June 1972 state DFL convention in Rochester, which elected delegates to the Democratic National Convention, Humphrey barely got a majority of the delegates (thirty-three out of sixty-four) from his home state.[4] The liberal wing of the party clearly tended toward McGovern.

The liberal convention delegates focused extensively, vocally, and visually (five hundred lavender armbands had been passed out by the Gay Rights Caucus and were being worn by the delegates) on social issues such as legalization of marijuana, gay rights, amnesty for draft evaders, and other non-bread-and-butter DFL issues.[5] Moe described the convention as "out of control." Dave Roe, president of the Minnesota AFL-CIO, used more colorful language, describing the party platform adopted by the delegates as "the platform of grass, ass, and amnesty."[6]

The actual workings on the convention floor that led to the platform were described by delegate Allan Spear (who would later go on to become a state senator and president of the senate) as follows:

But by Sunday, the Humphrey delegates, many of whom lived in northern and western Minnesota left early for the long drive home. In the last hours of the convention, three

planks were approved that represented everything the conservative Democrats feared: legalization of marijuana; un-
conditional amnesty for draft evaders; and full rights for gay
people. Including the right to marry. . . . The gay rights plank
passed right before the required time for adjournment. . . . I
[urged] people not to speak so we could come to a vote before the final gavel came down. We just made it.[7]

Moe and the associate chair, Ruth Cain, were so worried about the
party's image coming out of the convention that they issued a press
release saying they were "very disappointed" about how the convention had conducted its business. The release attempted to get the
focus back on issues Moe and Cain thought would play better with
the voters. The party leaders said,

No one should conclude from this misordering of priorities that the DFL . . . is any less concerned than it has ever
been about those problems which affect the vast majority of
Minnesotans. . . .
    It has always been and still is our intention to run our leg-
islative campaigns on a program calling for major reform of
our state's tax structure . . . equal educational opportunities . . .
more job opportunities in both the urban and rural areas,
tough environmental and consumer measures and reform of
the legislature itself.[8]

The release concluded that the DFL Party had a responsibility to place
these issues on the top of the priority list and stated that "we intend
to meet that responsibility."[9] Even Governor Anderson, the DFL's
top state official, risked the ire of the party's activist delegates and
disavowed the platform.[10]
    This very public schism between the convention delegates and
the candidates illustrates a tension often present in politics between
party activists, who write a party platform document, and candidates, who have to earn support and votes not only from those activists but also from less active and often skeptical voters who espouse
a broad spectrum of political views. The thirty-one-page platform
document acknowledged the tension but then went on to say that
the candidates should follow the delegates' position:

We [the delegates] recognize that public officials often have conflicting claims from constituents, from party and from conscience. All three cannot always be served; that is the dilemma inherent in representative government. . . .

Nonetheless, we adopt this platform in the expectation that those who carry our endorsement will support it.[11]

The frustrations in dealing with this tension would prove to be challenging for all. In general, the elected officials simply ignored the platform specifics and campaigned on issues they thought fit the interests and needs of their constituents.

Early in 1972, the DFL Party decided that the emphasis in the election should be on the house and senate legislative races. The party knew that getting party designation on legislative ballots would be of significant long-term help in the then Democratic-leaning state. Moe said the party recognized early on "the conundrum that we couldn't get party designation on the ballot without control of the legislature, and we couldn't get control of the legislature without party designation."[12]

Campaigns need strong candidates, and starting in the winter of 1972 and continuing through the summer, Moe talked several times a week with Minority Leaders Sabo and Coleman and Tom Kelm from the governor's staff to identify and recruit DFL candidates for the legislature. Slowly but surely the list of good candidates grew. The goal was to field a candidate in every district. There was no caucus staff at the time, so all activity went through the DFL Party. The party had an office, equipment, and a small field staff to help recruit and organize. But it was spread thin, and most of the nitty-gritty campaign work was done by the local candidates and their committees.

After Humphrey lost his bid for the presidency to McGovern in the summer of 1972, Humphrey and the DFL leadership realized the campaign still had an important asset that could be deployed in the effort to gain control of the legislature. Humphrey had a group of over thirty bright and dedicated students from various colleges in Minnesota who had worked throughout the country on his campaign. Bill McGrann, a top aide to Humphrey, had worked with this group of "kids" on political matters for over a year, and knew them and their political talents very well. McGrann, Kelm, Mike Berman (a key aide to Senator Mondale), Moe, Sabo, and Coleman decided the students should be deployed to help coordinate the many legislative campaigns. Money was raised, and each student was assigned two or three campaigns to coordinate and report regularly to McGrann. They performed well and played a significant and unheralded role in getting a DFL majority.[13]

Money was always a problem, as neither the DFL Party nor the Liberal Caucus had very much. Candidates were generally on their own to raise the needed funds for campaign materials and advertising. By current standards campaigns were cheap— $3,000 to $6,000 was the usual range—but that was a daunting amount at the time to most potential candidates. Sabo had a steering committee of about twelve caucus leaders and veterans who set priorities and doled out the $100 to $1,000 checks to candidates who had a realistic chance to win and who needed the funds.[14]

Sabo also had a strong and close relationship with the Minnesota AFL-CIO, led by its president, David Roe. The AFL-CIO and other labor unions would screen candidates and ask them to fill out a questionnaire expressing their views on a variety of topics important to organized labor. The unions would then endorse the candidates they liked and send them a financial contribution. Contributions were generally $200 or less. Sabo was well aware of the problems that had dogged the Good Government Committee and the Conservative Caucus for being too closely aligned, and he made sure the Liberal Caucus maintained its independence.[15]

In every election, many groups besides labor unions send questionnaires to candidates. The groups want to identify their legislative supporters and pin down the candidates. Some groups issue endorsements of candidates, and some, like labor, make financial contributions to the campaign. The questionnaires often make candidates and their campaign chairs very nervous. Questions on emotional and volatile issues such as gun control and abortion are particularly troublesome. In most cases, complex issues are boiled down into simple questions with no room for nuanced answers.[16] Some candidates simply refuse to answer all questionnaires, and others selectively respond. But candidates need support, and thus most answer at least some questionnaires. Candidates do their best to indicate support or opposition to an issue while keeping options open on specific questions until they have heard testimony at legislative hearings or studied an issue in more detail. No less than David Plouffe,

President Obama's campaign chair, said the Obama campaign got "boxed in" by a questionnaire in November 2007 from the Midwest Democracy Network. The Obama campaign had responded that it would give up private financing to take public money. When they later flip-flopped in the crucial issue and turned down public financing, Plouffe said, "We should have just said we would retain it as an option, which is what we really thought. Some kid screwed up a frickin' questionnaire. . . . I was furious that we filled out the damn questionnaire. . . . But that's campaigns."[17]

Grover Norquist, president of Americans for Tax Reform, has now taken the single-issue questionnaire concept to new heights. His organization asks that federal and state candidates sign a written pledge (with a copy sent to national headquarters so signers names can be posted on a Web site) stating that if elected, the candidate will "oppose and vote against any and all efforts to increase taxes." No exceptions are allowed.[18] As shown by the debt ceiling discussion at the federal level and the 2011 state government shutdown in Minnesota (see chapter 7), the effect on government of this pledge has been profound. A full-scale debate over "How prudent is it to take an irrevocable pledge about how to govern before one begins the actual work of governing?" is under way. Former Utah governor and presidential candidate Jon Huntsman found the answer to the question to be easy: "I don't sign pledges other than the Pledge of Allegiance and a pledge to my wife."[19]

In the brainstorming sessions held by the DFL leadership before the campaign, a key theme emerged relating to the legislative process. The theme took advantage of the 1971 amendments to the Permanent Rules of the legislature that had been proposed by the Liberal Caucuses.[20] Sabo felt that a part of what was needed to bring about what some were calling "legislative reform" was simply fair treatment for legislative minority caucus members. He knew from years of firsthand experience how frustrating it is to be an elected representative and be thwarted by not being able to be heard because of a procedural rule. The governor in his legislative days and Coleman as minority leader had also suffered under what they felt were unfair and oppressive Conservative Caucus rules. All thought this could be made into a winning political issue, particularly if connected to an allegation of excess influence of special business interests on the

Conservative Caucus and the need to open the process to more public scrutiny. The publicity from the 1971 session concerning the powerful Good Government Committee provided the DFL with strong evidence to support the allegation.

A multicolored brochure was created showing a drawing of the state capitol with padlocked doors. A big key was superimposed over the capitol with the words: "Your vote will turn the key! Open State Government to the people. Elect a DFL legislature in 1972." The fact that every Conservative Caucus member had voted against the Liberal's proposed rule changes in 1971 for recorded votes, tape recording of the sessions, and financial disclosure was highlighted. Two hundred thousand copies of this brochure were distributed by the DFL Party to its candidates. It was used extensively throughout the state. This theme was then developed further by various campaigns into slogans such as " no secrecy in government," "let the sunshine in," "legislative reform," and "openness in government."[21]

This theme was soon getting enough traction with voters that the Conservatives and Republicans thought they needed to respond. John Johnson, an assistant house Conservative Caucus leader, called the DFL rule amendment for open committee meetings "a double-talk meaningless amendment.... It was out and out deception." Republican Party chair David Krogseng said the secrecy issue was "a phony issue" and that "90 percent of the committees have been open." He went on to attack DFL Governor Anderson as having a "secret fund" used for "undisclosed purposes."[22] The DFL candidates ignored the counterattacks and continued to hammer away at the secrecy in government issues.

As part of the party's coordinating role, the DFL also prepared "sample ballots" to be distributed in each legislative district showing all the DFL candidates on the ballot that year. The Republican Party also sent out sample ballots to its voters. In an effort to make sure voters did not just vote for the more well-known candidates, like the presidential candidate McGovern or Senate candidate Mondale, and then skip most of the rest of the ballot, the DFL sample ballot in 1972 was significantly changed; it now had no pictures, except for a prominent picture of the state legislative candidates. This effort to reduce what campaign people call "voter fall off" was helpful.[23]

While the DFL dealt with its "out-of-control" convention in the summer, the Conservative Caucus was also having its problems. The public split over the role of business special-interest groups and the Good Government Committee continued to bedevil election coordinating efforts. Al France, an important legislator in the late 1960s, had served as the chief coordinator of legislative campaigns for the Republican Party. This role, as reported in the news media,

> brought him into indirect conflict with . . . [Majority Leader] Ernest Lindstrom. As a result of their private struggle, the embattled house Conservative caucus—already divided by the months-long feud between factions led by Lindstrom and Speaker Aubrey Dirlam—has encountered further obstacles to its 1972 campaign.
>
> Furthermore, Lindstrom's efforts to dislodge France from his party position have embroiled Republican Chairman David Krogseng in the caucus leader's campaign to curtail the influence of special interests on the house power structure.[24]

Thus, both parties were engaged in damage control while at the same time recruiting candidates and getting over two hundred individual campaigns started across the state.

As election day drew close, some of Minnesota's top business leaders were worried that the DFL might gain control of the legislature, particularly in the senate, where business interests had long wielded strong influence. Telegrams were sent on behalf of the chair of the board of 3M Company and Honeywell Inc., inviting top business leaders to an October meeting at the venerable Minneapolis Club. According to news accounts, about twenty-five "bankers, industrialists, and co-op executives" participated in the breakfast meeting. The Republican finance chair, John Pierson, and Conservative Senator George Pillsbury were also in attendance. The vice president of Northwest Bancorporation, who arranged the meeting, said no campaign funds were solicited but acknowledged that "contributions to Conservative candidates were understood to be desirable."[25] Meanwhile, the DFL candidates just kept on campaigning against "secrecy in government" and a variety of local issues.

In all campaigns the coordinating party apparatus can only do so much. The rest is up to the candidates and their campaign workers in the field. What makes election nights so exciting is that after months of slugging it out with an opponent at candidate forums and debates, enduring hours of travel, sitting through numerous campaign planning sessions and coffee parties, making fund-raising requests and handling rejections, placing hundreds of phone calls, and knocking on thousands of doors, a candidate never really knows for sure whether those efforts will translate into votes. When election night finally comes, the results pour in and suddenly it is over—usually in a matter of hours. Tears and cheers are frequent at that moment.

The values and political thoughts of the occupants of the farms and small towns near Wadena in north-central Minnesota were well known to Joe Graba, but he did not know the people in his new legislative district, and they did not know him. The federal court's reapportionment plan had left him with only three townships from the district he had won in 1970. All the rest were new territory with new voters.

Townships are common in the Midwest. Townships are typically a thirty-six-square-mile area used as a basic unit of government in rural areas. In the area where Graba lived, each township held 120 farms, give or take a few. There were thirty-nine townships in Graba's new district. In 1970, Graba had convinced fifteen to twenty farmers from his own township to go visit other farmers from neighboring townships to seek their support for his campaign. Often the campaigning farmers would bring their wives and make a daylong outing of their civic endeavor. The bedrock of his campaign had been this "farm-to-farm" effort, and it had earned Graba a victory in 1970 with 61 percent of the vote. It was obviously a time-consuming but successful way to campaign.

In late June 1972, after some serious review of the new legislative district boundaries, Graba called a meeting with his brothers and a number of longtime farmer friends and campaign leaders of the 1970 farm-to-farm campaign. Graba led off the discussion concerning the prospects of another campaign in the new Republican-leaning district. Roger Tellock, one of the farmers who had played a key role in the 1970 effort, looked at Graba and not so subtly told his friend to stop feeling sorry for himself and get on with it. Tellock said, "Look, it was all new territory last time. We'll just have to do it again." Then he teasingly told Graba, "Joe, you stay home, we do better when you aren't there." Graba got the message. He smiled, thanked his friend for the sound advice, and said he would run. The farmers got the pickup trucks up and running again, and the farmers and their wives were soon talking, drinking coffee, and campaigning hard in the new townships the campaign had inherited thanks to redistricting.

During the campaign, the DFL Party, Humphrey, and Mondale all offered to help Graba. Fearful of a backlash in the Republican district, Graba reluctantly turned down the offers. But Graba did use the DFL theme of openness. His campaign brochures asked: "Do You Know What Is Happening in State Government? Do you know that some Legislative Committees are not open to the public? . . . Joe Graba is working to change these procedures." This issue was effective with the farmers, who were always suspicious of what went on in the capitol in faraway downtown St. Paul.[26]

While Graba would later become the dean of the School of Education at Hamline University in St. Paul, he always retained the ability to talk the farm talk. When describing his 1972 campaign, he said, "We darn near drove the wheels right off those pickups." It all worked and worked well, as Graba again won big with 64 percent of the vote.[27]

In urban St. Paul, Ray Faricy's Republican opponent was a woman. As we have seen, women candidates were rare at the time. No one was sure just how to deal with the gender factor or how it would play out in the moderately conservative district. However, all knew it had the potential to be very tricky. Both Faricy and his opponent were opposed to legalization of abortion (pro-life in political vernacular), so that reduced the potential volatility on one issue that had special meaning for women.

Faricy generally campaigned no differently than he had two years earlier. Night after night, week after week, he would come home from work, grab a quick bite to eat, and head out the door. He worked hard at his traditional shoe-leather campaign of ringing doorbells, handing out his campaign materials, and asking for support from every dwelling unit in his district. When he received a favorable response, he asked for permission to put a small campaign lawn sign in the yard. Computers were not then a campaign staple, and Faricy had a three-by-five-inch note card for every dwelling he visited with the occupant's name and other information regarding issues important to the occupant. This was time consuming and led to a few dropped cards on doorsteps and street corners, but had proven to be effective in 1970.

Faricy did hold one meeting just on the gender issue with a group of DFL-leaning women from his district. He listened to stories about various forms of discrimination the women had endured. One issue in particular stood out, the inability of women to get credit in their own names. Credit would be issued only in the names of a husband or a father. Faricy told the group he would author legislation to end this practice. The meeting broke up with no promises of support, but Faricy came away thinking the meeting had gone well, and he detected no evidence of voting solely on the basis of gender.[28]

Faricy had voted against the Minnesota Miracle legislation and had a developing reputation as being an independent thinker. He used this vote as a talking point to support his independent approach in the Republican-leaning district.

Faricy did have one bastion of liberalism located in his district. Macalester College is a liberal arts college whose students and faculty make up almost an entire precinct in the district. Faricy was well aware of the college and, with the voting age now eighteen, its potential for new voters. In the late 1960s, he and two other lawyers had tried to help students establish residency on campus for voting purposes.

By 1972, Macalester was known as a school with a very liberal student body. The college had already implemented the more liberal living arrangements that were then becoming popular on America's college campuses: dormitories were no longer segregated by sex. Protests over the Vietnam War and other issues were common on and around the campus. Faricy campaigned door-to-door in the dorms as an incumbent member of the Liberal Caucus. This led to several interesting experiences for the then thirty-seven-year-old candidate. For example, Faricy repeatedly detected certain pungent fumes escaping from under the closed doors of some of the students' rooms. When he knocked on the door, he would sometimes hear sounds of scurrying around from behind the closed door, and then when the door slowly opened, smoke drifted out, but no cigarettes were seen. Faricy said that he would ask the occupants for their vote and leave. When asked in an interview, he said he never inhaled when he entered such rooms.[29] Faricy ended up winning big in that precinct and with 54 percent of the vote in the entire district.[30]

Across the Mississippi River in Minneapolis, Tom Berg had to begin his campaign by first fending off a challenge from within the

DFL Party from the new Gay Rights Caucus, which ran a candidate against him. This was the same group that had attacked Mondale, Humphrey, and Fraser and was involved at the state DFL convention in Rochester described earlier. Berg had always been a strong proponent of human and civil rights for all, and he felt he was being unfairly criticized. In fact, he had coauthored very controversial legislation carried by Young Turk Gary Flakne to amend the state's human rights law to prohibit discrimination based on sexual preference. However, the legislation never even made it out of committee. Berg won endorsement at his legislative district convention on the first ballot, 122 to 26.[31] Berg quickly moved to mend fences with the Gay Rights Caucus and continued to push for gay rights.

The multiple incumbent situation in the district was then clarified when Conservative Caucus freshman Arne Carlson moved to a district farther south in Minneapolis. However, this still left Berg facing a well-liked four-term Conservative Caucus incumbent. Berg ran a shoe-leather campaign like Faricy, and used the openness theme extensively. His opponent had voted against the rule changes proposed by the Liberals in 1971, and Berg described these votes at every coffee party and candidate forum. Berg also targeted the new eighteen-to-twenty-year-old voters who lived in the large number of apartment buildings in his district. He had sponsored legislation providing tenants with more rights in dealing with landlord-tenant disputes, and he trumpeted this issue in a large part of his district.

Even more important to Berg's campaign was an issue related to highway building and transportation. These topics were important at the time as the increasing number of metropolitan legislators sought more money for transit and opposed the new multilane freeways tearing up neighborhoods in their districts. The highway department had proposed to build new Interstate 394 through Berg's legislative district. Berg and his Liberal senate colleague Bob Tennessen both vigorously opposed the proposal. Both supported more mass transit.

Berg had even unsuccessfully tried to delete protected funding for highways from the state's constitution so that some of the funding could be used for mass transit. In the hearing on his bill, Berg learned the hard way about the need to talk to committee members about a bill before a hearing, and about the power of a committee chair. In the middle of the hearing, the chair of the Transportation Committee unceremoniously announced that Berg's proposed legislation contained a "revolutionary" concept, and killed the bill with a quick vote of the chair's supporters on the committee—leaving Berg sputtering at the podium with witnesses at his side still trying to explain his bill.[32] Berg tried to salvage something from his embarrassing performance by using the story in his campaign. He said it illustrated arrogance on the part of the Conservative majority.

In contrast to Berg's position on the freeway, his election opponent had authored legislation to authorize the new freeway. When Berg repeatedly made the differing positions on the freeway and highway funding a campaign issue, his opponent, on the eve of the election, wrote and distributed a rather strange open letter to the voters. The letter claimed that "one of the best ways to defeat legislation is to be its chief author." This argument did not sell, and Berg won comfortably with 58 percent of the vote.[33]

In Minnesota's Red River Valley region in northwestern Minnesota, Bill Kelly also campaigned hard. His opponent was both a farmer and a teacher, and had been a popular high school football coach in the area. Kelly beat him two years earlier by only four hundred votes, and his opponent had high name recognition. As often happens in legislative campaigns, geographical or neighborhood rivalries threaten to take interest away from the more general governmental policy issues. Kelly felt this was happening in his race. There were two main cities in the district, Crookston (population 8,312) and East Grand Forks (population 7,607), and Kelly was from East Grand Forks, and his opponent from Crookston. Kelly thought issues such as funding for education worked in his favor, and he worked closely with the Liberal senator from the district, Roger Moe, who was from Crookston, to get the voters to forget about geography and focus on public policy matters.

Kelly also had school-based contacts, as he had taught high school in the area for several years. Many of his students had gone on to college in the district, and many of his former students were instrumental in a strong get-out-the-vote effort, as well as in securing absentee votes for Kelly. As was shown in the 2008 U.S. Senate race in Minnesota between Al Franken and Norm Coleman and its recount, candidates at all levels are well advised to pay attention to absentee voters.[34]

Kelly, a Catholic, also had to deal with a religious undercurrent in the predominantly Lutheran district. His opponent attended a large and well-known Lutheran church. Kelly generally ignored the religion issue as he struggled to keep voters' attention on funding education and reforms to promote "openness in government." Kelly credits his campaign manager and salesman friend Bob Campbell for helping him effectively talk with voters by first "finding the handle" with a personal subject before moving on to the political issues that Kelly loved to talk about.

Kelly started his door-knocking campaign in the two cities in his district. After knocking on almost every door in these cities, he shifted to driving to the large farms that populated the flat and fertile valley, where wheat, sugar beets, and potatoes grow well. Kelly had a group of prominent and successful farmers on his team, and he used their names extensively to try and counteract his opponent's farm background.[35] Kelly, like Martin Olav Sabo a few years earlier, learned that a name and heritage can be meaningful in campaigns. So Kelly, the Irish Catholic, now used his middle name in his campaign materials. On election night, William Nelson Kelly won with 54 percent of the vote.[36]

Meanwhile, Sabo door-knocked his way to a 79 percent victory. He had not, however, been coasting. In addition to his time-consuming caucus coordinating duties, he had been working hard to elect a young University of Minnesota professor named Alan Spear to the senate and helping other house candidates throughout the state.[37]

Most nonstatewide candidates hold their own election night gatherings in their districts with friends and campaign workers. Campaign workers often call in the results from local precincts and then join the campaign event. In the Minneapolis–St. Paul area, once the outcome of their own race is known, many of the candidates and their supporters move on to the statewide election party, usually held in a downtown hotel.

On election night, Minority Leaders Sabo and Coleman, DFL Party chair Moe, and other DFL officials gathered at the Leamington Hotel in downtown Minneapolis to nervously await the returns. Governor Anderson, Senators Humphrey and Mondale, as well as representatives from all the major news media were present. Hopes were high, but these political veterans had all experienced the emotional ups and downs of politics before, and they were cautious. They noted with concern that presidential candidate McGovern was not faring well.

The real action, however, was in the legislative races. Berg and Faricy were among those who migrated to the crowded and noisy party at the Leamington after their own races were safely in the win column. On the TV screens at the Leamington, it became clear that Nixon was winning big. But it was also clear that Senator Mondale had been reelected, as had all eight of the state's members of Congress. Berg and Faricy were eager to see how their colleagues were doing and whether all the hard work would pay off with a legislative majority for their Liberal Caucus. There was extensive talk of whether Nixon or Mondale had the longest coattails.

One thing soon became clear: women candidates were making their mark. There had been a record forty-three women campaigning for legislative seats that year, and twelve had lost in a primary. Of the remaining thirty-one, six won senate legislative seats—four Liberals and two Conservatives. Helen McMillan, the only nonmetropolitan area woman candidate to win, credited the Minnesota Women's Political Caucus for recruiting the record number of female candidates. Five more women were elected to the house: Phyllis Kahn, who in 2011–12 is serving her twentieth term; Linda Berglin, who served a combined thirty-eight years in the house and senate before retiring in 2011; Joan Growe, who became Minnesota's secretary of state in 1974 and the DFL's candidate for the U.S. Senate in 1984; and Conservative Caucus members Mary Forsythe and Ernee McArthur.[38]

The 1972 election also increased racial diversity in the Minnesota Legislature. Two new suburban legislators were the first two African American members in the twentieth century: Ray Pleasant, a Conservative, was elected to the house from Bloomington, and B. Robert Lewis, a Liberal, was elected to the senate from St. Louis Park.[39]

Another fact that became clear was that voter turnout was high. Minnesota frequently leads the nation in the percentage of eligible voters who actually vote, and it appeared this would again hold true. Thanks to the Twenty-Sixth Amendment to the Constitution, this was the first time eighteen-to-twenty-year-olds could vote. With the Vietnam War and social issues being a big part of the national debate, it appeared this age group had joined other Minnesotans in voting heavily.[40]

The earliest returns were from the Twin Cities metropolitan area. They showed solid DFL voting in the legislative races. What this voting meant for control of the legislature first became clear in the senate. Four Conservative incumbents lost, and only two Liberal incumbents lost. By midnight it was certain that Coleman would be the leader of a new Liberal majority caucus. In the house, the Liberals also had a solid lead. As more returns came in and the scope of the DFL victory became known, the celebrating exploded. The band played "Happy Days Are Here Again," Humphrey, Mondale, and Governor Anderson each gave stem-winding speeches, and Sabo and Coleman were introduced as majority leaders. Moe kept pushing legislators on to the stage to be introduced to much cheering from all in attendance.

The next day's paper reported that the DFL was assured of controlling the senate, with three seats yet undecided. The paper also reported that "unofficial and incomplete returns . . . indicate that the DFL has a strong lead in the contest for control of the house, with its candidates leading in 70 of the 134 races."[41] It also reported that Sabo would likely be elected the next Speaker of the house at the first caucus meeting.[42] The fact that the DFL would control the house, the senate, and the governorship for the first time in the state's history was lost on no one. The McGovern loss had been expected and was quickly put aside in the euphoria of the moment. The DFL leads more than held up: the final house tally was seventy-seven Liberals and fifty-seven Conservatives, and the senate's was thirty-seven Liberals and thirty Conservatives.[43]

An analysis of the election results showed that the voters had sent a younger, less experienced, and more diverse group of legislators to St. Paul. There were thirty freshman elected in the house. Four of those freshman were still students at various schools in Minnesota, were in their early twenties, were Liberals, and had defeated veteran Conservative Caucus legislators.[44] The median age in the house would drop from forty-seven in 1963 to forty-one in the upcoming 1973 session. There was simply "a major generational turnover in the house." Not surprisingly, the level of experience in the house dropped along with the age. Experience went from an average of eight years or four terms in the 1971 session to slightly over seven years or three terms for the 1973 session. The experience drop in the senate was even more pronounced. Experience there fell from five-plus years to barely three years over the same time period.[45]

This change in experience was significant. Contrary to the "How Hard Can It Be?" 2008 campaign slogan used by Kinky Friedman, a country songwriter and colorful independent candidate for governor in Texas, good legislating is very difficult.[46] As we saw with the Minnesota Miracle legislation, effective legislating takes a certain combination of street savvy, wisdom, and hard work. When to persevere and when to compromise is one of the most difficult decisions a legislator must make. Majority Leader Lindstrom refused to compromise, while Majority Leader Holmquist, Governor Anderson, and Minority Leaders Sabo and Coleman did. The result was legislation that most people agree was good for Minnesota. Personal relationships, like the bipartisan kind between Governor Anderson and Majority Leader Holmquist, and the partisan kind, developing between Sabo, Kelly, Berg, Faricy, and Graba, take time to develop and often play a key role in creating and passing major legislation. A legislative body needs both experience and fresh ideas. The demographic changes buried in the election returns unfolding on the festive November night would cause Sabo and Coleman to think hard about committee chairmanships and caucus leaders within their relatively young and inexperienced caucuses.[47]

The analysis of the election returns also showed that the voters accepted the significant tax increases used to reduce disparities between school districts and to reduce property taxes. Of the seventy-seven legislators in the house that voted for the Minnesota Miracle legislation, fifty-nine ran for reelection, and of those fifty-nine, fifty-three, or 89.8 percent, were reelected. Of the fifty-eight legislators in the house that voted no, forty-nine ran for reelection and of those forty-nine, thirty-nine, or 79.6 percent, were reelected.[48]

The contrast between the Minnesota Miracle's public debate, bipartisan legislative vote, and public reaction and today's simplistic antitax attitude is stark. In the four-decade interval since those "miraculous" actions, a large portion of the voting public has lost faith in all political leaders and will not even listen to, much less discuss, how to pay for schools, parks, or wars.[49] As shown by the shutdown of state government in 2011 in Minnesota (see chapter 7), the "no new taxes" mantra is the easy way out, and many are taking it. The state legislatures and Congress must find a way with governors and the president to present and discuss both the expense (budget cutting) and the revenue (taxing) side of government budgets. If this discussion does not occur and economic and fiscal policy is not adapted to the changing world economy, domestic gridlock and economic stagnation for the lower and middle classes will continue or worsen, the country's debt to foreign nations will likely continue to grow, and other appropriate issues for government such as public health, environmental protection, education, and public safety will suffer.

Now that the Liberals finally had control, one of the first decisions Sabo needed to make was whether to run for majority leader or for Speaker. Despite his early reluctance to jump into the floor debate as a legislator, Sabo had come to enjoy the give-and-take of "life on the floor" and worried that he would miss it if he were presiding from the Speaker's rostrum. Sabo called an earlier Speaker, the Conservative Lloyd Duxbury, and asked for advice. True to form, the colorful "Dux" gave the advice quickly and succinctly: "You dumb son of a bitch, of course you should be Speaker." Sabo smiled at Dux's phrasing and thought, "Well, I did ask for the advice." The thirty-four-year-old Sabo mulled it over, and on November 10, 1972, announced he would be a candidate for Speaker of the house for the 1973–74 sessions of the legislature. Since the Liberals now had the majority, their November 25 caucus decision would control. No opposition was expected.[50]

Not only would life be changed for Sabo, it would also be very different for the Conservatives. As Republican Party chair David Krogseng put it, the loss of both houses was the "biggest disappointment of the election." He went on to note that the Conservatives would have to "assume the role of watchdogs the next two years."[51] Dirlam had survived a tough race, and Lindstrom had won reelection. But their special power as caucus leaders was gone. Carlson and Flakne and many Young Turks returned, but Lyall Schwarzkopf did not, as he had accepted an appointment to a position in Minneapolis city government and did not run. Most of the fifty-seven Conservatives would now see legislative life through a minority caucus lens for the first time.[52]

For the DFL, the openness themes had found a responsive electorate. The recruited candidates had creatively used this theme, while keeping the focus on the ever-critical local issues. Humphrey, Mondale, Anderson, and the other statewide candidates had stumped hard for the legislators. The money raised had been sufficient, and the campaign staffs of the DFL and in the victorious campaigns had performed well, even in the face of the loss of the presidency to Nixon. But now would come the real test: could the DFL legislators and the DFL governor, who would control both the executive branch and the legislative branch for the first time in the state's history, use this power to run their state in the manner contemplated by the Constitution in 1787 and expected by the voters who sent them to their state capitol 185 years later?

CHAPTER 6

Breakout Session

More important than winning the election is
governing . . . that is the test of a political party—
the acid, final test.

- Adlai Stevenson, 1952

"The newly elected DFL legislators 'are going to get an education' in the 1973 session. These young idealists are going to be frustrated. . . . They have a lot of new ideas and there isn't going to be any money to finance them."[1] The prediction was made by the retiring senate majority leader, Stanley Holmquist. The description of life for the new minority Conservative Caucus legislators (soon to be officially known as Republicans, with the passage of party designation for legislative elections) from outgoing Speaker of the House Aubrey Dirlam was more graphic: "Life in the minority is like relieving yourself in the wind and having it all blown back in your face."[2] Thus, the old guard handed over power and authority and painfully dealt with their defeat as the historic sixty-eighth session of the Minnesota Legislature began.

In fact, frustration was far from the minds of the DFL legislators as they elected Martin Sabo as Speaker of the house and Nick Coleman as senate majority leader. To replace Sabo as caucus leader, the DFL unanimously elected Irv Anderson, a naval aviator in World War II and a five-term legislator who worked as a quality-control inspector in a paper mill in the far north reaches of Minnesota. Anderson's district was the largest in terms of land area in Minnesota. It contained miles of wilderness area, many lakes, trees, moose, bear, and wolves, the city of International Falls (population 6,439), and a few towns.

On the Republican side of things, there were more signs of change. The outgoing majority leader, Ernie Lindstrom, announced he would not run for minority leader but would lead a personal crusade against what he called domination of the Minnesota Legislature by "certain powerful interest groups." His list included railroads, liquor, and mining industries. He also wanted to reduce the power of committee chairs and of the Speaker of the house. According to press reports, Lindstrom's actions "could hamper political unity of the conservatives."[3] Dirlam was elected minority leader.

Most of the DFL legislators were champing at the bit to get going since they had bills they wanted to pass and pass quickly. The liberal special-interest groups that had been shut out by the Conservatives for many years kept feeding the legislative urge to act quickly. Expectations were high on the part of many as new leadership took over and the legislature moved from right to left on the political spectrum.

Changing Procedures

With much public fanfare, the new majority began their efforts in earnest on January 2, 1973. They got off to a fast start. After Republican Secretary of State Arlen Erdahl called the house to order in accordance with the state constitution, Sabo was formally elected Speaker, legislation was passed by the house to implement the flexible-session amendment to allow the legislature to spread its 120-day limit over two years, and Senator Hubert Humphrey, who was in town to see his son, Hubert H. Humphrey III, be sworn in as a newly elected state senator, addressed the house. The next day, a happy Governor Anderson delivered his State of the State message to a joint session of the house and the senate.[4]

After the governor's address, Irv Anderson, as majority leader and chair of the Rules Committee, stood up and moved adoption of the proposed rules. He was recognized by Speaker Sabo and explained the new proposals. They included the DFL campaign promises of recording legislative debate, recording more votes on the floor of the house, and allowing minority caucus representation on the powerful Rules Committee. The proposed rules also opened all committees, including the Rules Committee, to the public.

The Republicans, trying to make political points as the DFLers had done two years earlier, offered amendments to the proposed rules to provide even more changes, such as written texts of the floor debates and provisions limiting the power of committee chairs.

The Republicans did not follow Sabo's idea of limiting the number of amendments but instead used the shotgun approach and offered more than a dozen amendments. The DFL argued against the proposals as being politically motivated and voted them down.[5] When the rules that govern conference committees (these committees consist of both house and senate members and attempt to reconcile differences between house and senate versions of the same legislation) were adopted later in the session, the DFL also opened these committees to the public.[6]

The DFL promptly made other changes to the legislative process as well. Sabo informed Dirlam of the committees that would be formed, and invited Dirlam to select the minority caucus members for those committees. Dirlam did, and Sabo accepted the choices. However, there was an issue concerning the Rules Committee. Dirlam did not submit even one name for this committee but complained his caucus was only allotted one-third of the members— despite the fact that two years earlier they had refused to give the then Liberal minority even one seat on the committee. Sabo and the DFL dismissed the claims as pure politics and assumed that the Republicans had internal disputes and could not agree on whom to recommend for this important committee. Sabo selected seven Republican members he thought were appropriate for the committee, including veterans Dirlam, Gary Flakne, Rod Searle, Tom Newcome, and Charlie Weaver.[7]

The length of committee hearings was expanded from one to two hours to allow for more testimony and deliberation, and schedules were changed so committees did not meet at the same time. In addition, the Regulated Industries Committee, which was supposed to regulate the liquor and various other industries, was abolished. Sabo thought the committee had been ineffective and wanted the regulatory power to be under the control of committees with broader jurisdiction.[8]

As the news media kept the DFLers' feet to the fire concerning their "openness" and "sunshine" campaign promises, Minority Leader Dirlam was ready with a quip on the DFL "sunshine" changes to the house rules. He conjured up a skeptical look and said he was sure that it was "still going to be partly cloudy."[9] But regardless of the political rhetoric about weather conditions, the legislative process had in fact irrevocably changed. Committee meetings and conference committees were open to the public, debates and additional votes were recorded, and the minority caucus had a greater say in how the legislature was run. These changes are still in effect in Minnesota, and the voting public has more reliable information on which to act. The changes led to plaudits for the state and criticism of the federal government. An editorial titled "Congress and Secrecy" said, "The public's business should be transacted in public. We wish Congress would follow the Minnesota example."[10]

This openness, or transparency as it is now called, has led to a new issue for citizens to face, at both the state and federal level: how to present the instantly available information to the electorate in a thoughtful, user-friendly manner. While timeliness and availability of information may not be the issues they once were, context, analysis, and appropriate balance certainly are. And reporting that solves these issues is in short supply. Partisan blogs and shouting TV commentators interested primarily in generating controversy and high advertising ratings are no substitute for good journalism. Mark Bowden, a veteran journalist, called the modern electronic reporting scene "post journalistic" and described its impact as follows:

> Without journalism, the public good is viewed only through a partisan lens, and politics becomes blood sport.
> Americans increasingly choose to listen only to their own side of the argument, to bloggers and commentators who reinforce their convictions and paint the world only in acceptable, comfortable colors. . . . The other side is no longer the honorable opposition, maybe partly right; but rather always wrong, stupid, criminal, even downright evil.[11]

Right after the 2010 election, *New York Times* writer David Carr, who covers the media as it intersects with culture, business, and government, said,

> the idea of objective journalism has been on a pretty rough ride . . . with viewers deciding to align themselves with outlets that share their points of view—warts, agendas and all. . . .
> Now news anchors lecture the federal government on its response to disasters, cable networks function as propaganda machines for political parties and newspaper writers throw

aside neutrality to tell readers what is really going on behind the headlines.[12]

Discussing the changed news industry in the era of the Internet and social media, the *Economist* weighed in with plain talk on the business aspects of reporting the news: "Successful media organizations will . . . need to reorient themselves towards serving readers rather than advertisers, embrace social features and collaboration, get off political and moral high horses and stop trying to erect barriers around journalism to protect their position."[13]

Whatever the business models, the changing approach to news and politics is a serious issue that needs to be understood by readers, listeners, and viewers if our relatively complex federal system of government is to function properly. Without accurate reporting and critical listening and thinking by the voters, the political polarization that now prevails will continue to paralyze both the states and the federal government. Countries with a better sense of unity and purpose will move forward, while America's federal system will continue to splinter into partisan camps and be limited by political gridlock.

Changing Priorities

The DFL wanted to make a quick public statement that things had indeed changed, not only in the critical but somewhat arcane areas of rules and legislative process, but also in the types of interests that would at least be considered. The DFLers began by passing House File No. 3 on the eighth day of the session, making Minnesota the twenty-sixth state in the nation to ratify the proposed equal rights amendment to the U.S. Constitution. The ratification bill, authored by Bill Kelly, passed with bipartisan support 104 to 28.[14] Consumer protection bills and various bills to aid the physically disabled were also promptly introduced and passed.[15]

The new majority also quickly changed how Minnesotans would elect their representatives to the legislature. One bill eliminated the fiction that the Minnesota Legislature was not a partisan body. In a "truth in advertising" bill, the DFL majority provided that the legislative candidates should be located on the partisan area of the ballot with the congressional, gubernatorial, and other statewide candidates.[16] In a more controversial move, the DFL made the same change for the mayors and city council candidates for Minnesota's three largest cities: Minneapolis, St. Paul, and Duluth.[17] Minneapolis DFLer James Rice, a colorful veteran political warrior who had been the secretary to former DFL governor Karl Rolvaag from 1963 to 1965, authored the bill. Rice simply argued that "the same reasons for party designation for legislators also apply to the executive officers and council members of our major cities."[18] All knew that these cities had a majority of DFL voters and that this change would help the DFL. In addition, the legislature provided for same-day voter registration.[19]

State senator and GOP party chair Robert Brown attacked the election changes, saying that the DFL was adopting a "deliberate pattern" in election bills to give the DFL unfair advantages. As examples, Brown cited same-day voter registration and legislation to allow for transportation of voters to the polls. Brown said, "It is easy to visualize the buses lined up . . . and people herded in to vote as they are told. . . . These two bills would make Chicago look like Shangri-La by comparison."[20] The DFL countered with statements about the fundamental importance in a democracy of making it convenient for citizens to vote and pointed out to the Republicans that not every citizen owned a car.[21]

All of these bills passed early in the session, and the new controlling party felt good about its actions as the legislative session fell into a routine.

Changing Legislation

As the session progressed and legislation began moving, it was as if lumberjacks had freed a logjam in a river. The environment, education, consumer affairs, election laws, and labor legislation were all addressed by a torrent of legislation that started flowing out of committees on its way to the governor's desk for signing (see Appendix A for a list of significant legislation).

Environment

Significant legislative changes were made concerning the stewardship of Minnesota's environment. Environmental planning received strong emphasis. A new Environmental Policy Act required the state to consider the balance between nature and human requirements in its building plans. Environmental impact statements were required for projects of more than local significance. An Environmental Quality Council was created to coordinate environmental planning. A $1.5 million grant program to fund comprehensive solid waste recycling programs and a Critical Areas Act to protect areas of unusual scenic and recreational values were adopted. Criteria for locating power plants were developed, civil penalties were established for polluters, bonding authority was granted for sewage treatment, procedures were put in place to battle tree diseases that threatened to wipe out the urban forest in Minnesota's major cities, and hazardous waste controls were created. In addition, to ensure that future generations would understand environmental issues, an Environmental Education Council was established.[22]

Several Republicans joined in, and all of these changes passed with bipartisan support. Henry Savelkoul, a third-term Republican, coauthored many of these bills, and he and Republicans Searle and Arne Carlson provided strong support from their positions as veteran members of the minority caucus.

The chief architect of all of this environmental legislation was a nine-term veteran from Duluth, Willard Munger. He was named by Sabo to chair the Environmental Preservation and Natural Resources Committee (Environment). Munger was one of the more senior members and was soft-spoken and often mumbled on the house floor. He had cut his teeth on politics during the Depression. Unlike many of the new, young legislators, he not only knew the history of the DFL Party, he had lived through it. Describing one of his early days in politics, Munger said, "I ran out of money because I used my last two and a half dollars to go out and listen to a debate between Norman Thomas and Huey Long."[23] Munger began his environmental work in the late 1940s, long before becoming a legislator, by opposing the earliest efforts by Reserve Mining, a large iron ore mining company, to dump its waste "tailings" into Lake Superior.[24] Despite his liberal background and strong environmental views, he was one of the legislature's most popular members. His legacy lives on in Minnesota through many fine environmental programs, a clean Lake Superior, a swimmable St. Louis River, and the Willard Munger State Trail in northern Minnesota.

Joe Graba was also heavily involved in the work of the Environment Committee as the chair of its game and fish subcommittee. In the outdoor-loving Minnesota, this was an important and difficult assignment, as many people and organizations take their hunting and fishing rights very seriously. The relevant legislation is frequently hotly debated. To the consternation of some, the propriety of two-line fishing, the spearing of game fish, and deciding whether the state should require deer hunters to wear blaze orange took many hours of legislative time to resolve. Graba's steady hand was important to the resolution.[25]

K–12 Education

In addition to work on the Environment Committee, Graba immersed himself in numbers and schoolkids. He had been named by Sabo to be on the Education Committee chaired by a veteran legislator and future lieutenant governor candidate, Carl Johnson.[26] Tom Berg was named the vice chair of the committee. Graba chaired the school aids subcommittee, which determined how much school aid goes to which districts. It produced the largest spending bill in the legislature. Johnson helped train both Graba and Berg in the ways of running a major committee.

As we saw in chapter 4, the Minnesota Miracle legislation of 1971 significantly lowered real estate taxes, increased aid to K–12 education, and reduced the spending disparity between districts. The 1973 session appropriated $1.3 billion to support public elementary and secondary education and revised the school aid formulas further to complete the 1971 reform efforts. The revisions included extra aid for fast-growing districts and districts such as Minneapolis and St. Paul, with a heavy concentration of students from families receiving welfare aid. It also provided more money for special education and furthered the goal of equal educational opportunity for all school districts.[27] In the process of guiding all this through the legislature, Graba firmly established himself as the go-to guy in the house for questions and answers concerning the use of tax dollars for education.

Higher Education and Appropriations

Ray Faricy continued his work on the Appropriations Committee as vice chair of the Education Division. The chair of the full Appropriations Committee was Fred Norton, a key leader in the DFL Caucus and a future Speaker of the house.[28] The Education Division had jurisdiction over appropriations for the University of Minnesota and all other state colleges.

The Appropriations Committee and its three divisions had a tradition of working out their recommendations in committee deliberations, and then, to bring some discipline to the process, when the bill was brought before the full house, all members would circle their wagons and vote against any efforts to change the legislation. It was a rare day when an appropriation bill was amended by persons outside of the committee. This bipartisan procedure, the committee members, and their disciplined approach were held in high regard by other legislators of both parties. One of the bills passed using this procedure during the 1973–74 session was a new student loan program financed by $30 million in bonds.[29]

Faricy also began work on fulfilling his campaign promise to the woman who had attended his campaign meeting and raised the issue of inability to obtain credit in her own name. He authored legislation to prohibit discrimination in the extension of credit on the basis of sex. Other authors on the bill included two new women legislators, Linda Berglin and Joan Growe. When the bill was passed and ready to be signed into law, Faricy invited the constituent from his campaign meeting to the bill-signing ceremony with Governor Anderson. She attended along with the authors and was thrilled to have been a part of making feminist history.[30]

Metropolitan Area Issues

Berg was named by Sabo to serve on the Metropolitan and Urban Affairs Committee, which had jurisdiction over the Metropolitan Council and metropolitan agencies in charge of airports, transit, and sewers. In another example of the changed approach to legislation, Berg successfully authored a bill to strengthen the Metropolitan Council by giving it approval power over the construction of certain major highways in the metropolitan area. Highway personnel had always had complete control over where and how to build highways, and they were not happy about the change. The legislation also allowed the council to suspend any public or private development project of "metropolitan significance" for a time period to bring about coordinated land-use planning in the metropolitan area.[31]

Funding for metropolitan parks and mass transit was substantially increased. Extensive discussions were begun concerning the type of mass transit to be used in the Minneapolis–St. Paul area and how to pay for it.[32]

Crime

Berg also authored a handgun control bill that had been proposed by Attorney General Warren Spannaus. Majority Leader Nick Coleman was the senate author of the bill. Governor Anderson urged the bill's passage and indicated he would sign it. In the hunting and fishing state of Minnesota, this bill was politically dangerous, and after getting through several committees, it was sent to an unfavorable committee and defeated, primarily by rural legislators. The news headlines announced, "Handgun bill dies with a whimper." Spannaus, Coleman, Berg, and their allies said they would keep working on the bill and bring it back with a bang in subsequent sessions.[33]

Taxes

The session held the line on taxes. The DFL was well aware of the significant increases in income and sales taxes in the 1971 session and wanted to provide the voters with a period of fiscal stability. One tax change was made to help the business community by eliminating a tax on "huge and ponderous equipment." A portion of the business community had for years been trying to remove that tax and had not been able to get it done under Conservative control. This change provided the DFL an opportunity to soften its antibusiness image. The lost revenue was offset with a tax on payrolls, supported by both labor and business.

A pet project of Senator Coleman eliminated the taxes on what Coleman referred to as the "working poor." This allowed working people with low incomes to have tax-free income equal to what they would receive from welfare. In another move in keeping with the tastes of the legislators and the DFL's working-class image, the legislature exempted the first eighty thousand barrels of beer brewed by each Minnesota brewery from any state tax.[34] Despite all the new activity, the DFL fiscal policies for the 1973 and 1974 sessions resulted in a surplus in the state's coffers at the end of 1974.[35]

Labor

Irv Anderson described the views of organized labor at the start of the session: "labor . . . legislation will be big in this session, because labor groups obviously had been shunted aside . . . they're going to be coming out."[36] In addition to the unemployment compensation legislation passed in the first few days, Faricy carried a bill that set a general statewide minimum wage and required time-and-a-half pay for work over forty-eight hours in a week. This was another bipartisan effort, with strong assistance from Republicans Arne Carlson and Ray Pleasant.[37]

The importance of several of these laws to ordinary citizens was described thirty-eight years later by David Roe, who was president of the AFL-CIO during the 1973–74 legislative sessions. Speaking at the capitol in 2011, Roe recognized Faricy and senate author John Milton for their work on minimum wage legislation and spoke movingly about the 1973–74 legislative sessions as being the first since statehood where "working people were able to achieve any meaningful legislative victories." In a strong but emotional eighty-one-year-old voice, Roe told how much those sessions meant to organized labor and thanked the legislators for their work on behalf of "thousands of working people throughout the state."[38]

In legislation that directly dealt with the federal question of the proper role of state government, Irv Anderson authored an enforcement statute for the federal Occupational Safety and Health Act (OSHA). The previously enacted OSHA legislation allowed for either state or federal enforcement of OSHA, and Anderson's bill provided that the state should assume OSHA enforcement.[39] Sabo, after serving twenty-eight years in the U.S. Congress, said this act by the legislature was "one of the best examples I have seen as to how federalism should work." He described the combination of federal and state legislation as providing "for strong and uniform national standards so business could efficiently plan and implement its actions across state lines, but state enforcement of those standards permits both business and labor to be heard and disputes resolved in the local area."[40]

Election and Campaign Finances

The sixty-eighth session also enacted one of the nation's most comprehensive ethics and election reform bills. This legislation was in part the outgrowth of the early discussions between Kelly and Berg in 1971 concerning the strong influence of lobbyists. Detailed work started on this legislation in early 1973, before the Watergate Committee hearings in May of that year became big news, but those hearings and their aftermath provided stark evidence of the need for the legislation and helped its passage. Berg carried this legislation with his friend Harry Sieben, a fellow second-term legislator and future Speaker of the house. The bill was introduced on March 5, 1973, and was another example of bipartisan work, as Republicans Savelkoul and Bob Ferderer coauthored the legislation along with DFLer Stan Fudro.[41]

Legislators pay a great deal of attention to proposed legislative changes that affect their reelection. Since this bill dramatically changed the election system they were familiar with and had generally mastered, many would have liked to see the bill die a quiet death in a committee. But if the bill ever reached the house floor for a final vote, the support would likely be overwhelming, as there was a "good government" aura about the bill that would make it very difficult to oppose. Berg and the coauthors were well aware of this, and they all worked together with a strong coalition of "watchdog" groups for over a year to keep the legislation moving through the various committees. In addition to groups such as the Joint Religious Legislative Coalition, the League of Women Voters, and Common Cause, Governor Anderson, Sabo, Senator Coleman, and senate authors Steve Keefe, Robert North, and Robert Ashbach were critical in the pushing and prodding necessary to keep this legislation on track.

The bill did many things: it established a bipartisan commission to administer the law, required lobbyists to report the money spent on lobbying, and required legislators, statewide elected officials, and top appointed officials to disclose the type and approximate amounts of economic interests they owned. These persons were also required to report all conflicts of interest to the commission. In addition, the bill provided for the disclosure of all campaign contributions above $50 to legislative candidates and above $100 to statewide candidates.

Campaign spending was limited by candidates in return for partial public funding of their campaigns. The public funding was financed in part by either a tax credit or a checkoff on the tax return, allowing taxpayers to contribute a dollar of their tax money to one of the major parties or to a general campaign fund that was split evenly between the candidates.[42] This portion of the bill was very controversial, as many Republicans believed it would take away an advantage they had in raising money. There were also constitutional arguments on claimed restrictions on free speech and a host of other arguments against the partial public funding and limits on spending. The supporters remained adamant that these provisions were crucial to the proper workings of the legislation, and the partial public funding and limits stayed in the bill.

Once the bill had cleared all the committees and the full house and the senate, it was necessary to reconcile the differences between the house and senate versions. A six-person conference committee cochaired by Berg and Keefe met and argued for five days, often far into the night, without agreement on the final provisions. Tempers grew short and frustration increased. Senator Ashbach expressed his frustration, saying the bill was like a marshmallow: "You punch it here, and it comes out over there." Berg and his friend Senator Bob Tennessen sparred over the constitutionality of one of the provisions. Tennessen noted that the Senate Counsel's office felt the provision was unconstitutional. Berg sharply said, "They don't vote [on the committee]." Tennessen shot back, "The court votes." Finally, Berg and Keefe got fed up with the bickering and lack of progress and went out to dinner by themselves at the Blue Horse restaurant near the capitol. In an example of the limits of openness and transparency, about two hours later they came up with a package that was agreeable to all. The final bill passed in March 1974. The vote in the house was 118 to 10, and in the senate the vote was 41 to 17. The bill was promptly signed by the governor.[43]

The underlying purpose of the legislation was to bring greater public confidence to the legislative process. The methods used to accomplish that purpose were to reduce the impact of special-interest money, provide more openness about the flow of money in campaigns, and let the voters decide the propriety of a candidate's fundraising actions and the existence and importance of any conflicts of interest. It worked well for a number of years, but as fund-raising and costs escalated, the solutions needed to change. The Supreme Court decisions in 2010 (throwing out legislative prohibitions on certain corporate and labor spending as unconstitutional violations of the First Amendment's right to free speech and stopping Arizona from paying matching public funds to candidates under its campaign finance law) make it clear this vexing problem is far from solved.[44]

Housing

Governor Anderson grew up in the working-class neighborhood known as the East Side of St. Paul and proudly represented the area as a state senator. The governor's parents still lived there when he was governor, and he always kept in close touch with his old neighborhood. In an example of how things can work when key players are of like mind, the governor challenged the executive director of the Minnesota Housing Finance Agency, Jim Dlugosch, and Jim Solem and others in the State Planning Agency to develop a home-improvement loan program using the state's bonding authority to help working-class neighborhoods throughout the state. Wall Street told Dlugosch and Solem it could not be done, as no one would buy such bonds.

In December 1973, Solem, Bruce Vento, then the state representative from the area, and a few community activists took a very cold walking tour of the East Side. They wanted to see the area firsthand, and they stopped at the governor's favorite coffee shop for pie and coffee. To the surprise of no one, the governor showed up. This walk and talk and some creative financial thinking led to a bill aimed at low- and moderate-income families. The legislature passed and the governor proudly signed the nation's first home-improvement loan program using state bonding authority. The legislation provide $100 million of bonding authority for such purposes and over $400 million for home purchase loans.[45]

As all this legislation was being debated, humor was found to be helpful in dealing with the long and sometimes tedious sessions on the house floor. A "streaking" incident at a Minnesota college led to a bit of horseplay involving a veteran legislator, Neil Haugerud, and Berg. On a cold Monday in March, about seventy-five college students performed "streaking incidents" in various places on their campus, earning their college the title of the streaking capital of Minnesota.

The streakers wore nothing but ski masks and tennis shoes. A few days later, Berg and Haugerud, noting the general boredom in the house, picked an innocuous bill and prepared and offered an amendment to the bill to regulate the "profession of streaking." As the clerk started to read the amendment, house members began to pay attention. The amendment defined a streaker as anyone "who moves at a high speed . . . without sartorial adornment as a nymph." The amendment imposed a two-dollar tax on streakers or streaker peekers (a defined term that included all members of the legislature) and a twenty-five-cent tax on ski masks and sneakers. The amendment concluded by requiring special safety equipment for the streakers: "every streaker when streaking at night shall be equipped with a lamp on the front and a red reflector on the rear." The amendment earned the authors robust laughs from everyone except the Speaker. Sabo directed his best Norwegian frown at Haugerud and Berg. The amendment was withdrawn to audible groans from house members, and the house returned to tedium.[46]

LEAP

Governor Anderson had convinced a number of major Minnesota corporations to "loan" executives to the state at no cost to review and make suggestions for improving the efficiency of state government. Jim Pederson, administrative assistant to the governor, played a significant role in training and coordinating the executives and their actions. Prominent and well-regarded businessman Doug Dayton was the chair of the group of executives. This "Loaned Executive Action Program" (LEAP) was well received by the legislature. Twenty-eight LEAP recommendations required legislative approval, and twenty-seven of these recommendations were passed and signed into law. Two of the recommendations involved major changes to the organization of state government. A new department of finance and a new department of personnel were created. Annual savings from the LEAP recommendations were expected to exceed $65 million.[47]

Sunshine Law

In furtherance of the openness-in-government theme from the past campaign, a "sunshine," or open meeting, law was passed. This law significantly expanded requirements that meetings of school boards, city councils, and other local units of government be open to the public. The new law added state agencies, boards, and commissions as well as committees and subcommittees of both the state agencies and local governments to the list of groups that must open their meetings to the public. An exception was made for individual personnel discussions. Joan Growe was the chief author, and the legislation had Republican coauthors and support.[48]

The openness resulting from this far-reaching bill at first caused much consternation among officials who had been used to doing their work outside of public view. The law was, and still is, difficult to administer. For example, is it a "meeting" when a majority of city council members get together for coffee at 10:00 a.m. in the local coffee shop? The answer is generally yes, and over time the rules have become well known to officials, who are usually careful to do the public's business in public.

The extensive use of e-mails and texting is a current example of potential compliance problems with the concept of transparency. If decisions are in fact made by elected officials electronically outside of the public's view, does this constitute a "virtual meeting" and thus violate the open meeting law? In certain circumstances the answer again is yes.[49] This situation well illustrates the need for constant vigilance by both public officials, the media, and others concerned about openness, and the need for possible change in government procedures and regulations to enforce transparency as technology advances.

Privacy

On the flip side of transparency is the vexing issue of privacy. Computers were beginning to hum in larger numbers in various state agencies, and Dan Magraw, the assistant commissioner of Administration in charge of the relatively new area of computers and data collection, began to worry about all the personal data being collected. Two legislators had similar worries and were drafting legislation to deal with their concerns.

Freshman DFL legislator John Lindstrom began to research the sparse body of existing law that dealt with the topic. He found a Swedish law that he liked. He had a bill drafted based on the Swedish model, introduced it, and passed it through the house. Senator Tennessen had also held a long-standing concern about "the government sticking its nose into people's business, and seeking information it doesn't need and doesn't use."[50] Tennessen had followed the work of a 1973 federal commission that had developed five "Principles of Fair Information Practice."[51] He thought the principles were well thought out and had them drafted into legislative form.

The Minnesota Newspaper Association and others monitor legislative efforts to keep information private, and they became concerned about the legislators' efforts. John Finnegan, then president of the association and executive editor of the *St. Paul Pioneer Press,* contacted Lindstrom and Tennessen and expressed his concerns. In a series of discussions, meetings, and phone calls with Finnegan and other relevant parties, Lindstrom and Tennessen agreed on wording for a bill that they thought met the needs of all.[52] This was then incorporated into Lindstrom's bill, which then passed and became known as the Data Privacy Law.[53]

The law established various requirements for state and local governments, including that the collecting government tell citizens for what purpose the collected data will be used, and whether the person is legally required to supply the data. It also provided procedures for citizens to see data about themselves and to correct any errors.[54] The bill passed easily but caused great angst in bureaucratic circles. "No one knows what's going to happen when this hits. . . . Heaven help us all," said Magraw.[55] The bureaucracy figured it out, and the law and its procedures were refined over several legislative sessions. A provision from the first statute concerning the consequences of not providing the data is still known by lawyers working in this field as a "Tennessen warning." These warnings and the modified statute continue to help provide individuals with protections from today's massive data-collecting sinks.[56]

Planning for the Future

During this session and in producing the Minnesota Miracle, a common theme relating to fiscal policy, education, the environment, housing, and land-use decisions was the importance of enacting long-term, sustainable solutions. A bill spelling out the need for this approach for the state as a whole was authored by Kelly. The legislation grew out of concerns that the state was not doing enough "big picture" analysis of the impact of its policies. Key players in raising this concern and working on Kelly's bill were the State Planning Agency and its head, Jerry Christenson; the Citizens League; a business group known as the Upper Midwest Council; and a distinguished geography professor from the University of Minnesota, John Borchert. Kelly's bill was also strongly supported by the governor, who had a special concern for the economic future of the nonmetropolitan areas of the state. Under the bill, the governor was to appoint a "Commission on Minnesota's Future," consisting of forty members from all parts of the state, whose job was to analyze growth and development policies for Minnesota. The commission began work with staff assistance from the State Planning Agency.[57]

Another bill, which did not receive much publicity but would have a long-lasting impact on planning, was also initiated by Christenson and guided to passage by Senate Majority Leader Coleman. Coleman's bill created a position within the State Planning Agency for a state demographer.[58] The bill passed, and Hazel Reinhardt was hired to gather demographic data and prepare population projections for use by the legislature and others in state government.

A LEAP nuts-and-bolts recommendation was the creation of a Legislative Audit Commission. This commission was to oversee "performance audits" (as opposed to the more traditional fiscal audits) of various state agencies and programs. Minnesota had never had this type of oversight before, and some were nervous about what it might uncover, particularly in an election year. Nevertheless, the legislature established the commission in 1973 and expanded it in 1975.[59] As we will see, this commission proved to be very effective and continues to be an important part of the legislative branch's efforts to reduce wasteful spending and ensure wise and effective use of government resources.[60]

Legislative Pay

As the 1974 session was about to adjourn, the house had finished its business and was waiting for the senate to complete its last bit of business when Ed Gearty, a senior DFL senator, knocked on the door of the press corps' offices in the basement of the capitol. Gearty found Sabo playing bridge with a couple of news reporters. As the door opened, Sabo looked up and was surprised to see Gearty. Sabo excused himself and stepped out into the hall to talk with the senator. Gearty said that he was planning to offer an amendment to a routine bill the next morning (the last day of the session) to raise legislative pay from $700 a month to $1,000 a month, a 43 percent increase. Gearty asked Sabo if he thought the house would concur. Legislative pay is always a touchy political subject with voters and is usually handled carefully. In this instance, however, the tired Sabo just said, "Probably," and went back to his bridge game. The reporters never asked about the conversation, and Sabo volunteered nothing. Despite the fact that Sabo spent several hours with two of the governor's top aides later that night, neither he nor Gearty mentioned the potential pay raise to the governor or members of his staff.[61]

The next day the senate passed Gearty's amendment thirty-eight to seventeen and sent the bill to the house. Majority Leader Irv Anderson made a motion for the house to concur, but the motion failed by the overwhelming margin of thirty to eighty-nine. Sabo and Anderson were stunned. As other business continued, hurried private discussions were held among worried legislators concerning pay, politics, and procedural options. Finally, a motion to reconsider the vote on the senate's pay bill was made by Republican Tom Newcome. The house grew quiet as Newcome addressed his colleagues: "This isn't something that's easy to do. But . . . everybody here deserves a pay increase. You . . . ought to have the courage to . . . vote for it." The reconsideration motion passed, and then the bill passed sixty-nine to fifty-four, with thirty-nine members changing their votes from Anderson's earlier motion to concur.[62]

Then the firestorm hit. The governor's office was deluged with calls and letters demanding a veto. News headlines described the scene: "Legislative pay-raise protests thunder in," and "Governor faces bombshell over legislative pay hikes."[63] The governor was caught by surprise, and the legislature clearly looked bad. The governor sensed a political opportunity and waited a few days to let things build and then vetoed the bill.[64] Sabo acknowledged that "I really screwed up by not telling the governor or his staff."[65] However, the vote to support the last-minute pay raise was bipartisan, and despite the fervor generated at the end of the legislative session, this never became a significant issue in the next campaign.

Changing the Constitution

The vexing problem of partisan politics has been present from the very beginning in Minnesota. In 1857, when the Republican and Democratic delegates to the constitutional convention drafting the Minnesota Constitution met, they refused to meet in the same room. Each party drafted separate but similar documents, and the delegates never even acted in a joint meeting during the entire convention. One document was signed by the Republicans, and one by the Democrats. Both were approved by the voters and Congress.[66]

In the early 1970s, this questionable drafting and approval process and the outdated verbiage of the document caused the League of Women Voters and others to push for a state constitutional convention to prepare an updated constitution. A commission had been established in 1971 to study this issue. The governor appointed former Republican governor Elmer L. Andersen to chair the commission.[67] The prospect of a constitutional convention got Jack Davies, a DFL state senator and law professor, stirred up. He realized that a constitutional convention could do as much harm as good.

Davies argued it would be better to simply combine the existing documents into one and correct the grammar and outdated verbiage. Instead of a convention, Davies proposed that the commission adopt a neutral "form and structure" amendment to the constitution.[68] The commission agreed, and Davies, Justice James Otis from the Minnesota Supreme Court, and Republican legislator Lon Heinitz were named by the commission to a subcommittee to work on the project.

Davies had the laboring oar and promptly went to work, cutting and pasting from the 1857 verbiage and cleaning up outdated language. The resulting "scotch tape constitution," as Davies calls it, was readily approved by Otis, Heinitz, and the full commission.[69] A bill was introduced in the legislature to place the amendment before the voters. Support grew, the legislation passed, and in 1974 the amendment was approved by the voters.[70] Hundreds of judges and lawyers who have to deal with the state constitution from time to time remain grateful to the law professor and his colleagues for their countless hours of work cleaning up an interesting example of ridiculous partisanship.

Adding Staff

As the workload increased for the majority party legislators, they realized that more staff were needed to achieve their legislative goals. Several talented new persons joined the House Research staff. One was fiscal analyst Eileen Baumgartner, who left the executive branch and State Planning Agency to join the legislative branch. Baumgartner's work on the Minnesota Miracle legislation and research on sales taxes and the state's system for local government aid provided the legislators with a sound source of information, both for analyzing financial projections provided by the executive branch and lobbyists, and for determining the impact of spending and taxing decisions.

Another key staff addition in 1972 was the current legislative auditor, Jim Nobles. Nobles came to House Research as a young intern from the University of Minnesota's School of Public Affairs seeking to fulfill an internship requirement to obtain his master's degree. In 1973, after the DFL took control, Nobles said:

> There was a lot of buzz about whether or not this . . . non-partisan office [House Research] was going to be embraced by the new leadership. . . . The signal went out from the new leadership, which was Martin Sabo and Irv Anderson, that they really did want House Research to stay nonpartisan with an exception or two.[71]

Nobles described his first contact with the new controlling party: "I went to Irv Anderson, who didn't know me from Adam, and I just said, 'Representative Anderson, I'm an intern from House Research . . . and I'd kind of like to stay here. . . .'" Anderson replied, "Fine, we don't want to kick anybody out other than what we've already done, so you've got a job." Nobles was assigned to the Governmental Operations Committee, which dealt with changes in state governmental structure and procedures, and stayed there for six years before moving on as a staff member to the Office of the Legislative Auditor.[72]

The staff at House Research was proud of its work and its independence from partisan politics. As Kevin Kenny, who joined House Research in the early 1970s, put it, "House Research thought of itself as a small university."[73] The work of this "small university" was critical to much of what was accomplished by the legislature during the 1970s. Nobles described that period as "a time of . . . real energy and ideas and reform." He said LEAP deserves some credit for this as it was "one of the best efforts from the outside that I've ever seen, . . . it was a real working group of midlevel executives from the public and private sectors who . . . really spent a lot of time in state government and came up with some really good recommendations."[74]

In addition to the innovative changes from the LEAP program, Nobles said,

> many forces were coming together to really strengthen
> the state legislature. . . . this was happening all across the
> country. . . . It was no longer enough for them to just be these
> sneaky places where lawyers and farmers came . . . in their off
> time to . . . be an old boys' club—that it was getting to be seri-
> ous business, there was real money on the table, there were
> real issues that states needed to handle and you needed a
> much more professional legislature in many ways.
>   Watergate starts coming along around this time. That had a
> big impact too, in . . . focusing people's attention on the struc-
> ture of government accountability, kind of who we are, what
> kind of government do we have. It was a time of real interest
> in governmental process and a real swing toward reform to
> create good government.[75]

As the legislature grew in independence from the executive branch and lobbyists and became a source of information in its own right, legislators found they were getting more requests from businesses, local elected officials, nonprofit groups, and constituents for information and help. Since such requests can be important to reelection, the need for more partisan caucus staff to deal with the requests became apparent.

Also, Sabo, Anderson, and other leaders realized that there were partisan issues that needed critical analysis and program design that should not be performed by the nonpartisan House Research staff. These leaders wanted to keep the "small university" free from any perceived or real taint from partisan politics. As a result, a small caucus research staff was established for each of the two party caucuses.[76]

In summer 1973, Sabo and Anderson interviewed Ed Dirkswager for a position with a new group to be called "House DFL Caucus Research." Dirkswager was then a State Planning Agency employee working for Jerry Christenson. He had graduated in physics from St. John's University in Minnesota and studied astrophysics at Yale. After deciding astrophysics was not in his future, he received a degree in religious education at Catholic University in Washington, D.C., and eventually went to the School of Public Affairs at the University of Minnesota. There he worked with his friend, future legislator John Brandl. At the State Planning Agency, Dirkswager put his academic skills to work on gathering information for a small fact-filled book containing population data, graphs, and projections to be used by legislators and other state policy makers. This *Pocket Data Book* helped guide the work of the Commission on Minnesota's Future and helped governors and legislators for many years plan and allocate financial resources based not on guesswork or biased statistical analysis produced by a lobbying group but on accurate data and projections.[77] Dirkswager also served as the staff person for the Commission on Minnesota's Future.

Sabo and Anderson appreciated Dirkswager's strong academic and policy-development background and asked him to direct the new House DFL Caucus Research staff. Dirkswager agreed and soon organized a staff of five to help the DFL Caucus with research, constituent service, speech writing, development of policy papers, and the like. The Republican Caucus had a similar arrangement to perform its research functions.[78]

Adding Space

Kelly was named by Sabo to be the vice chair of the Rules Committee, chaired by Irv Anderson. This committee's jurisdiction included legislative office space. As a result of growing complaints from legislators about lack of decent office space, Anderson appointed a five-person space subcommittee of the Rules Committee to be chaired by

Kelly. The DFL members were Kelly, Anderson, and Sabo, and the Republican members were Newcome and Searle. During summer 1973, the subcommittee looked at all state buildings in the capitol area complex and decided that the best and most efficient space for legislative offices would be in what was known as the State Office Building, often not so affectionately called SOB. The building was right next to the capitol and was connected by a tunnel to the capitol. Plans were made and implemented to remodel the building to provide hearing rooms and individual offices for most of the legislators. (The controlling DFL senators had offices in the capitol, and they refused to move.) During the subcommittee's process, it was noted by Kelly and others that certain minor changes in design and procedures for office assignments were at times made by Majority Leader Anderson after the subcommittee meetings. Such unilateral conduct by Anderson became a growing concern for Kelly and others as time went on.[79] The new offices were ready in early 1974 and were a huge improvement for the legislators and their staff.

Gaining Perspective

As minority leader, Sabo had been active in an organization known as the National Legislative Conference (NLC), a group of legislative leaders from around the country. Sabo began to work with these other legislators on ways to improve the performance and effectiveness of state legislatures in our federal system. He played a significant role in establishing a new organization, which included the NLC and two other organizations concerned about improving state government. The new organization was called the National Conference of State Legislatures (NCSL), which formally came into existence on January 1, 1975.[80] All the discussions, conferences, and meetings that were involved in establishing the NCSL broadened Sabo's legislative perspective, sharpened his ideas on ways to improve state government, and clarified his thinking on how state government should work within the federal system. Sabo was elected the third president of the NCSL in 1976. The NCSL continues to be a strong and growing organization dedicated to improving state legislatures.

Sabo's perspective also changed regarding the increased news coverage he received as Speaker. On at least one occasion his normal, even-keel personality gave way. Early on a cold winter morning in 1973, before heading to the capitol, he was enjoying a cigarette, a cup of coffee, and the morning paper, when he read a news report strongly criticizing one of his favorite topics. He angrily grabbed his coat, hat, and gloves and jumped into his car and headed to the capitol to issue a hard-hitting response. He did not get very far.

Sabo lived in a modest home with an unheated garage, and always plugged his car engine into an electric heater, which warmed the oil in the engine so it would start on Minnesota's below-zero mornings. As Sabo slammed the car into reverse and backed out of his garage, he heard a loud crack. He looked up and noticed the electrical outlet, the cord, and a portion of his garage wall traveling with him. A bit sheepish, Sabo got out of the car, unplugged the heater cord, and tried to put his garage back together. He eventually made it to the capitol and decided to deal with less controversial topics for the rest of the morning.[81]

As the session continued, Kelly, Faricy, Graba, and Berg also gained additional perspective and continued to climb the legislative learning curve. Each had successfully carried major legislation, had worked closely with strong and experienced committee chairs, and had spent hours meeting with top staff from the governor's office and local officials. They had held public "town hall" meetings with their constituents about a variety of problems. (In Kelly and Graba's case, some of these meetings were literally in town halls.) As a result, they developed a feel for many of the problems of their constituents. They began to appreciate the complexity of their task and the critical importance of top-quality staff work to analyze constituent problems and determine if a legislative solution made sense. Each had developed a strong relationship with the staff of both DFL Caucus Research and House Research, and they used that staff extensively.

Their second-term education also involved learning the differences between the senate and the house. Rivalry between groups working side by side on the same problems is common in many contexts, and the house and senate were no exception. House members looked jealously at the four-year term of the senators. And after the forty-plus years of continuous Conservative control, the senate had developed a certain paternalistic attitude toward governmental matters. The senators prided themselves in being fiercely independent— of the governor, their leaders, and certainly the house. This institutional attitude was adopted by some of the individual DFL senators as they exercised control for the first time in history. However, house members also had experience in governing, and they did not appreciate being patronized by their senate colleagues. Egos clashed, and the word *arrogant* was often used by house members to describe certain senators. For the senate's part, they thought that some house members were myopic and too close to Governor Anderson and that the house suffered from a serious lack of decorum. All of this caused significant friction from time to time and was another factor that needed to be dealt with to get legislation all the way to the governor's desk.

The sophomores were also learning that civility, personal friendships, and trust needed to be maintained. In the real world of legislating, all these things play an important part in bridging gaps among rural, urban, and suburban interests and in political philosophies. In a good example of the importance of maintaining a civil approach while fighting over political philosophy, Lindstrom, besides continuing to challenge the DFL on many matters, kept talking privately throughout the 1973 session to DFL legislators about the need for change in liquor laws to promote competition and lower prices. Finally, on the last day of the 1973 session, many of Lindstrom's liquor-reform ideas were enacted with significant help from house DFLers Faricy and Jim Casserly and from the DFL-controlled senate. The governor, whom Lindstrom had attacked so vigorously, readily signed the bill.[82]

As the 1974 session continued, concerns were voiced among a small group of house DFLers about Anderson's uneven performance as majority leader. There was even some limited talk within the DFL Caucus of running someone against Anderson for the position next session. However, the talk never made it into public view, and no contest against Anderson occurred.

In a news analysis of the session, Faricy and Berg were listed as "controversialists" along with Phyllis Kahn, Flakne, a young Republican from Duluth, Jim Ulland, and a few others. The article listed handgun control, election campaign reform, "ban the can" (requiring a deposit on throwaway beer and soda containers), and allowing the open sale of contraceptives in stores as examples of controversial bills these legislators had pushed as authors. The article described the impact of the demographic change under way in the legislature: "These and other young aggressive legislators have moved into a gap created by the ouster of the Republicans from power and the advancement of more-senior DFLers into committee chairmanships."[83] While not all these controversial bills made it to final passage, their progress at the committee level showed that by the end of the 1974 session a new era had arrived at the capitol. *Responsive* was now an adjective that could at times be said to describe state government in Minnesota.

At the end of the 1974 session, Senator Allan Spear made an announcement that was noted throughout the country and helped change the perspective of many. In a speech on the senate floor, Spear announced that he was gay. He thus became one of the first openly gay legislators in the country. Spear was a smart, funny, and popular senator who continued to win reelection by large margins. He was an associate professor of history at the University of Minnesota with a Ph.D. in history from Yale. He served twenty-eight years until he retired in 2000.[84]

In 1993, Spear successfully authored an amendment to change the Minnesota Human Rights Act to prevent discrimination against persons because of their sexual orientation. In a dramatic speech to his skeptical colleagues Spear said, "I'm fifty-five years old, this is not a phase I'm going through." In the house, Karen Clark succeeded in getting the bill passed. As Clark noted, "It was one of those watershed moments. . . . I don't think people realized that twenty years of work had gone into that moment."[85] The bill was similar to the bill first introduced by Young Turk Flakne and coauthored by Berg in 1971 (see chapter 5).

At the start of the 1973 session, Berg, Kelly, and Republican Richard Anderson were charged with presenting an orientation session to the many new legislators. The session, completed in a few hours, covered such things as the mechanics of legislating, decorum, and staff services available. It generally did not go beyond day-to-day problems. The following summer, Berg and Kelly attended a NCSL conference where Dan Rather of CBS News gave the luncheon speech. Rather strongly challenged the several hundred legislators in attendance to do a better job of fulfilling their role in America's federal system. Berg and Kelly continued to think about Rather's comments, their own experience as second-term legislators, and the legislative institution in which they were spending many interesting and difficult days.

They developed the idea for a legislative retreat to be attended only by legislators. The idea was that legislators should have some time when they could stop thinking about their next meeting or the next election and instead think seriously about what it meant to be a legislator. Berg and Kelly wanted to share their views and hear from others about what it means to represent thousands of people, with the authority and responsibility to tax them, to define which of their activities are legal and which are not, and to decide how much money goes to their children's school and which powers their county, city, and township governments should be allowed to exercise. Berg and Kelly approached Sabo with the idea, and he concurred, made some suggestions, and asked that they continue with the detailed planning. Republican Richard Anderson was brought into the discussion, and he also readily concurred with the idea.

This group thought an outside perspective was critical, and they contacted Dan Rather to see if he would be available to speak to the retreat. He was not. They then invited another CBS newsman, Phil Jones, who had previously covered the Minnesota Legislature, and Charles Bailey, editor of the *Minneapolis Tribune*. Both newsmen accepted.[86]

St. John's University was chosen as the retreat site, and two days in December were selected as the dates. St. John's is a well-regarded Benedictine liberal arts college with impressive architecture located on many acres of wooded hills in rural Minnesota, a little over an hour from the state capital. (It is also a short distance from the purported site of Garrison Keillor's Lake Wobegon.) As word got out about the planning, objections were raised by some members of the Republican Caucus. Some did not like the idea of Rather being invited, and others thought it a "boondoggle in a rural area." Still others thought this was merely a ploy to allow legislators to receive another $33 per diem payment for their attendance. Republican Arne Carlson said the idea had received a "very divided" response from the Republican Caucus, but he encouraged his caucus members to attend. He said the objections were "at best, short sighted." Berg continued to push the event as being "much needed . . . [to determine] what kind of changes are going to be required of the legislature to meet future problems."[87] On December 13, legislators climbed on buses and retreated to St. John's. Attendance was excellent from both the Republican and DFL Caucuses.

Newsmen Jones and Bailey used their outsider perspective to urge legislators to step back for a moment and think about their role in America's government. Jones in particular was harsh in his assessment of state legislative performance throughout history and noted the rise in the relative importance of the federal government with this metaphor: "People have long been dismayed . . . puzzled . . . disappointed in state government. Like the long-suffering wife of a habitually faithless husband, they hang onto the shadow of the old dream until the end, but also like the disappointed spouse, they turn elsewhere for comfort and support."

Jones ended his remarks with a serious and haunting question for the Minnesota legislators: "Is your legislature what people have died for on many a battlefield?"[88] The question was met with silence. It was a valid question then, and it is now. It is also one that should be asked repeatedly not only of state legislators but of members of Congress as well.

Changing Time Spent Governing

The 1973 session started on January 2 and ended on May 21. During these 139 calendar days, 66 "legislative days," as defined by the legislature in accordance with the newly passed flexible-session amendment, were used. This left 54 "legislative days" for the 1974 session in accordance with the constitution's 120-day legislative limit. Two thousand five hundred bills had been introduced in the house in 1973, and 783 were passed by both the house and the senate and signed by the governor. Sixty-two bills that had passed the committee process were left on the house calendar ready to be acted on by the house in 1974.[89]

The legislature wanted to use the pending period between the "full" sessions of the legislature, which were held at the beginning of each year, to study problems and listen to voters. The DFL decided to hold "mini-sessions" during the interim period from May 26, 1973, to the reconvening date of January 15, 1974. These mini-sessions began in July and consisted of formal committee hearings for one week each month. Legislation could be officially introduced during the interim period, and committees had legal authority to recommend bills for passage, as they did during the regular session. The full legislature did not meet during this interim period.[90]

The mini-sessions were a mixed bag. Some committees worked hard and gained significant understanding of problems; others seldom met or dealt only with minor issues. One editorial, titled "Not All Good, Not All Bad," summed up the mini-sessions: "DFLers generally praise the mini-session idea. Republicans express doubts as to the benefits, but are not entirely condemnatory."[91]

When the legislative session reconvened on January 15, 1974, in addition to the sixty-two bills still on the legislative calendar from 1973, forty-six new bills had been recommended by committees during the interim period.[92] After the session adjourned on March 29, 1974, having used fifty of the allowable fifty-four days, some people questioned whether the flexible-session amendment and the mini-sessions were good ideas. Many argued that the flexible-session amendment provided needed time to study and reach more fair, efficient, and long-lasting solutions. Supporters of the change and the use of mini-sessions argued that constituents had a greater chance of being heard and that people gained more confidence that their state government was listening. Others argued it was not a meaningful change in procedures and that the added time and cost were simply not worth the effort.

After the mini-sessions, Sabo was asked by an editorial writer to discuss the additional time spent by legislators at the capitol, the improved procedures, and the increase in staff and office space. Sabo responded, "it's clear we're going through some very fundamental changes in the Legislature in terms of the time that we spend working at the process. The question is, . . . what's the role of the Legislature?" He went on to partially answer his own question: "It is of 'prime importance' that the Legislature be 'much more involved' in state government." However, he acknowledged that he was worried that the legislature may "step out of its [proper] role as policy-maker," and "become too involved in administrative responsibilities which . . . are more properly left to state, local, and metropolitan agencies."[93]

This changed legislature was not to Ernie Lindstrom's liking. He decided to retire from the legislature and said the "part-time citizen legislator" is being replaced by the "full-time professional politician." Republican leaders Newcome and Weaver made similar comments as they also announced their retirements. In addition, Dirlam announced his retirement. Thus, all the Republican Caucus leaders were retiring at the end of the session.[94]

A view contrary to that expressed by the retiring Republicans was put forth by a first-term state senator, John Milton. In a 1974 interview he noted that "to describe the issue as a choice between a 'part-time citizen' legislature versus a 'full-time professional' Legislature is to load the question. These words 'connote good and evil.'" Milton argued that the "Legislature has to be full-time to carry out its responsibility as the key policy-maker for the state" and to properly oversee the bureaucracy. He concluded by noting that lobbyists, administrators, and the bureaucracy are full-time. "Is anybody else (besides the legislator) part-time or amateur or citizen? How can you have a check and balance if one is part-time, with hands tied behind their backs . . . ?"[95]

This debate about full- or part-time state legislators continues to this day throughout the country.[96]

Changing Campaign Positions

As the 1974 session came to an end, both political parties adjusted their upcoming campaign strategy to reflect the change in roles caused by the 1972 election. Running as the party in control is different from running as a challenger. The DFL, with all its statewide officeholders up for reelection and having controlled the machinery of state government, now had to present and defend its record to the voters. The Republicans had to criticize the DFL record and its candidates and talk about Republican alternatives. While defending a record can be difficult, as the Republicans found in 1972, the advantages of incumbency in such things as name recognition and fund-raising are great. Even more important, the DFL thought it had done a good job of governing. While the number of bills passed is not usually a good way to measure the effectiveness or success of a legislature (or a legislator), a quantitative analysis does help show the breadth and depth of the issues addressed during this historic session. Over 3,700 bills were introduced in the house, and of these, 1,366 were passed and became law. This was several hundred more than in either the previous 1971 or the subsequent 1975–76 sessions.[97] The incumbent DFL members were proud of their historic two-year record and more than happy to debate it with the Republicans.

In any election where a governor is running, most of the media attention focuses on that race. The other statewide candidates— lieutenant governor, attorney general, secretary of state, auditor, and treasurer—and individual legislators share the remaining media coverage allotted to politics.

The Republicans knew this, and in June went on the attack, focusing on the governor's office. Their candidate for governor was a state legislator from Minneapolis who had a good Scandinavian name for Minnesota politics, John Johnson. He said there were "indictable offenses that have been committed" and alleged that Polar Panel, a company where Tom Kelm, the governor's executive secretary, was president, had improperly provided corporate credit and jobs for DFL campaigners in 1970 and then filed bankruptcy. Lindstrom joined in by alleging that there were "unaccounted-for slush funds and coercive fund-raising." State Senator Bob Brown, Republican Party chair, jumped into the fray, claiming the DFL had allowed "boss rule in this state" to develop.[98] These attacks were not working very well. One article described Anderson as having a

> commanding lead among Minnesota voters . . . 67% of the electorate preferred Anderson, while 12% chose Johnson [the GOP candidate], and 21% were undecided. . . .
>
> 42% of the eligible voters considered themselves DFLers and 23% thought of themselves as Republicans.
>
> As if these figures did not make Republican prospects bleak enough, the poll indicated that Anderson holds the support of almost 90% of the DFLers and also wins about two-thirds of the independents, and almost one-third of the Republicans.[99]

In the legislative races, the DFL had recruited candidates for every district in the state but one. They also had thirty-seven DFL senators who were not up for reelection and who could help campaign. The Republicans did not even field a candidate in fourteen districts.[100] In addition, the Republicans had to face the general mood of the country after the Watergate scandals. By the fall, the resignation of President Nixon in August 1974 and the subsequent Ford pardon of Nixon in September had made things even tougher for the GOP. In addition, the party of candidates would now be designated on ballots, and that change would likely help the DFL candidates.

As the summer and fall wore on, the Republicans continued their efforts to portray the state as scandal ridden, with the governor's executive secretary bearing the brunt of the charges. Kelm was a bit heavyset, had a reputation for being a tough task master, and fit many people's image of a hard-nosed politico—an image that also served as a flack catcher to protect the governor. He thus made a favorite target for Republican attacks. None of these charges stuck, and as a headline read a few days before the election, "Except for Kelm issue, Wendy's campaign serene."[101] To make matters even tougher for the Republicans, in August it was announced that the state had a $224 million surplus and that the surplus might well reach $300 million by the end of the fiscal year, June 30, 1975. The DFL was proud of its record of financial stewardship, but the Republican candidate for treasurer, Robert Stassen, alleged that the surplus was because of "sleight of hand expenses shifts," and long-term borrowing for current expenses. The state's revenue commissioner then noted that the country's economy was doing well, and at least twenty-eight other states also had large surpluses. Stassen's allegations had little impact.[102]

On election night there was another DFL victory party at the Leamington Hotel. Unlike two years earlier, there was much less suspense for most of the participants. Governor Anderson and Lieutenant Governor Rudy Perpich led a huge victory by carrying every county in the state. All other DFL statewide candidates won as well. Joan Growe became Minnesota's secretary of state with 52.3 percent of the vote, and Warren Spannaus, despite his sponsorship of the controversial handgun control legislation, won reelection as attorney general with 64 percent of the vote. Two state legislators were elected to Congress: Tom Hagedorn, a Republican, and Richard Nolan, a DFLer. This meant the DFL held five of Minnesota's eight congressional seats, the first time the DFL had held a majority since 1956.[103] The DFLers were very happy.

The DFL also gained 26 seats in the house. The final tally for the house was 103 for the DFL and 31 for the GOP. Sabo had been unopposed, and Berg, Faricy, Graba, and Kelly all won with relative ease.[104] Flakne, who had left the legislature in 1973 after being named county attorney for the state's largest county, survived the DFL onslaught and won election to county attorney.[105]

Republican Party chair Brown explained the results by saying, "We were caught in a down cycle . . . which was compounded by the troubles of the National party." Others blamed Brown, and said he had polarized the party over his opposition to abortion.[106] Arne Carlson, long after his legislative service and eight-year service as a

Republican governor, reflected on the 1973 session and said, "The DFL recognized these new tides, these new forces of consumerism and environmentalism."[107]

The election results gave the DFL legislators increased confidence that their program of change to more-progressive taxation, stronger environmental protections, and continuing efforts to provide equal educational opportunity for K–12 students regardless of the property wealth of a particular school district was supported by the voters. The results also reinforced a belief that the extensive changes to the legislative process—more transparency, staff, offices, and time spent governing—were not only sound public policy, they were also good politics. In any event, it was clear that state government had changed dramatically from the 1960s and that the DFL had continued its dominance of state politics.

Despite concerns by some about Irv Anderson's credibility, after the big electoral win, he and Sabo were easily reelected as leaders of the DFL Caucus for the 1975–76 sessions. Sabo promptly began the process of deciding which committees to keep and which to change, selecting chairs for the committees, and figuring out how best to use the permitted 120 legislative days. With a presidential election coming in the fall of 1976 and the ongoing turmoil of a war that was not going well, it was clear that the next two years would be a turbulent period in the country. The legislators would need to work hard to keep focused on the business of governing their state.

CHAPTER 7

Presidential Politics and Musical Chairs

> As Governor, there isn't a lot I can do . . . to crack down
> on crime. Law enforcement is really a local issue. It's the
> cops' job to tighten down on criminals.
>
> ▪ Jesse Ventura, *I Ain't Got Time to Bleed*

The beginning of the annual John Beargrease sled dog race along Minnesota's North Shore of Lake Superior is a lot like the beginning of the annual legislative sessions taking place at the same time two hundred miles away in St. Paul.[1] As the dogs sense that the race is about to begin and are released from their cages, they jump around, bark loudly, occasionally snarl at one another, and frequently get tangled in their harnesses. The mushers line them up to travel as a team to pull their heavy loads in the right direction. So it was with Speaker Martin Sabo and Majority Leaders Irv Anderson and Nick Coleman, as they tried to get their huge majorities lined up and pulling in the same direction on January 7, 1975. When the legislative starting gun went off at noon that day, newly elected Secretary of State Joan Growe proudly convened the house. The majority legislators stopped barking for the moment and got into their harnesses, which had been pointed in a common direction by Sabo, Anderson, and Coleman. Whether these legislators would pull together as a team or end up barking at each other and getting tangled in their harnesses remained to be seen.

The thirty-one-member Republican Caucus regrouped after their election loss and selected Henry Savelkoul as its minority leader. Savelkoul, age thirty-five, had just been elected to his fourth term. He had been a classmate of Tom Berg's in law school, and like Sabo and Ernie Lindstrom, Savelkoul had grown up in North Dakota. He and his wife, Margaret, liked the rural life, and they settled down in Albert Lea, a city of 19,418 in the southern farm belt of Minnesota, a few miles from the Iowa border. Savelkoul took his Young Republican ideas and his accounting and law degrees and joined a law firm that included David Graven, a DFL Party activist who ran for Congress in 1962 and for the Democratic nomination for governor in 1970.[2]

During the 1973–74 sessions, Savelkoul had shown an ability to work with the new DFL majority legislators. He enjoyed the outdoors, had worked well with Willard Munger, and, along with Republican Arne Carlson, coauthored much of the DFL's environmental legislation. Savelkoul was also a coauthor of the election law reform package authored by Berg and Harry Sieben. He had been very helpful in gathering and holding Republican votes for that bill. Carlson was elected an assistant minority leader. In a tacit admission of the weakness of their caucus and perhaps feeling that Sabo would treat the members of their caucus fairly, the Republicans offered no candidate for the position of Speaker. In a further gesture of good will, Savelkoul and ranking Republican Rod Searle seconded Sabo's nomination. In his seconding speech Savelkoul urged members to "do away with partisanship for partisanship's sake." Sabo was elected unanimously.[3]

Sabo had earlier tried to set a more restrained tone for the 1975–76 sessions. He wanted to use the interim period between the annual sessions to study and develop legislation: "I hope that we slow the process down . . . and that our agenda is not as large [as 1973–74]." In a statement that said a great deal about Sabo's views of the legislative process and foretold much about the upcoming legislative session, Sabo said that "the most crucial problem is to handle fiscal matters." He agreed with the governor's promise not to increase the sales or total income taxes but said there could be "internal revisions" in the tax system. Senate Majority Leader Coleman generally agreed, and both Sabo and Coleman gingerly raised the possibility of a legislative pay raise.[4]

Sabo's announcement of the appointment of new committee chairs raised a few eyebrows around the capitol. He appointed legislators who had served only two terms to chair three major committees. Sieben was named chair of the Government Operations Committee, Bill Kelly was named chair of the Tax Committee, and Berg was named chair of a new Local and Urban Affairs Committee, which was a combination of three previously existing committees. Kelly had not even served on the Tax Committee during his first two terms.[5]

This was also an interesting time on the national political scene. A few months earlier President Gerald Ford had pardoned former president Nixon from any federal crimes he may have committed, and Congress had just confirmed Nelson Rockefeller as vice president.[6] Inflation was rampant with an 11 percent increase in the consumer price index in 1974, and lines were beginning to form at gas stations as gasoline became scarce, and energy costs rose sharply.[7] Ronald Reagan was getting ready to challenge Ford for the Republican presidential nomination in 1976.[8] Governor Wendell Anderson was paying attention to all this as he got ready to give his second inaugural address.

The speech was not the usual inaugural speech from a governor about his plans for the state for the next four years. Yes, there was quite a bit about education, the need for catastrophic health insurance, more property tax relief, and the like, but there was more. As the media reported, Anderson "came down hard against sending more dollars to the Arabs, to . . . South Korea or to South Vietnam." He also quoted political columnist Walter Lippmann on "the stern virtues by which civilization is made."[9] Thus began the speculation that the governor had "his eyes on the Democratic national ticket in 1976."[10] For the next twenty-three months, national politics and the ambitions and opportunities for Anderson, Lieutenant Governor Perpich, and Senator Walter Mondale would play out with far-reaching consequences for Minnesota and both major political parties.

A few days after the governor's address, the house and senate, instead of arguing over specific bills, went to school—literally. They attended three half-day sessions of "Minnesota Horizons" presentations at a nearby school. These presentations were data-filled background sessions about the state's population, its fiscal position, its local governmental structure, and its business and industrial base. The sessions were run by Jerry Christenson's State Planning Agency. Ed Dirkswager's *Pocket Data Book* was used extensively, as was information developed by the Commission on Minnesota's Future and Minnesota's new demographer. The concept of using accurate data instead of anecdotal evidence to drive policy was pushed hard, as Christenson tried to implement his notion that "planning has to be linked to power."[11] In today's buzz words, the sessions would be said to be calling for "evidence-based public policy making." The sessions were well received and were broadcast into schools and over public radio and television.[12]

Federalism Revisited

To understand the why and how of much of the legislation that was passed in the 1970s in general and in this session in particular, we need to take another quick look at how federalism and the delivery of government services have evolved over the 220-plus years since the Constitution was drafted and adopted. As shown in chapter 1, the Constitution established a unique system of federalism with two sovereign units of government: the federal government and the states. However, this "dual federalism" does not explain the role and authority of local units of government such as counties, cities, townships, and school districts, which have become crucial to governing a crowded and diverse country.

These local units are not sovereign; that is, they do not get their power—their authority and ability to tax—from the people directly; they get it from the states. The power to govern runs from the people to the sovereign governments and then back to the local units of government in such amounts as the sovereigns specify. States via their legislatures and governors have passed laws to establish and enable counties, cities, school districts, and a variety of other local governments to govern.[13] The state has granted these local units of government authority to tax and spend, sometimes within certain limits, and to deliver services, such as education, health care, recreation, police and fire, and the like.

In the largely agrarian America of the 1800s and continuing to the 1930s, the state was the main sovereign government providing the authority for and sometimes help with financial resources for the local governments. As the country expanded geographically and became more entangled in international affairs, the other sovereign, the federal government, began to take a more active role in state and local matters. This process increased during the Depression and World War II and accelerated in the mid-1950s and 1960s, with the interstate highway program and more socially and economically based programs such as the War on Poverty and Head Start. The Social Security Act was amended in 1965 to include Medicaid, a critically important and jointly administered state and federal program for health care for low-income people. These programs provided authority and significant money directly to states and local governments.

As was briefly discussed earlier, some of that federal money in the 1970s came in the form of revenue sharing, by which two-thirds of the money bypassed the states and went directly to the local units of government. But there was also a major expansion of programs and "categorical" and "block" grant making from the federal government. During the Johnson, Nixon, Ford, and Carter administrations, the federal aid programs increased from 181 in 1964 to 539 in 1981. And the grants were not small. For example, in 1980, the amount of grants to states and local governments was $94 billion. Many of these grants had "performance guidelines" or "standards" attached, which required certain results. Thus, by using its revenue-raising and revenue-distribution capabilities, the federal government strengthened its position in the modern version of dual federalism.[14]

Congress has continued to flex its muscles by increasing its use of the "preemption doctrine," which allows Congress to "preempt" a particular state or local law or regulation or even an entire "field" of legislation. When something is "preempted" by Congress, the state or local government cannot get involved.[15] The Employee Retirement Income Security Act (ERISA) defining employee benefit plans is an example of Congress preempting a particular field.[16] Another power, sometimes referred to by political scientists as a "subset of federal preemptions," are "mandates." Mandates are actions that Congress, using its financial leverage (often based on its power to regulate commerce), wants the states to take.[17] The No Child Left Behind Act of 2001 contains a number of mandates. This controversial statute is an example of congressional muscle flexing designed to push state governments to act in a manner Congress believes is in the best interest of the nation.[18]

The power of Congress to preempt, mandate, and use its financial powers to achieve certain state action has been present since the Constitution was adopted, but its use has significantly expanded since the mid-1960s. This expansion has "produced fundamental changes in the nature of the federal system."[19] Both good and bad consequences have resulted from these changes. For example, ERISA's uniform standards across fifty states helped many plan and implement employee benefit plans, but it also caused major headaches for state legislators (including, as we will see, those in Minnesota who were trying to pass some innovative health-care legislation during the 1975–76 sessions), governors, state health and insurance regulators, and judges, who have to sort out what has been preempted and what has not.

The ERISA statute and federal regulations use very general wording to accomplish preemption. These vague words have kept a small army of lawyers employed for many years trying to interpret what exactly Congress meant. Sabo, after his experiences in trying to develop health-care legislation at the state level and his twenty-eight years in Congress, referred to the ERISA preemption statute as "poorly thought-out" and "needlessly causing expense and curtailing creativity in approaches to sensibly develop health-care legislation."[20]

The No Child Left Behind Act is also an example of what can happen when the federal mandated answer does not match up with the states' answers as to how to solve the problem. In 2011, several states refused to comply with some of the testing provisions of the federal statute. The secretary of education, who also did not like the federal statute, developed a waiver policy to help the states. As one professor described these actions, "This is a big federalist chess game. Until now, Washington has had the stronger position. Going forward, states will be stronger." Waivers from the mandate that requires 100 percent proficiency in math and reading—a target many educators believe is impossible—were granted in 2012 to ten states including Minnesota.[21]

The 2012 Supreme Court decisions involving the federal government's Patient Protection and Affordable Care Act (ACA) and Arizona's legislative actions on immigration matters make clear the continuing importance of federalism.[22] The cases also illustrate the importance of legislative, presidential, and judicial leadership and the significance of our system of checks and balances. The Arizona case shows that despite the lack of action by Congress, the federal government, and only the federal government, can take certain actions regarding immigration policy. But the case with the most potential impact in many years on federalism is the ACA case.

The tortuous history of the ACA through Congress and its passage through the court system in *National Federation of Independent Business v. Sebelius* sheds light on how politics and federalism work in today's world. The case started immediately after Congress passed the legislation in 2010 as the elected attorneys-general of thirteen sovereign states challenged the constitutional power of the sovereign federal government to take various actions regarding the cost, payment, and delivery of health care. The judicial branch of the federal government, being the final arbiter of such matters, heard evidence and arguments about the ACA over two years as thirteen other states, the National Federation of Independent Business, and several individuals subsequently joined the case. After analyzing the respective powers of the states and the federal goverment under various clauses of the Constitution, including the commerce and tax clauses, a majority of the Supreme Court decided that the "individual mandate" provision (which requires most people to have "minimum essential" health insurance) of the ACA was not within the constitutional power of the federal government under the commerce clause, but to the surprise of many, it was within the federal government's power "to lay and collect taxes." Thus the Court continued the practice started in the 1930s of upholding major social legislation passed by Congress—but under a potentially significant changed rationale.[23]

In ruling on the other "key provision" of the ACA, which establishes a major expansion of Medicaid to begin in 2014, the Court found the application of a long-standing practice of the federal government to "encourage" the states to adopt federal policies to be unconstitutional. As noted above, the federal government has for many years used financial incentives to get the states to adopt certain policies that are not within the powers of the federal government. This practice has generally been found to be constitutional. However, in the ACA case, the Court expressed concern that at some point such incentives amount to federal coercion of the states and, quoting an earlier case, noted that "the Constitution has never been understood to confer upon Congress the ability to require the states to govern according to Congress' instructions." The Court then zeroed in on the portion of the ACA that allowed the federal government to withdraw all federal Medicaid funding (not just the funding for the expansion) if a state did not agree to expand the Medicaid program. It found this provision unconstitutional and agreed with the challenging states that this huge fiscal threat " 'crossed the line distinguishing encouragement from coercion.' " The Court said the threat was "much more than 'relatively mild encouragement' [to the states]—it is a gun to the head. . . . The threatened loss of over 10 percent of a state's overall budget . . . is economic dragooning that leaves the states with no real option but to acquiesce in the Medicaid expansion."[24]

While this decision will certainly be a major topic of discussion for those interested in the delivery of health care and in federalism, it remains to be seen how large an impact it will actually have as Congress and the states decide what to do about Medicaid before the scheduled 2014 expansion.

A more detailed constitutional analysis of the power of Congress to use the preemption doctrine, mandates, and its fiscal power to cause state action is beyond the scope of this book, but readers should be aware that the judicial branch continues to grant strong deference to the legislative branch and its powers of preemption and mandates. According to the bipartisan Advisory Commission on Intergovernmental Relations (ACIR), the Court has "given the congress substantial freedom to interpret its own constitutional powers, checked only by the voters and the political muscle of state and local governments in the national political process."[25] Thus, the Court has largely left it up to members of the U.S. House and Senate to exercise their wisdom and discretion in using this power, and to voters and state legislatures to push back when they think Washington has acted imprudently. The majority opinion in the ACA case generally follows this long line of judicial reasoning by ending with the following: "The Court does not express any opinion on the wisdom of the ACA. Under the Constitution that judgment is reserved to the people."[26] Thus the vitality of federalism and the intertwined roles of the courts and legislatures continue in American government.

There is one additional point about the Court's actions starting in the 1950s that needs to be mentioned. At about the same time as much of the expansion of federal power by the legislative and executive branches described above, the judicial branch of the federal government began to be more frequently drawn in to deciding the propriety of the actions and inactions of states and local governments. These decisions were based on key constitutional protections of individual liberties and had significant fiscal and social impact on how the country was to be governed. Starting with *Brown v. Board of Education of Topeka* in 1954 and continuing through the 1970s, the Supreme Court struck down various programs run by state and local governments. In *Brown* and a related case in the District of Columbia, the Court determined that racially segregated schools under the doctrine of separate but equal were not fair to all. The Court struck down the local school board's actions as violating the Constitution's equal protection and due process provisions of the Fourteenth Amendment.[27] This decision and those that followed led to busing of students and violent clashes of citizens reacting to school desegregation.

In the decades following, the Court and lower federal courts found that the constitutional violations of certain state and local government programs were so egregious that their actions were not only struck down, but the lower federal courts in some cases actually took over the direct supervision of the programs. Examples of these situations included housing, crowded mental health institutions, and prisons.[28] The 2011 Supreme Court decision forcing California to make "the choice of shrinking its prison population drastically or make sufficient room for the prisoners" shows the Court will remain active in requiring the states and local governments to act in a manner the Court believes is necessary to protect the individual rights of citizens.[29]

As described above, the roles of the federal, state, and local governments will inevitably continue to change. In explaining these changing governmental relationships, political scientists, judges, and politicians have used a variety of adjectives (including dual, cooperative, creative, and horizontal) to define federalism as it works in practice. But as the American Political Science Association recognized, there is still work to be done. In a 2005 symposium, it noted "the current inadequacies of the theories of dual and cooperative federalism and the need for a broader theory."[30] While academics and think tanks develop and articulate a revised theory to explain what is happening, the day-to-day work of governing marches on.

The expanded role of the federal government had an impact on all, but none more so than on state and local officials, who were often in the front lines of controversy over the delivery of preempted or judicially modified government services. Making sense of the expanded federal role was critical to the three new committee chairs appointed by Sabo. These committees had jurisdiction over much of the subject matter in which the federal government was becoming so active.

The new Local and Urban Affairs Committee, chaired by Berg, was asked to deal with the eighty-seven counties, 855 cities and municipalities, thirteen regional development commissions, 1,798 townships, and hundreds of special districts in Minnesota in a manner that was both coherent and consistent with the dictates of federalism. The Governmental Operations Committee, chaired by Sieben, was asked to similarly deal with the state's twenty-one departments, almost a hundred boards, committees, councils, and authorities, and their operation.

The Tax Committee, chaired by Kelly, was to raise the billions of dollars in revenue necessary to balance the state's budget, to oversee the taxing authority given to the various local units of government, and along with the Appropriations Committee, to pay attention to the federal government's activities concerning revenue sharing and grant making. The state revenue included the state money that goes to local school districts via the school aid formula that Joe Graba and the School Aids Committee developed and the appropriations to higher education institutions that Ray Faricy and his Appropriations Committee colleagues found to be necessary.

With this background, we look at some of the topics dealt with during the 1975–76 sessions of the legislature, including developing a "circuit breaker" for taxes, considering ways to improve local government, adopting laws for the changing role of women in society, dealing with gun control, expanding health-care insurance and programs, designing a new transit system for the Minneapolis–St. Paul area, and building a new home for the Vikings, Twins, and University of Minnesota Gophers (see Appendix A for a list of significant legislation).

Taxing and Spending, 1975–76

The Basics of Taxes and Revenue Distribution

In dealing with fiscal matters, the constitutional ground rules are different for our two sets of sovereign governments. State governments do not have as much wiggle room as the federal government. All state constitutions, except Vermont's, require a balanced operating budget for every budget cycle.[31] The federal government, however, can print or borrow money as it sees fit, subject only to international market and political forces.[32] The difference is due to the possibility of wars, major natural disasters, and national and worldwide economic problems that are so large that federal flexibility in fiscal and monetary policy is necessary.

The state's balanced budget requirements can cause significant problems for legislatures, governors, and courts. For example, the Minnesota Supreme Court decided a case near the end of the 2010 legislative session involving the veto by Minnesota's Republican Governor Tim Pawlenty of a tax increase bill passed by the DFL-controlled legislature in the 2009 session. The bill would have balanced the budget. It was passed at the end of the legislative session, and the legislature then adjourned in May. About six weeks later, on the first day of the next fiscal year, the governor unilaterally "unalloted" approximately $2.5 billion of previously approved legislative spending in order to get to his idea of a balanced budget. The governor has authority to "unallot" in certain situations.

In a decision about one year later, after a case had worked its way through the courts, the Minnesota Supreme Court discussed the balanced budget requirement and separation of powers doctrine and stated that "the Legislature has the primary responsibility to establish the spending priorities for the state. . . . The executive branch has a limited . . . role in the budget process." The court noted that the governor did not call a special session of the legislature, and then found that the governor's actions were invalid and not in accord with the unallotment statute.[33]

The legislature was in session in 2010 when the decision was announced. The decision had the effect of adding billions of dollars to the budget gap then facing the state. The argument between the "no new taxes" stance of Governor Pawlenty, who was not seeking reelection but was busy on the national scene exploring a presidential race, and the legislature's "balanced approach" (some increase in taxes and some cuts) continued for a couple of weeks after the court's decision.[34] The legislature, where Speaker of the House Margaret Anderson Kelliher was the DFL-endorsed candidate to replace Pawlenty as governor in the coming election and where the Republican nominee, Representative Tom Emmer, was a key player, decided the best thing was to accept most of the governor's attempted cuts. The legislature also exercised its rights as a sovereign power and postponed the payment of many local government and school aids, thus technically balancing the current budget. The legislators and candidates for governor then hit the campaign trail.

The problem with this deal was that it really did not fix anything; it merely moved the problem down the road and increased the projected deficit for the next two-year budget cycle. This expensive problem would need to be faced by a new governor, a new legislature, and hundreds of local government officials who had to figure out how to deliver services to voters without the revenue they had been led to expect. The voters would need to sort out this mess.

In November 2010 they did—sort of—with gubernatorial candidate Kelliher not surviving the primary, and Emmer losing a very close general election to DFLer Mark Dayton. Dayton's winning campaign was based on a platform of "tax the rich," and he squeaked past Emmer, who campaigned on the "no new taxes" idea. However, the Republicans, in a major surprise, wrested legislative control from the DFL. Thus, the state was left with a divided government, no clear-cut answer to how to meet its balanced budget requirement, and a projected deficit of over $6 billion.[35]

In 2011, DFL Governor Dayton and the Republican-controlled legislature locked horns for six months over how to fund the inherited deficit and a balanced budget for the next two-year budget cycle. The stalemate resulted in the longest (twenty days) shutdown of a state in U.S. history and a lower credit rating, which means higher interest costs.[36] The painful, costly, and disruptive shutdown finally came to an end when the governor concluded that the Republican legislators (of which in the house, 47 percent were freshman, and where the Speaker of the house and over 18 percent of his Republican colleagues had previously pledged in writing to the Americans for Tax Reform to not vote for any tax increases) would never compromise on the "no new taxes" issue.[37]

The governor reluctantly accepted the concept of more borrowing to fund the budget, and the Republicans agreed to $1.4 billion in additional spending over their previously passed and vetoed $34.1 billion budget.[38] Governor Dayton said the additional funds were required to avoid "draconian cuts" in services and payments to the citizens of the state.[39] The borrowing included shifting an additional $700 million in school aid payments to the next budget cycle.[40] One deplorable result of the "deals" of 2010 and 2011 is that the state is obligated to the school districts for $2.1 billion, with no plan for repayment.[41] This deep fiscal hole will be faced by the legislature and the governor in 2013, as they again wrestle with the balanced budget requirement and a new two-year budget cycle. As the headlines in the state's largest paper put it, "Painful deal delays day of reckoning."[42] It was clear that the time spent in talking and political posturing to reach these "deals" was not the state's finest hour.

In dealing with the constitutionally mandated balanced budget requirement, whether in 1975 or in 2011, every legislature faces tough questions regarding spending and taxes. The Appropriations and School Aids Committees and their senate counterparts do the initial heavy lifting by listening to the state's citizens in legislative hearings, analyzing the effectiveness of existing programs, and deciding which needs and programs are appropriate for funding. The Tax Committee defines the tax policy to be adopted to pay the bill. Early in the process these committees listen to the governor to hear what the executive branch says about spending and taxes. In the 1975–76 sessions, Governor Anderson said that in his opinion the spending number was $5 billion.[43] As the legislative process moved forward, the debate focused on two essential questions: how much should the state spend, and who should pay the taxes?

Sabo had always found the budgeting process interesting and challenging, and he knew the importance of the answers to the questions of how much and who pays—both from a fairness to the taxpayers perspective and a political perspective. He had been a key legislative player in determining the all-important answers since 1970. As Speaker, Sabo met periodically with the relevant committee chairs and discussed the need to coordinate their efforts, to be fair, and to keep an eye on the political ball.

This group of committee chairs and Sabo considered many things, including the existing and often politically entrenched tax and spend structure, the location of certain high-value properties such as key shopping centers, power plants, and Minnesota's iron ore mines, the state's credit rating, its outstanding indebtedness, and general economic base—all of which Kelly referred to as "givens," and all of which were difficult to change. They also considered the types of taxpayers: individuals, corporations, partnerships, cooperatives, and so on, as well as the impact of possible tax changes on job creation, the environment, and the business climate. Based on these discussions and the ever-present dose of politics, the group began to decide how much it thought was necessary to run the state properly, and how much the state could afford. They then began to decide who should pay how much in order to balance the budget and at the same time maintain a sense of overall fairness in tax policy.

The process was fluid, and as the session went on, the financial targets were adjusted. The theory was that toward the end of the legislative session, all this would come together in a balanced and fair budget. In practice, however, history had shown that the complicated public process, the divergent views of the citizenry and their elected officials, and the strong egos and personalities involved made the chance that practice would follow theory highly problematic.

In deciding these fiscal policy questions, legislators need to understand the impact on people and policies of the various possible taxes. Since persons with lower incomes usually spend a greater percentage of their income on housing and other necessities, property and sales taxes take a greater percentage of income from those persons than from persons with higher incomes. These types of taxes are called "regressive." Under a typical income tax, the rate goes up as income rises, and thus income taxes take a greater percentage of income from persons with higher incomes. This type of tax is said to be "progressive." Not surprisingly, persons with lower income tend to favor progressive taxes, and persons with higher incomes tend to favor regressive taxes.

The regressive property tax, usually set by local government officials, is a very visible tax to property owners—both businesses and individuals. As inflation raises property values (as it generally did in the 1970s), the property tax goes up along with the property's value, assuming the tax rate (mill levy, as it is called in tax terminology) stays the same. For many senior citizens and others living on a fixed income, inflation means a greater share of their income goes to pay property taxes. These citizens are soon talking to their elected officials about "being taxed out of our homes." A business owner may face a similar problem, as the tax goes up whether or not the business is making money. As any legislator, county commissioner, or city council member with many businesses or senior citizens in their district will tell you, this is not idle talk. It is talk that carries political power. Tax Committee members hear a great deal from all sides in determining who pays and how much.

Sabo, Coleman, and Governor Anderson, all veterans of the Minnesota Miracle marathon discussions in 1971, were well aware of the problems caused for many by the link between taxes on real estate and taxes on income. As discussed earlier, to address these problems, previous legislatures had transferred state money to local units of government by means of school and local government aids to help lower property taxes. Additional property tax relief via a more targeted tax break had also been provided. Thus, there was a "homestead credit" for homeowners, a "renters' credit," a "disabled persons' credit," and a "senior citizens' credit." The legislature's practice of adding credits was, in the opinion of the Citizens League, "patching and remodeling and adding-on . . . without any overall plan or sense of direction about the objectives of a well-thought-out state policy."[44]

A fifteen-member Tax Study Commission had been established in the 1971 tax act to continue to "examine Minnesota's total tax structure, its equity and distribution." Governor Anderson made five appointments, and the house and senate each appointed five members. The governor appointed the president of Honeywell, the dean of the Graduate School of the University of Minnesota, a leader of the United Auto Workers, the general counsel from Land O'Lakes agricultural cooperative, and Sabo.[45] In other words, the executive and legislative branches of government were asking for help from some of the state's top business, academic, and labor leaders in deciding who pays and how much they pay.

The governor listened to the Tax Study Commission, and in his inaugural and budget addresses, he recommended combining the homestead, renters', senior citizens', and disabled persons' credit into a "single income-adjusted property tax relief system." The total increase in cost to the state for this proposed system of lowering property taxes was $50 million.[46]

The Circuit Breaker, Tax Philosophy, and the Aftermath

Eileen Baumgartner had now joined House Research, the "small university," and was assigned to the Tax Committee. She worked closely with Sabo, Kelly, Tax Study Commission staff Ron Rainey, and John Haynes from the governor's office. They were charged with analyzing how best to implement the system of relating property tax relief to income. Their recommendation was to adopt the concepts developed by the Tax Study Commission and the governor. This involved phasing out the various property tax credits (homestead, seniors, etc.) and replacing them with a "circuit breaker." Under this proposal, if property taxes exceeded a certain percentage of income, the state "broke the circuit" of income and property tax and provided a refund to the property tax payer. Sabo, Kelly, and the house generally agreed with these concepts. Senator Alec Olson, a member of the Tax Study Commission, also agreed, but many other senators had reservations about the idea.[47]

As with many things, the devil was in the details. Those details led to disputes between legislators who were usually political allies. Sabo, Kelly, and Olson found the details in the governor's proposal "unworkable." They refused to pass it. The unworkable feature related to the timing of the payments and the governor's insistence on also developing a $150 million "rainy-day" reserve fund for future contingencies.[48] The house generally supported the concept of a rainy-day fund but was concerned that there was not enough money in the state coffers to provide both sufficient property tax relief under the circuit breaker and a rainy-day fund. Baumgartner and her colleagues ran numerous "what if" calculations to find a workable solution.

The senate leadership was not enamored with either the circuit breaker or the rainy-day fund. Senate Majority Leader Coleman said the governor's proposal for the circuit breaker "was pretty expensive," and he and others, such as Assistant Majority Leader George Conzemius, had alternative uses for the money required for the circuit breaker.[49] The alternatives included a one-time rebate to taxpayers, tax rate cuts, an increase in school aids, and having the state take over part of the costs of funding welfare programs. The latter two alternatives would help lower property taxes, as the costs of schools and county-run welfare programs took a large share of the property tax revenues raised by local school boards and counties.

In general terms, Sabo's political philosophy included a pay-as-you-go approach for operating costs, and he was successful in imparting it to most of his house colleagues. This approach resulted in tax increases from time to time (such as the Minnesota Miracle in 1971) but did not result in deficits that future legislatures or generations had to address. Sabo and the house DFLers were skeptical about the senate's rebate idea and other new programs that had a long "tail" and thus would require a future legislature to borrow, cut other programs, or raise taxes. The governor generally agreed with Sabo and the house. The governor was also concerned about overly optimistic revenue projections and said, "We must be careful. . . . We must not allow ourselves to indulge in excessive optimism [with revenue projections] which would result in defaulting on our commitments."[50] This cautious fiscal philosophy was to become the central sticking point in tough and colorful battles with the senate DFL in upcoming months.

Meanwhile, the School Aids and Appropriations Committees were taking testimony on how much money was needed for schools, welfare, and other programs and services. A strong commitment to education led Graba and the School Aids Committee to develop the largest single spending bill at that time in legislative history: $1.6 billion for the state's share of K–12 school costs. The bill provided more targeted aids for school districts with rapidly changing enrollments and for districts with a high percentage of students from homes receiving public assistance.[51]

The Appropriations Committee's major bills and other ongoing appropriations called for another $3.4 billion. Thus, the final legislative answer in the house to the question of how much was close to the governor's $5 billion.

Federalism, 1972 style. Cartoon by Dan Dowling, *Kansas City Star,*
January 9, 1972. Reprinted with permission.

The transfer of power is under way as former governor Harold LeVander *(left)* leaves the governor's residence with new governor Wendell Anderson, January 1971. Photograph by Earl Seubert. Courtesy of the *Star Tribune*/Minneapolis–St. Paul, 2011.

Governor-elect Wendell Anderson *(left)* receives congratulations from State Senator Nick Coleman *(center)* and U.S. Senator Hubert Humphrey, December 1970. Photograph by Mike Zerby. Courtesy of the *Star Tribune*/Minneapolis–St. Paul, 2011.

Governor-elect Wendell Anderson *(left)* with newly appointed executive secretary Tom Kelm *(center)* and administrative assistant Jim Pederson, December 1970. Photograph by Donald Black. Courtesy of the *Star Tribune*/Minneapolis–St. Paul, 2011.

Newly elected Majority Leader Ernie Lindstrom *(left)* confers with fellow Conservative legislator Charlie Weaver in the 1971 legislative session. Photograph courtesy of the *Star Tribune*/Minneapolis–St. Paul, 2011.

Citizens protest high property taxes outside the state capitol in 1971. Photograph courtesy of the Minnesota Historical Society.

Key legislators talk taxes and revenue sharing, leading to the 1971 "Minnesota Miracle" legislation: Governor Wendell Anderson *(back to camera)*; from left: Senate Majority Leader Stanley Holmquist, House Minority Leader Martin Sabo, House Speaker Aubrey Dirlam, and Senate Minority Leader Nick Coleman. Photograph by Powell Krugar. Courtesy of the *Star Tribune*/Minneapolis–St. Paul, 2011.

Reapportionment confusion. Cartoon by Roy Justus, *Minneapolis Star,* May 5, 1972. Courtesy of the *Star Tribune*/Minneapolis–St. Paul, 2011. Image courtesy of the Roy Justus Papers, Special Collections Research Center, Syracuse University Library.

DATES TO REMEMBER

SEPTEMBER 12
PRIMARY ELECTION

OCTOBER 17
LAST DAY TO REGISTER
FOR GENERAL ELECTION

NOVEMBER 7
GENERAL ELECTION

DFL LEGISLATURE

Prepared and circulated by the Minnesota DFL Central Committee,
Richard Moe, Chairman, 730 East 38th Street, Minneapolis.

Your Key To Open Government

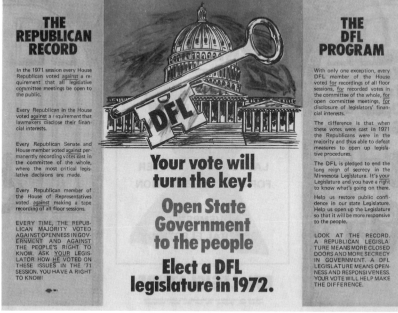

THE REPUBLICAN RECORD

In the 1971 session every House Republican voted against a requirement that all legislative committee meetings be open to the public.

Every Republican in the House voted against a requirement that lawmakers disclose their financial interests.

Every Republican Senate and House member voted against permanently recording votes cast in the committee of the whole, where the most critical legislative decisions are made.

Every Republican member of the House of Representatives voted against making a tape recording of all floor sessions.

EVERY TIME, THE REPUBLICAN MAJORITY VOTED AGAINST OPENNESS IN GOVERNMENT AND AGAINST THE PEOPLE'S RIGHT TO KNOW. ASK YOUR LEGISLATOR HOW HE VOTED ON THESE ISSUES IN THE '71 SESSION. YOU HAVE A RIGHT TO KNOW!

Your vote will turn the key!

Open State Government to the people

Elect a DFL legislature in 1972.

THE DFL PROGRAM

With only one exception, every DFL member of the House voted for recordings of all floor sessions, for recorded votes in the committee of the whole, for open committee meetings, for disclosure of legislators' financial interests.

The difference is that when these votes were cast in 1971 the Republicans were in the majority and thus able to defeat measures to open up legislative procedures.

The DFL is pledged to end the long reign of secrecy in the Minnesota Legislature. It's your Legislature and you have a right to know what's going on there.

Help us restore public confidence in our state Legislature. Help us open up the Legislature so that it will be more responsive to the people.

LOOK AT THE RECORD. A REPUBLICAN LEGISLATURE MEANS MORE CLOSED DOORS AND MORE SECRECY IN GOVERNMENT. A DFL LEGISLATURE MEANS OPENNESS AND RESPONSIVENESS. YOUR VOTE WILL HELP MAKE THE DIFFERENCE.

The DFL election brochure that played a key role in the historic 1972 DFL legislative victory. Courtesy of the Minnesota Historical Society.

History is made. Cartoon by Jerry Fearing, *St. Paul Pioneer Press,*
November 9, 1972. Reprinted with permission.

Newly reelected legislator Tom Berg *(center)* is introduced to the
DFL victory party on election night 1972 by Hubert Humphrey
and Walter Mondale. Photograph by Charles Bjorgen and Roger
Nystrom. Courtesy of the *Star Tribune*/Minneapolis–St. Paul, 2011.

Newly elected Speaker
of the House Martin
Sabo presides in 1973
with longtime Chief
Clerk Ed Burdick *(cen-
ter)* at his usual post at
the podium with as-
sistant Hazel Johnson
(left). Photograph by
Minnesota House of
Representatives/Tom
Olmscheid.

Second-term legislator Ray Faricy speaking on the house floor. Photograph by Minnesota House of Representatives/Tom Olmscheid.

Newly elected legislators at an orientation session after the 1972 election. The new legislators included five women, which increased the number of women in the legislature from one to six. Four of the new women are pictured: Phyllis Kahn, back row; Linda Berglin, lower left; and Mary Forysthe and Ernee McArthur, left to right in front row. Newly elected legislator Joan Growe was absent from the picture. Photograph by Donald Black. Courtesy of the *Star Tribune*/Minneapolis–St. Paul, 2011.

Time magazine August 13, 1973. The country's leading news magazine takes note of a place and time when government and politics worked well—and when the fishing was good.

Newly elected Republican Minority Leader Henry Savelkoul *(left)* with newly elected Speaker of the House Martin Sabo. Photograph by Minnesota House of Representatives/Tom Olmscheid.

House Minority Caucus leaders, 1975–76: *(left to right)* Rodney Searle, James Ulland, Henry Savelkoul, Arne Carlson, and Salisbury Adams. Photograph by Minnesota House of Representatives/ Tom Olmscheid, from *Minnesota Legislative Manual, 1975–1976.*

Governor Wendell Anderson in his office with legislators discussing tax-rebate plan proposed by Senator Nick Coleman, March 1976. *Left to right:* Anderson, House Speaker Martin Sabo, Leslie Danford and Tom Kelm of the governor's staff, Senator Alec Olson, Representative Bill Kelly, Representative John Lindstrom, and Coleman, March 1976. Photograph by Kent Kobertsteen. Courtesy of the *Star Tribune*/Minneapolis–St. Paul, 2011.

Deputy Education Commissioner Joe Graba shortly after leaving the legislature, 1978. Photograph by Earl Seubert. Courtesy of the *Star Tribune*/ Minneapolis– St. Paul, 2011.

GOP sees gains if DFL brawls

A view of the potential shake-up in Minnesota politics in 1976 and beyond if U.S. Senator Walter Mondale becomes vice president. Cartoon by Craig MacIntosh, *Minneapolis Star,* August 9, 1976. Courtesy of the *Star Tribune*/Minneapolis–St. Paul, 2011.

Charles "Chuck" Slocum, chairman of the Minnesota Independent Republican Party; 2. U.S. Senator Walter Mondale; 3. U.S. Representative Bill Frenzel; 4. Rudy Boschwitz, Republican National Committeeman; 5. Attorney General Warren Spannaus; 6. Lieutenant Governor Rudy Perpich; 7. Governor Wendell Anderson; 8. U.S. Representative Don Fraser; 9. House Speaker Martin Sabo.

Governor Rudy Perpich signs Handgun Control Act legislation. *Left to right:* house author Tom Berg, senate author Bill McCutcheon, Perpich, Robert Hentges (aide to Attorney General Warren Spannaus), Spannaus, and senate coauthor Nick Coleman. Photograph by Minnesota House of Representatives/Tom Olmscheid.

In a rare visit by a governor to the house floor, Governor Rudy Perpich and Tax Committee Chair Bill Kelly discuss tax policy in 1977. Photograph by Minnesota House of Representatives/Tom Olmscheid.

Vice President Walter Mondale with newly appointed Senator (and candidate for election) Wendell Anderson and Senate candidate Robert Short *(right)* aboard Air Force Two just before the "Minnesota Massacre" in October 1978. Photograph by Kent Kobertsteen. Courtesy of the *Star Tribune*/Minneapolis–St. Paul, 2011.

Gubernatorial candidate Al Quie *(right)*, AFL-CIO President David Roe *(center)*, and Governor Rudy Perpich at AFL-CIO Convention just before the 1978 election. Photograph by Charles Bjorgen. Courtesy of the *Star Tribune*/Minneapolis–St. Paul, 2011.

Former House Majority Leader Irv Anderson *(center)* with Representative Carl Johnson *(left)* contemplating how to make the 1979 legislature work with sixty-seven Democrats and sixty-seven Republicans, shortly after the "Minnesota Massacre" election, December 1978. Courtesy of the *Star Tribune*/Minneapolis–St. Paul, 2011.

Newly reelected Secretary of State Joan Growe is ready to convene the 1979 session of the legislature, January 1979. Courtesy of the *Star Tribune*/Minneapolis–St. Paul, 2011.

Outgoing Congressman Donald Fraser *(left)* with newly elected
Congressman Martin Sabo in 1978. Photograph by Minnesota House
of Representatives/Tom Olmscheid.

Federalism, 2010 style. Cartoon by Jack Ohman, *The Oregonian,*
August 10, 2010. Reprinted with permission.

Several weeks before the end of the session, Kelly and the Tax Committee brought their legislation stating who should pay this $5 billion to the house floor. Their answer to who pays was, in general terms, that those who pay income and sales taxes should pay the same as they had been paying, those who bought taconite (iron ore) should pay $0.39 a ton more, and persons of low and moderate income should pay less in property taxes via the circuit-breaker mechanism.[52]

Explaining to the legislature and the public the why and how of spending and taxing legislation is a miserable task. It is the lot of the chairs of the Tax, School Aids, and Appropriations Committees to perform this task. It includes delivering a combination of boring and unpleasant news. Legislators and constituents alike nod favorably when they hear about the spending for programs they believe are necessary, and frown or shout bad words when they hear about program cuts or the taxes necessary to pay for the spending. John Haynes, the governor's chief fiscal advisor, would help explain the governor's perspective by periodically walking down to the capitol basement where the press corps was housed, and visiting one-on-one with reporters. The majority leader and the Speaker also played a role in defending the proposals from the ever-present political attacks, but the nitty-gritty of explaining the details falls on the committee chairs. Tax Committee Chair Kelly had to use all his diplomatic skills and Irish wit to explain the complicated circuit breaker and to deliver the "who pays and how much?" message on the house floor. Graba assisted when the discussion turned to the relationship of property taxes to school aids.

The discussion that took place over the next couple of weeks about taxes was generally not different from other debates in other years over fiscal policy. Simple slogans, platitudes, and clichés such as "fiscal responsibility," "tax and spend," "invest for the future," and "live within your means" peppered the discussion by legislators, reporters, editorialists, commentators, and constituents alike. These smooth-sounding phrases add little or nothing to the analysis of the impact of legislation. They lull the mind and allow people to gloss over unpleasant truths about what is actually happening to people in their businesses, classrooms, homes, and farms. The search for a more complete and accurate way to engage the public in a thoughtful discussion of fiscal issues remains a major task for our democratic system. Bringing policy wonk ideas to the TV sets, computer screens, kitchen tables, boardrooms, and labor halls in the country is a difficult task that few perform well. But cliché-ridden or not, the debate came to an end, and Kelly got the job done. The house passed the 1975 omnibus tax bill with bipartisan support and sent it to the senate.[53]

As the legislative session moved toward adjournment, another important bill relating to taxes headed for passage. Who pays and how much? were at the forefront of the debate on this bill as well. Al Patton, a quiet and effective legislator from Sartell in central Minnesota, carried a controversial bill raising the tax on gasoline $0.02 per gallon. The bill also addressed the high costs of freeways and the shift in state policy away from building more and bigger urban highways to providing other methods of moving people in and between cities and suburbs. Included in the bill were a moratorium on building specified freeways in the Minneapolis–St. Paul area, appropriations for mass transit, and a requirement to build sound barriers along freeways in residential neighborhoods. Sabo named Berg and Bill Schreiber, a Republican and a member of the Local and Urban Affairs Committee, which was then wrestling with issues involving billions of dollars of transit proposals, to the Gas Tax Conference Committee.[54]

Reaching agreement on the spending part of this bill involved another example of the human and unforeseen factors in the legislative process. As the conference committee argued about the impact of freeways on neighborhoods, the house pushed hard for its position to force the Highway Department to build sound barriers along new freeways that ran through residential neighborhoods. This was contentious since many rural legislators, particularly in the senate, did not want precious gas tax dollars spent on expensive noise barriers—especially since the money could be used to build bigger and better "farm-to-market roads."

The legislative adjournment date and thus the deadline for the conference committee was May 20, which is also close to Mother Nature's deadline for planting corn in Minnesota. As the last scheduled meeting of the conference committee dragged on past midnight on Saturday night, May 18, senator and farmer Clarence Purfeerst, the chief senate author of the bill, announced he had to leave the meeting as he was planting corn shortly after sunrise about five hours hence. Purfeerst was a vociferous opponent of the noise barriers. When he left the meeting, the house negotiators promptly moved that the house position on noise barriers be adopted. Without Purfeerst present, the urban senators felt more comfortable supporting their urban house colleagues, and the house position was adopted. As the house negotiators walked out of the capitol on Sunday morning just as the dawn broke and the birds started chirping, they were asked by a reporter how they managed the noise barrier legislative legerdemain. They grinned and told the perplexed reporter, "God was on our side."[55]

While the gas tax negotiators found common ground, the omnibus tax bill conferees struggled. The senate conferees continued to push for direct tax relief for income tax payers. The house liked the idea of tax relief and recognized there was a projected state surplus, but members were worried about the future impact of the proposed permanent tax cuts. Around the country, severe fiscal problems were occurring, and local units of government were close to bankruptcy. New York City got so close to bankruptcy that fall that its lawyers "were in the State Supreme Court filing a bankruptcy petition and police cars were mobilized to serve the papers on the banks."[56] This crisis around the country got people's attention, and the financial solvency of local units of government became a national concern. The house, led by Sabo, noted this and kept preaching fiscal prudence. The governor continued to support the house position.

Finally a compromise was reached, and the 1975 omnibus tax bill passed and was signed by the governor. According to one editorial, the final bill was a "compromise in the best sense."[57] It included a $50 million circuit breaker for property tax relief, retained the homestead and renters' credits, merged the senior citizens' and disabled persons' credits into the circuit breaker, and, in accordance with senate wishes, provided for the partial state takeover of welfare costs.[58] The circuit breaker continues to this day to work well in Minnesota. In 2010, the House Rules Committee passed a resolution commemorating thirty-five years of the circuit breaker (now called the Property Tax Refund Program and the Renters Credit Program) and called it a "model of public policy throughout the last 35 years." The resolution passed with strong bipartisan support.[59]

The time and energy spent on resolving the underlying fiscal dispute between the house and senate caused other problems to develop. Despite a frantic last-minute rush in the senate, several important bills, including a major appropriation bill, did not pass before the constitutionally mandated time for adjournment. Both the senate and the house DFL caucuses looked bad. Minority Leader Savelkoul wasted no time in accusing the DFL majority of having left the legislative business "in near shambles," and alleging that there was a "circus atmosphere" at the end of the session. Even Majority Leader Irv Anderson agreed there had been problems, as the news media blared, "House leaders agree logjam worst ever."[60]

The media was particularly hard on the senate, which had "dallied on the floor most of the [last] day."[61] When the senate finally realized it was running out of time before the midnight deadline, it had to suspend its rules to get the key bills passed just to keep the state running. But since the DFL had only thirty-nine of the forty-five votes required to suspend the rules, at least six Republican votes were needed. Senate Republican leader Robert Ashbach said, "We had it in the palm of our hand to force a special session. . . . But we [the Republican Caucus] decided that wouldn't be responsible." Republican Robert Stassen saw it a bit differently. "We chickened out," he said.[62] But whatever the motivation, after making the DFL majority squirm, the Republicans did help by voting to suspend the rules. The scene was not pretty as the "Majority DFLers lost control in the State Senate Monday night. . . . Chaos reigned as the Senate adjourned a few minutes after midnight. . . . Coleman stood somewhat red-faced and shaken."[63] While most of the critical bills got passed by the deadline, the facts were clear to all: the DFL had not been able to get its act together on fiscal issues. The net result for managing the work flow in May 1975 was some bad press for the DFL, a number of upset legislators, and continued disagreement between house and senate DFLers on a variety of topics.

The result for overall policy, however, was more positive for the DFL, as the session was called "hard-working and generally productive."[64] In addition to the circuit breaker and partial takeover of welfare costs, school aids were substantially increased, and a surplus was projected for the state treasury. The governor decided that any problems caused by the unpassed bills were not great enough to warrant a special session, and thus solutions to any fiscal problems that developed in the interim period between sessions as well as the governor's request for a formal reserve, or "rainy-day fund," would need to wait for the 1976 session.[65]

The Republicans not only gained political ammunition about DFL mismanagement of the session, they could show that it was the Republicans that had acted conscientiously to avoid any special session. In today's political climate it is hard to imagine either party acting as responsibly as the Republican senators did in 1975.

Local Governments

The house recognized the increasingly entangled structure of federal, state, and local governments in the delivery of government services, and began to deal with it in a comprehensive way during the 1975–76 sessions.

Expanding Power

The Minneapolis–St. Paul metropolitan area contains many lakes, rivers, and streams, but none is large enough to form a natural barrier to stop real estate development. As in so many areas across the country, urban sprawl was becoming a major problem in the 1960s and 1970s. Building roads, sewers, and parks through the several different cities, counties, school districts, and watershed districts that make up the metropolitan area was complex, confusing, and costly. The Metropolitan Council had been established by the legislature in 1967 to deal with such problems and to help coordinate some of the new federal housing, transit, and other grant-in-aid programs then being implemented. The Metropolitan Council had been given further powers in 1974 under the Metropolitan Reorganization Act to help shape development and control expensive sprawl.

Two additional bills were passed in 1976 to supplement the Metropolitan Council's authority. The first described the type of projects that were of "Metropolitan Significance" and thus subject to Metropolitan Council scrutiny pursuant to the 1974 Metropolitan Reorganization Act. The second, known as the Metropolitan Land Planning Act, required local units of government in the metropolitan area to develop land-use plans and submit them to the Metropolitan Council for review. The bill gave the Metropolitan Council the power to require the counties, towns, or cities to modify their plans to make them consistent with the council's own metropolitan plan and other relevant local plans. This ruffled many feathers in local government circles. An appeal process to address the concerns of local government officials was developed by Harry Sieben and pushed through on the house floor over Berg's objections.

This planning legislation was at the cutting edge of land-use planning in the country. The National Conference of State Legislatures (NCSL) thought the legislation would be a good vehicle to show

how innovative legislation is in fact developed. The NCSL sponsored a thirty-minute documentary that was filmed in the Minnesota Legislature in 1976 about the process and the human side of legislating. Berg, Sabo, Graba, Sieben, and others were filmed in a variety of settings, and the film was shown on television and around the country to schools and civic groups.[66]

Joint Powers

A bill that passed without much fanfare but had much potential expanded the authority of local units of government to negotiate and enter into "joint power agreements." These agreements allow two or more local units of government the flexibility to negotiate and deliver services, such as police or fire services, to citizens across often outdated governmental boundaries without having to get state approval. This mechanism is a good example of a state wisely using its sovereign power to enable local governments to solve problems. Joint power agreements continue to be an effective tool to deliver a variety of services.[67] Interstate compacts are an example of a similar sensible technique at the state level.[68]

Oversight

The establishment of the Local and Urban Affairs Committee in the place of three previously existing committees (each of which had jurisdiction over just one part of the local government structure, e.g., cities), provided an opportunity for the house to better analyze the interrelationships among all levels of local government: townships, cities, counties, special purpose districts, the newly established regional development commissions, and the federal government. Berg, as chair of the new committee, met with Jim Solem of the Office of Local and Urban Affairs of the State Planning Agency and Gary Currie from House Research in early 1975 to develop ideas to make maximum use of the new committee structure. Sabo also wanted to use the committee's legislative oversight perspective to study the revenues and expenditures of the central cities of Minneapolis and St. Paul to see how they compared to each other and other large cities in the state. As a result, studies on big-city finances and the demographics of local government officials were begun, which, as described in the next chapter, led to further legislative controversies.

Women's Issues

In January 1975, a few days before Nancy Brataas, a former Republican state chair, won a special election and became the second woman ever elected to the senate, two women house members, Linda Berglin and Janet Clark, joined Representative Wesley Skoglund for what they thought would be a routine lunch.[69] The lunch ended up tearing down a barrier to equal treatment for women and ensuring that women legislators could join their male counterparts at a popular legislative lunch stop.

In the 1970s, when bans on gifts to legislators were much less strict than in today's world, all legislators received a complimentary right to use the athletic and dining facilities at the St. Paul Athletic Club, a private club. (The legislators had to pay for their food and beverages.) Berglin, Clark, and Skoglund stopped for lunch at the cafeteria in the club and were promptly told, "Women aren't allowed in here." Skoglund showed the hostess his complimentary card and said he was told he could bring guests. However, the women servers refused to serve the food, while men "went around the trio" and were served. Meanwhile, the hostess scurried to find the manager. About five minutes later, "word came from upstairs to serve the women." The three finally got their food and were offered a table by two men who were just leaving. Skoglund was disgusted and said he planned to introduce a bill to make such discrimination illegal. The board of directors of the club said a change in the policy was "being considered."[70] It was not only considered, it was implemented, and Brataas, Berglin, Clark, and the other women legislators could henceforth dine hassle free.

House DFL member Phyllis Kahn led the way to broader progress for women with several pieces of legislation. One provided for equal opportunity for girls and boys in school athletics, another provided that a woman may keep her maiden name when marrying, and a third established a Council on the Economic Status of Women. This council would go on to play a significant role in successfully pushing for legislation to require pay equity for women.[71]

Crime

As promised at the end of the previous session, Attorney General Warren Spannaus, Berg, and Senate Majority Leader Coleman brought the Handgun Control Act back to the legislature to try again

to get statewide regulation of handguns in Minnesota. The tortuous process of House File 679 during this session well illustrates
the legislative process as it deals with public conflicts and regional
and cultural differences in an emotionally and politically charged
atmosphere.

Cosmetic and substantive changes were made to the bill's 1973
version. The substantive changes related to sentencing of criminals
and permits for gun dealers. These helped reduce objections to the
bill, but only slightly. The changes had no impact on opponents who
believed that all gun control is bad or that it is unconstitutional. Bob
Hentges, the top legislative aid to Spannaus, directed the drafting
and worked closely with Berg and Coleman to round up the necessary votes.

Coauthors were picked with care. Ray Faricy again agreed to coauthor the bill, along with a Democrat from Duluth, Mike Jaros. Ted
Suss, a DFLer from the southern part of the Minneapolis–St. Paul
metropolitan area, and Jerry Knickerbocker, a Republican from the
western suburbs of the metropolitan area, were other coauthors. In the
senate, Coleman was the chief author along with Harmon Ogdahl, a
Republican from Minneapolis, and Bill McCutcheon, a DFLer and a
police officer from St. Paul.[72]

On February 25, 1975, the eighteen-page House File 679 was introduced. Senate File 625, a slightly different version of the bill, was
introduced two days later. The bills covered only handguns. They
prohibited five categories of persons from possessing handguns:
convicted felons, juveniles, persons with adjudicated mental illness,
and known alcoholics or drug users. The bills provided a fourteen-
day "cooling-off" period before a handgun could be bought, required
gun dealers to be licensed, prevented carrying a handgun in a public
place, and banned the cheap "Saturday night specials" that had no
real purpose other than to kill people.[73]

A lesson Berg had learned the hard way in the 1973 session was the
need for specific statistical evidence to support the general claims
that the bill would save lives. At Berg's request, a detailed study, conducted by Margaret Dostal with help from Ron Duffy from the DFL
Caucus Research staff, reviewed every one of the 155 handgun deaths
in the state from 1972 through 1974. Thousands of pages of records
were found and searched. A strong correlation between handgun
deaths and the use of handguns by the five categories of people prohibited from owning handguns by the bill was found.[74] The study, an

example of the importance of good staff work, received widespread media circulation including a seven-part series in the state's largest newspaper.[75] Berg, Coleman, Hentges, and their allies used the study data extensively in their quest for votes.

The first hearing on either bill was before the House Committee on Crime Prevention and Corrections on March 4, 1975. Several hundred noisy people, many carrying placards in opposition to any form of gun control, crowded into Room Five, a hearing room in the State Office Building. The chair of the committee, Don Moe, a third-term legislator from St. Paul and a supporter of the bill, anticipated a large crowd and had arranged for extra State Patrol personnel to be on hand as security. Moe explained at the outset that there would be three hearings on the bill: the first to explain the bill and for proponents to testify, the second for the opponents to testify, and the third for the committee to deliberate and vote.

Berg began by explaining the bill and introducing witnesses favorable to the bill. These included Attorney General Spannaus, the chief of police from Hibbing (a city located in the heart of the anti-gun control territory of northern Minnesota's Iron Range), the chief of police from Minneapolis, and former Young Turk Gary Flakne, now the Hennepin County attorney. Two witnesses who had had loved ones killed in shootings involving handguns also testified. Supporting statements from former Republican governor Elmer L. Andersen, the superintendent of the Minnesota Bureau of Criminal Apprehension, and others were placed in the record.[76]

Berg's wife, Margit, attended the hearing and was quietly sitting in the midst of a group of vocal opponents. As the hearing continued, Berg kept going to the podium and introducing each witness to the committee. About halfway through the witnesses as Berg rose to go to the podium, an opponent of the bill sitting next to Margit asked out loud to no one in particular, "Who is that dumb shit, anyhow?" Margit turned to the man, smiled, and said, "my husband." She reported there were no more audible comments from her area of the hearing room during the rest of the testimony. Later in the legislative process, however, she did receive a threatening call at home that bothered her significantly. A number of supporters also received hate mail and threats.

On March 11 the opponents of the legislation then had their turn at the podium. The most articulate opposition came from a group known as the Committee for Effective Crime Control. Their spokesperson said the group "thinks of itself as a civil-rights group. . . . We defend the basic right to have and use arms by honest citizens."[77] The forty-six witnesses who spoke against the bill during the next several hours were from all parts of the state. One opponent argued that the bill would not keep handguns away from dangerous people as anyone can simply make a pistol with readily available pipe fittings. He displayed the materials to the committee, proceeded to screw the fittings together, and then reached into his pocket and pulled out a .22 caliber bullet. Committee Chair Moe pounded his gavel, sternly told the witness that he had made his point, and that if he proceeded any further with his demonstration, he would be escorted out of the room by the State Patrol. Moe was booed by the crowd, but the witness sat down saying, "May God punish the evildoer that punishes the innocent citizen."[78] After one more hearing a week later and a variety of amendments, a roll call vote was taken on a motion to pass the bill. House File 679 was recommended to pass and was sent to the house floor by a vote of eleven to six.[79]

Pursuant to procedures then in effect, the first time a bill was debated on the house floor, the house was said to be acting as a "Committee of the Whole." Any amendments that were germane to the bill were allowed. A simple majority was needed to adopt an amendment, to send the bill back to a committee, or to recommend that the bill pass. If the bill was recommended to pass, the bill was "laid over" for a day and then taken up for "final passage." In this second debate, no amendments were allowed, and at least sixty-eight votes from the 134-member house were needed to pass the bill.

On April 3, the bill came up for debate by the house acting as a Committee of the Whole. Opponents promptly tried to send the bill to the same committee that had killed the bill in 1973. This time the motion was defeated forty-seven to eighty-four.[80]

Numerous amendments were offered, and Berg and other supporters of the bill were able to fend off most of them. Then, after hours of debate, a motion was made to send the bill to the Appropriations Committee, which was to hear all bills involving the expenditures of state funds. There were small administrative costs involved in processing the permits required by the bill. Proponents argued the amounts were so small as to be inconsequential. They lost. The motion passed sixty-six to thirty-three, and House File 679 traveled backwards to the Appropriations Committee.[81]

Six days later the Appropriations Committee heard the bill. The hearing was limited to the fiscal impact of the proposed legislation. After much arguing, coauthor Faricy, a member of the committee, moved that the bill be recommended to pass. On another roll call vote, the motion passed, and House File 679 headed back to the House Chamber for still another round of arguments.[82]

On April 21 the bill again came before the house acting as a Committee of the Whole. This time a very tired Berg with assistance from an equally tired Hentges had counted votes carefully, and they thought they had commitments for the necessary votes. The debate started in earnest, as opponents once again made a motion to refer the bill to an unfavorable committee, this time the rural-dominated Agricultural Committee. The motion failed.[83] Majority Leader Irv Anderson, who represented the hunting and fishing area of northern Minnesota and was a vocal opponent of the bill, then offered an amendment to limit the bill to the Minneapolis–St. Paul metropolitan area. Berg argued strenuously against this amendment, and it was defeated fifty-five to seventy-seven.[84] As the debate wound down, Berg was even more tired and very worried but realized it was now or never and moved that the bill be recommended to pass. The vote was taken, and the motion passed sixty-eight to sixty-four.[85]

Now Berg, Spannaus, and Hentges needed to hold the votes for twenty-four hours, when the bill would again be voted on for final passage and transmission to the senate. Everyone knew that arms would be twisted, and threats and promises made to get at least one of the sixty-eight to switch from voting "Aye" to voting "No" on the final vote. An Associated Press news account said the upcoming vote "rank[ed] near the top in sheer emotionalism" for legislation ever considered by the legislature.[86]

To make matters worse for Berg and his allies, one of the staunch yes votes, Jim Rice, was hospitalized that night with pneumonia. The two members who were absent on the sixty-eight to sixty-four vote were likely to return and were solid no votes. Ron Sieloff, one of only nine Republicans to vote for the bill, told Berg he had changed his mind and would vote no. Willard Munger, who had voted no, was vacillating. Berg and Spannaus were both allies of Munger on environmental legislation and thought they had a chance to get Munger to support the bill and offset the possible loss of Sieloff's vote. On the day of the vote for final passage, Berg visited with Munger twice, Spannaus called him, as did Munger's brother, an attorney in Duluth, who was a friend of Spannaus and supported the bill. Munger played it close to the vest, and no one was sure how he would ultimately vote. Kelly told Berg he would vote for the bill only if needed, as this was a difficult vote for him with many of his constituents being vocal opponents of gun control.

When the house convened for the final vote, Berg, feeling the tension and knowing every vote was critical, requested a "call of the house." This is a procedure that requires that all legislators attend and vote unless formally excused. No one except Rice had been excused. As the debate was under way, Berg nodded appreciatively to Rice when he arrived from the hospital, shuffled down the center aisle of the House Chamber, and slowly eased himself into his chair.

Then a new problem developed. Another yes vote as of the day before, Republican Salisbury Adams, went to Berg and said, "I'm sorry, but I have to leave to pick up my eighty-five-year-old mother, who is arriving at the airport in about half an hour." Berg looked incredulously at Adams and said as nicely as he could, "No way," and asked him to please wait a minute. He thought for a moment and then had a page bring a note to his wife, who was watching the proceedings from the gallery. She responded to her husband's plea with a note: "Sure, I'll gladly go pick her up—it's getting a bit boring anyway." Adams gave Berg's wife the flight information and a description of his mother and went back to his seat. About an hour later Adams walked back to Berg's desk and said his mother was up in the gallery, enjoying the debate, and had said to "tell that young man [Berg] to keep fighting."

The voting tally board in the House Chamber is a large board listing each member of the legislature with a red and a green light after the member's name. Each member has a red and a green button to push indicating their vote. No totals show at the bottom of the board. Thus, it is difficult to get a quick and accurate count just by looking at the 134 colored lights on the board. However, the Speaker has an electronic tally in front of him at the Speaker's rostrum, so he can always tell the vote. The voting board remains open, and legislators can switch their votes until the Speaker exercises his discretion and directs the clerk to "close the roll." The vote is then closed, and no more voting changes can occur. On close bills, it is not uncommon for the voting board to remain open for several minutes to allow the authors a chance to round up the necessary votes. So it was with House File 679. Despite all the counting and cross-checking, Berg only had 67 of the 134 votes.

The chairs of the Tax and Appropriations Committees, as well as the majority and minority leaders, have phones at their desks on the house floor, so they can communicate with each other and the Speaker during a debate. Tax Committee Chair Kelly sat next to Berg on the house floor, and after several minutes with no vote switching going on, Kelly's phone rang. It was Sabo, who told Kelly, "I want to talk to Tom." Kelly handed the phone to Berg. Sabo said the tally was sixty-seven in favor and sixty-seven against. Berg said, "Yeah, I know, give me a couple more minutes." Sabo said, "Okay," and hung up. Berg told Kelly what Sabo had said. Kelly said nothing and immediately reached across the desk to his voting buttons and quickly switched from "No" to "Aye." As soon as the vote opposite his name switched from red to green on the tally board, Sabo ordered, "The clerk will close the roll." The chamber and visitors' gallery suddenly grew silent as the electronic tally clicked away, and all eyes shifted to a separate electronic screen that shows the bill number and the votes for and against. A few agonizing seconds later the board flashed: "HF 679, 68 Aye, 66 No." As Sabo announced, "The bill has passed and its title agreed to," a cheer arose from the gallery, where supporters had gathered. Berg breathed a sigh of relief, turned to Kelly and simply said, "Thank you, my friend."[87]

The cheers quickly gave way to frowns and curses as word arrived that Senate File 625, the senate companion bill, was not doing well. The bill had been amended substantially in the Senate Judiciary Committee and had been sent to the Finance Committee (similar to the House Appropriations Committee). After much maneuvering and more amendments in that committee, Coleman convinced the committee to send the bill to the Senate Rules Committee, which Coleman, as majority leader, chaired. Since committees usually support their chair, Coleman thought this was his best chance to get a strong bill to the senate floor. The Rules Committee did send the bill to the senate floor—but without any recommendation to pass.[88]

On the senate floor, Coleman knew that he did not have the votes to pass his weakened bill, much less the stronger bill that had squeaked by the house. He amended his bill further to delete the fourteen-day waiting period and certain other provisions that several senators found objectionable. When even this bill was eight votes short of passage, Coleman maneuvered to reconsider the vote the next day. He did so and further amended his bill. After this final round of amendments, Coleman was able to pick up the needed votes, and the bill passed, thirty-four to thirty-two.[89] It then went back to the house.

The house could either accept the bill as the senate had passed it, or refuse to concur and send the bill to a conference committee to reconcile the two bills. The reconciled bill would then have to go back to both the house and the senate for another vote. The decision as to what to do was up to Berg as the chief author.

Berg was disappointed that the senate had severely weakened the bill for which he had fought so hard and for which a number of legislators had taken very tough votes. It was clear that the senate would accept no changes to their version of the bill. In reality he faced the difficult choice of accepting the bill as passed by the senate or of starting over again in the next session after new elections. He discussed all this with Spannaus and Hentges and finally agreed he had to compromise one more time to make any progress. He agreed to the senate version, and the house readily passed it.[90] Governor Anderson signed Minnesota's first handgun control bill on June 4, 1975.[91]

The final bill banned Saturday night specials, required a permit to carry a handgun, and made it illegal for five categories of persons to possess a handgun: persons eighteen years of age or younger, unless they had completed an approved handgun safety class, persons mentally ill as defined in the bill, persons that abuse alcohol or drugs as defined in the bill, and all convicted felons. The final bill did not license gun dealers or provide for a waiting period before being able to buy a gun.[92]

Spannaus, Berg, Coleman, and their supporters doggedly said they planned to try to get at least the license provisions and the waiting period into the law in the 1977–78 sessions.[93]

Health Care

Smoking

In an interesting and amusing change to the House Rules, Phyllis Kahn, with strong support from Kelly, proposed a change to the rules to prohibit smoking in the House Chamber. Kelly had authored a similar proposal in an earlier session, which was defeated on a tie vote in the Rules Committee. Speaker Sabo was then a chain-smoker, and it was widely rumored that he did not want a smoking ban. In presenting her proposal on the house floor, Kahn showed sympathy toward the popular Sabo and exempted the Speaker's platform from the smoking ban. As Kahn put it with a smile on her face, "Even though I ask for justice, . . . I see nothing wrong with justice tempered by mercy." Kelly was not buying it. He asked for the floor, was recognized by Sabo, and offered an amendment to include the Speaker's platform in the no-smoking area. As Sabo puffed on a cigarette, Kelly simply argued, "I don't see why any area of the chamber should be excluded." After much discussion and quizzical looks from Sabo and Kahn, Kelly's amendment passed overwhelmingly—with Kahn, the antismoking advocate, voting against it. Sabo sighed, put out his cigarette, and told house members to put away all cigarettes and pipes.[94]

Several months later, the nation's first statewide antismoking bill was passed under the tenacious leadership of Kahn. Her bill prohibited smoking indoors in public places and at public meetings throughout the state, except in designated smoking areas. Sabo was a coauthor on the legislation.[95]

Health Insurance

The governor in his 1975 inaugural address proposed that the state provide a program of catastrophic health insurance to protect families from financial ruin due to major health problems.[96] Sabo reviewed the governor's proposal and thought it would not withstand the legislative and public scrutiny it would surely face. Sabo, whose job outside of the legislature was selling health and other insurance, convinced the governor that the proposal was not ready for prime time and that they should use the interim period between the 1975 and 1976 sessions to prepare more expansive and well-thought-out legislation. During the summer, Sabo convened a group of top staff people, including Ed Dirkswager from Caucus Research, Larry Fredrickson from the senate research staff, John Turner from Northwestern National Life, and Kevin Kenny from House Research, to help work on the legislation.

Sabo knew how insurance worked in practice and the issues it presented for working families, individuals, and small businesses. He knew that some could not purchase insurance due to preexisting conditions. He also knew that he wanted at least three things in the bill: the ability for every individual and small business to have the option to buy insurance at a reasonable premium, some cost-control provisions, and catastrophic coverage for illnesses that resulted in out-of-pocket costs in excess of certain thresholds. Sabo directed the project, while Dirkswager and Kenny began to research and draft the exact wording of the legislation.[97]

When the bill was finished in December 1975, it was remarkably similar in concept to the so-called public option that was proposed, and ultimately withdrawn, in the 2009–10 bill before the U.S. Congress. The 1975 Minnesota bill established a Comprehensive Health Association (CHA), a nonprofit membership organization governed by and consisting of all entities licensed to sell health insurance in the state as well as self-insurers. All individuals, including dependents, and all employers with less than fifty employees were eligible to buy insurance. Preexisting conditions were not covered for six months if any treatment had been required in the last ninety days. Premiums were determined by a committee of actuaries so as to make the association self-supporting, and CHA was to develop a detailed plan of operation. Both the premiums and the operational plan were subject to approval by the state's insurance commissioner. Any CHA losses were to be shared by the members on a pro-rata basis. The bill specified three levels of coverage, which had to be offered to all by insurance companies selling policies in the state.

As cost-control measures, no more than 12.5 percent of the premiums could be used for expenses of administration of CHA, and hospital rates were to be made public and subject to review and comment by the state's health commissioner.

Catastrophic health insurance was defined, and all employers were required to offer at least a standard coverage for such insurance to their employees. Another provision provided that the state pay the excess costs for every person or household that had exceeded a very high threshold of health-care expenses in a twelve-month period. This provision would not come into play for those with private insurance, but it did provide at least some protection from financial devastation for everyone.[98]

Sabo asked Jim Swanson, chair of the Health and Welfare Committee, to carry the bill, and Swanson readily agreed. As the bill was scrutinized by four different committees and in the conference committee after house passage, the effect of the recently enacted federal Employee Retirement Income Security Act (ERISA) became more clear. Simply put, the state could no longer have much impact on plans defined as "employee benefit plans" by ERISA, as state action on such plans was preempted. Since the ERISA definition included almost all of the large employers' health plans in the state, the impact on the expansive original house bill was large and adverse. As a result of the ERISA preemption issues and changes by the senate, Sabo and the house had to drop many of the important provisions of their bill. The bill that was ultimately signed by the governor was significant but not as far-reaching as Sabo and colleagues had hoped. The final bill created a comprehensive plan for persons who could not otherwise get insurance due to their health history and provided catastrophic coverage with very high thresholds.[99] The state thus became one of the first in the country to provide a mechanism to "insure the uninsurable," and the program has continued to provide insurance for people in difficult situations for over thirty-five years.[100]

Certificate of Need

Like now, both public and private health-care costs were rising at an alarming rate in the 1970s, and the legislature, after hearings and study, concluded there was excessive capital spending on various health-care facilities and equipment. They also concluded that this was a significant factor in the high cost of health care. The legislature decided the mechanism of the market place was not adequately controlling the costs for necessary health-care services. New regulations were authorized, procedures developed, and requirements established to require a state-issued "certificate of need" before building a health-care facility or acquiring any equipment covered by the bill.[101]

Community Health Services

The passage of the Community Health Services Act illustrates the flexibility available to state and local governments in creating and implementing programs. The act provided for a system of community health services to be available to qualified persons throughout the state. In actions reminiscent of some federal programs started in the 1960s, the services had to meet state guidelines and standards, but the programs were to be administered by local governments. The services included public health, nursing, family planning, nutrition, emergency medical services, and health education. The legislature provided several options for administering the program: a local "human services board," the county board, a new local health board, or city councils in Minnesota's largest counties. The state board of health had to approve the local plans. A pilot program for community mental health centers was also passed with a strong emphasis on enabling people to live independently without hospitalization.[102] All these health-care bills passed with bipartisan support.[103]

Transit

The 1970s were exciting times for urban planners and transit technology experts. The federal government was putting significant time, money, and effort into new transit technology throughout the country, and Minnesota was a major player in the process. Proposals ranged from traditional heavy railcar systems to futuristic personalized rapid transit (PRT), a system of little cars on an extensive system of guideways that would zip people from their neighborhoods to their place of work or shopping and back. In downtown areas, "people movers" were proposed—a sort of horizontal elevator placed on the outside of buildings with stops at the major buildings. Various rubber-tired vehicles ranging from large articulated buses to jitneys and small vans for organized carpools ("paratransit") were being discussed as well. Big money, from $1 to $2 billion, was the price tag associated with implementation of many of the systems.[104]

The Citizens League weighed in to the debate with solid questions about what it was the legislature was trying to accomplish with the $1 to $2 billion: Was it more ridership, shaping residential or commercial development, or reducing dependence on gasoline? The Citizens League also asked which unit of local government—the Metropolitan Council, with its more general responsibility for development in the metropolitan area, or the Metropolitan Transit Commission (MTC), which was charged with delivering transit service—should decide the best system to recommend to the legislature.[105] Various experts from the University of Minnesota and Jerry Christenson and Jim Solem at the State Planning Agency were heavily involved in helping the legislature understand the options and related costs and benefits.

Discussion of these transit proposals had begun during the 1973–74 sessions. The house and senate each had a committee (Metropolitan and Urban Affairs) that dealt extensively with these issues. The house committee was chaired by John Salchert, from Minneapolis, and the senate committee was chaired by John Chenoweth, from St. Paul. The two chairs did not get along. Berg, a member of the house committee, acted as a peacemaker between the two chairs to get action on some metropolitan planning bills, but friction between the chairs played a major role in stalling the transit bill and others.[106]

The Metropolitan Council and the MTC also did not see eye to eye on which transit system to propose to the legislature. Doug Kelm, brother of the governor's executive secretary, had been appointed by the governor to a four-year term as chair of the MTC in 1971. Kelm was a forceful advocate of a fifty-seven-mile system of traditional heavy-rail fixed guideways with forty passenger vehicles, at a projected cost of approximately $1 billion. The Metropolitan Council opposed that solution, and the two agencies continued to battle over which transit system should be recommended to the legislature.

In 1973, right in the middle of the controversy, Governor Anderson appointed John Boland to be the chair of the Metropolitan Council. Boland was a DFL state representative, first elected to the house in 1970 and reelected in 1972 from a St. Paul suburb. Boland had worked closely with Berg, Sabo, and a number of St. Paul senators who were key players in the transit battles. The governor, ever mindful of the importance of personal relationships in legislating, hoped Boland's knowledge of the legislature and his relationships with Senators Coleman, Chenoweth, and Bob North and former house colleagues Sabo and Berg would help settle the legislative turbulence over the transit issue.[107]

During the 1973–74 sessions, the house, led by John Tomlinson, a legislator from St. Paul, had supported Kelm and the MTC proposal, but the senate adamantly refused to do so. After being rebuffed by the senate, Tomlinson compromised with Chenoweth and the other key senators. Legislation was passed ordering the MTC to prepare "plans" for the senate-favored transit system using the smaller vehicle (PRT) technology generally favored by Chenoweth and several other senators. The plans were to be submitted to the Metropolitan Council for review and were to be ready by the 1975 session.[108] As the plans were being prepared, Salchert announced his retirement. Berg took over as chair of the newly constituted Local and Urban Affairs Committee at the start of the 1975 session.

In 1975, but before the PRT plans were completed, the governor appointed Kelm to a second term as MTC chair, an appointment subject to senate confirmation. The senate refused to confirm—at least initially. Members of the Senate Metropolitan Affairs Committee voted not to confirm, because they were "angry at Kelm for his efforts to generate public support for the MTC's rail transit plan."

Majority Leader Coleman weighed in, saying Kelm "ought to real-ize that he is an impediment to the development of mass transit and gracefully step aside." However, Committee Chair Chenoweth held up the final issuance of his committee's negative report on Kelm to "see if he changes his ways."[109]

Thus, the transit controversy was front and center as the 1975 session began work in earnest on the transit question, with the ex-perienced players, the units of government directly involved, and the house and senate all going in different directions.

Chenoweth remained very interested in PRT, and said in Feb-ruary 1975 that he hoped preliminary engineering could begin on a PRT system as early as June.[110] Berg was uncertain about which transit technology plan to support, although he had earlier voted for the MTC plan. Berg signaled his concern about the cost of the transit proposals in a talk he gave to the Citizens League early in the 1975 session. Berg noted the huge price tag associated with the MTC plan and said, "We have the capability to bankrupt the whole metro-politan area." He also continued his criticism of the highway depart-ment's efforts, saying that the "massive urban freeway construction of the 1950's was a mistake because social, environmental, and eco-nomic costs were not given adequate consideration."[111]

Berg's skepticism about the PRT proposal grew, and he and the Local and Urban Affairs Committee decided to make their own anal-ysis of the transit issue. Berg appointed a subcommittee to develop a recommendation on what should be done, naming a neighboring suburban legislator, Pete Petrafeso, to be chair. Petrafeso, like Berg, favored transit and was skeptical of building more freeways through established neighborhoods.

Berg and Petrafeso turned to House Research, the "small univer-sity," to help them analyze the complicated and expensive options. Tom Todd, a young, talented member of House Research, had been assigned to assist the Local and Urban Affairs Committee. Todd, a graduate of Carleton College in Minnesota and of the University of Chicago Law School, had helped arrange numerous hearings on the transit issue. Berg and Petrafeso asked Todd to put his academic skills to work and write a report setting forth their findings, recom-mendations, and accompanying rationale. In view of the significant fiscal and potential political impacts of the transit decision, Sabo was kept closely apprised.

The final thirty-seven-page report was issued by Berg and Petrafeso in May 1975. It caused a stir because it flatly rejected PRT, favored by many of the senators, and the technology favored by the MTC. The report discussed the six alternative transit systems that had been seriously proposed and studied extensively. Five of these were "fixed-guideway (rail) or exclusive right-of-way systems," and one was an all-bus alternative without corridor freeways. The latter proposal was a new one developed by the Metropolitan Council under Boland's leadership. It contained eighty-three fewer miles of metropolitan area freeways than the council's earlier proposal. The report noted that the population projection of runaway growth for the metropolitan area had recently been substantially revised downward from when the planning had begun for the proposed fixed-guideway transit alternatives. The report also considered the alleged ancillary benefits, such as reductions in congestion, energy use, the need for more freeways, and the total costs of the proposals. Berg and Petrafeso rejected the fixed-guideway approach and recommended the Metropolitan Council's approach. Their rationale was clear:

> This recommendation rests on many considerations, all of them relate to one central judgment: that the transportation problems we might solve and the ancillary benefits we might derive from building one of these systems . . . are all out of proportion to the costs we would incur. . . .
> The transportation problems faced by the metropolitan area are neither so profound as to warrant investment in the guideways nor so simple to be solved by them. . . .
> We cannot any longer justify large plans originally developed to cope with a rate of growth almost three times greater than we now expect. . . .
> The Metropolitan council has estimated that the capital costs of building a fixed guideway system . . . might well triple the public debt and threaten the credit of every local and regional governmental unit in the metropolitan area.[112]

The report concluded by saying that the area must continue to plan and monitor new developments in transportation and that by not building the fixed-guideway rail system now, the area would have the fiscal flexibility to "respond to an uncertain future."[113]

To Berg's pleasant surprise, Senator Chenoweth "hailed the report as demonstrating essential agreement among the two key legislative committees and the Metropolitan Council." The report that Todd had written was well received—"anybody interested in resolving the long-standing metro transit dispute should read and heed the report"—and was praised as "exceptionally well written."[114]

With general agreement reached on the type of transit, the house and senate were able over the next fifteen months to reconcile remaining differences over transit and metropolitan issues. As part of the gas tax legislation described earlier, the legislature put a moratorium on some interstate freeway development in the metropolitan area, required sound barriers on certain freeways, and approved $28 million for the MTC to improve mass transit via buses and paratransit alternatives.[115] The powers of the Metropolitan Council were strengthened, and, most importantly, in a bill that passed through the Governmental Operations Committee, chaired by Harry Sieben, a new Department of Transportation (DOT) was created that made the highway department but one group within the new agency, in order to "provide a balanced transportation system."[116]

The end result was that the 1975–76 legislative sessions significantly modified the effect of public transportation on the development and livability of cities, suburbs, and towns. The changed governmental structure also made those responsible for planning and implementing major and expensive public transit decisions more responsive and accountable to a broader group of people.

These transit decisions continue to affect life in the Minneapolis–St. Paul metropolitan area today. As part of the 1970s transit debate, the Minnesota Highway Department had proposed a new limited-access freeway along a major avenue (Hiawatha) in South Minneapolis. After many local hearings over how to best use this corridor in a manner consistent with a neighboring park, the local forces arguing for a "Boulevard Yes—Freeway No!" approach carried the day. A strong argument made by the local group was that this corridor should not be a highway but should be used for light-rail transit (LRT). For twenty-five years, no highway was built, and Hiawatha Avenue became a wide boulevard, with space reserved for possible LRT use.[117]

In 2001, the Minneapolis–St. Paul metropolitan area began building a modern LRT system. Hennepin County, led by Commissioner Peter McLaughlin, and using significant funding obtained from the federal government with the help of then Congressman Sabo, a senior member of the House Appropriations Committee, played a key role in getting the project going. The first leg of that system, the Hiawatha Line, runs along the boulevard. Ridership on the system is high, and a second leg of the system connecting the downtowns of St. Paul and Minneapolis is scheduled to be completed in 2014.[118] A third leg is in the advanced planning stage. This LRT system and the Northstar Commuter Rail line are good examples of local units of government coming together under joint powers agreements and working with the Metropolitan Council and the state and federal governments to build and operate a transit system crossing multiple municipal and county boundaries.

Sports Stadiums and Taxes

Yogi Berra framed it well when he said, "If people don't want to go to the ballpark, how are you going to stop them?" The answer, according to many in Minnesota in 1976, was to build a bigger and better stadium—and put a roof on it. As with many of the issues in this book, Yogi's question remains relevant. The drumbeat for new stadiums has continued from 1976 to the present. Since 2000, new baseball stadiums have been built in thirteen cities.[119] In Minnesota, the Twins and University of Minnesota Gophers each convinced the state legislature in 2008 to build stadiums for them, and to build them without roofs or domes, so nature's elements may be enjoyed by players and fans alike. In 2012 the Minnesota Vikings and the National Football League persuaded the legislature, the governor, and the mayor and city council of Minneapolis to chip in and help the team replace the thirty-one-year-old Metrodome. In an interesting comment on the increasingly pervasive use of taxpayer subsidies for professional sports facilities, *Sports Illustrated* noted the $184 million contract the Twins signed in 2010 with All-Star catcher Joe Mauer and said, "This contract is exactly what teams should do when *given* [emphasis added] a taxpayer-funded ballpark: invest their new revenues in their superstars."[120]

"If you build it, they will come" proved true, as major league sports arrived in Minnesota in 1961. The then Washington Senators moved to Minnesota to play in a stadium that had been built for baseball in 1956 and currently housed the minor league Minneapolis

Millers. The stadium was on the edge of a cornfield in Bloomington, just south of Minneapolis. The Minnesota Vikings also landed
in Minnesota in 1961, as an NFL franchise had been granted in 1960.
Both teams played in the 41,200-seat Metropolitan Stadium.[121]

The Vikings under coach Norm Van Brocklin and led by rookie
quarterback Fran Tarkenton made a colorful splash in Minnesota,
surprising everyone by beating the Chicago Bears in the Viking's first
regular season game. The Twins also prospered and were in their
first World Series just four years later, where they lost to Sandy Kou-
fax and the Los Angles Dodgers in seven games.

It can get very cold in Minnesota in November and December,
and the stories are legion about Viking coach Bud Grant (who had
played football at the University of Minnesota and coached at Winni-
peg, Canada) refusing to use heaters on the sidelines, telling his players that cold was "just a state of mind." Tailgating was undertaken in
snowmobile suits, and "antifreeze," carried in flasks, was often consumed by the Viking faithful. A rivalry with equally cold Green Bay
soon developed.

The cold weather and success on the field led to agitation by both
the Twins and the Vikings for a new and larger stadium with a roof.
It began in earnest in the 1970s, as leases for the Twins and the Vikings were set to expire in 1975. Competition to be the site for a new
stadium among the fast-growing Bloomington and the two central
cities of Minneapolis and St. Paul began at the same time. Since these
cities could not fund a major facility under existing tax and bonding authority, they turned to the sovereign government, the state,
for more authority and money. The teams signed year-to-year leases,
and the legislature took up the issue in 1976.[122]

A Select Joint Sports Facilities Committee made up of legislators
from both the house and senate had been reviewing options since
July 1975.[123] In February 1976, the joint committee approved a draft
bill giving the Metropolitan Parks, Arts and Recreation Commission bonding authority of up to $46.5 million to acquire property
and build a stadium "within one-half mile of the intersection of 12th
avenue and 2nd street in the city of Minneapolis" (an area known as
Industry Square). John Tomlinson was the chief author with Sabo,
Minority Leader Savelkoul, Republican Bill Dean, and DFLer Jim
Casserly the other authors. Tomlinson was from St. Paul, Savelkoul from southern Minnesota, and Sabo, Casserly, and Dean from

Minneapolis. The bill was sent to the Local and Urban Affairs Committee chaired by Berg, also from Minneapolis.[124]

Berg and Sabo had a significant disagreement over the bill. Berg's position was that he was open to the possibility of a stadium but if a stadium was going to be built with significant public money involved, the state should also spend some money for Minnesota's dynamic arts community. Sabo had serious reservations about money for the arts. (It should be noted that Berg had more arts organizations located in his district than did Sabo.) At a meeting in Sabo's office before the bill was introduced, Berg told Sabo that meaningful arts funding was his price for supporting a stadium. Sabo was not happy. He responded with a cold and noncommittal "We'll see," as the meeting ended.

Hearings started with intense lobbying by the Vikings and Twins, the Minneapolis Chamber of Commerce, and organized labor. All were in favor. The media in general, and sportswriters in particular, were also in favor. Bloomington and many other suburbs were opposed, as were a variety of taxpayer and citizen groups. All were vocal about their position, and Sabo almost lost his party's endorsement for reelection because of his support for a stadium.[125]

Over the next several months, the bill had a tortuous history involving many amendments and many committees. At one point in March 1976, even U.S. Senator Hubert Humphrey got into the act with a phrase that lives on in local lore: "Without professional sports teams, the Twin Cities would be just a cold Omaha."[126]

Berg succeeded on a close vote with help from some Republican legislators in adding an amendment to the bill providing $2.8 million to the arts community. Recognizing that the arts are meaningful for all and the political value of a statewide approach, his amendment specified that the arts funding should be distributed statewide and not just to the large establishment arts organizations located in the large cities. With support from Bill Kelly, who was always a strong proponent of rural Minnesota, the amendment was written to use the existing State Arts Council and Regional Development Commissions as vehicles to distribute the funding to arts organizations throughout the state.[127]

The bill with funding for a stadium finally passed the house toward the end of the session. (Funding for the arts was cut and moved to a separate appropriation bill, which ultimately passed.)[128] The senate was wrestling with the stadium issue at the same time, and with only three days to go in the session, it passed a separate version of the bill. In fact, the senate passed two versions, but each version made support for the stadium contingent on the passage of income tax relief measures that had been discussed and rejected by the house a year earlier in the discussion leading up to the 1975 omnibus tax bill.[129]

Cutting deals is a part of the legislative process that is tricky at best. It takes an accurate reading of support for the terms of the deal from the relevant forces outside the legislature, and a thorough knowledge of the legislators with whom one is dealing. Making a deal on two separate bills, each one dealing with high-profile issues that are only marginally related, is a high-wire act without a safety net. In this case the senate miscalculated on their ability to make the deal connecting a new stadium and income tax policy. The resulting slip and fall was fatal to the stadium.

The house negotiators on the income tax relief measures based their concern on the country's economy and on the impact the senate's proposed tax relief measures would have on future budgets. Sabo consistently reminded the senators that he had been talking about the need to leave a surplus for months and that he had pointed out that the then projected $200 million state surplus, while a lot of money, was less than 4 percent of the state's budget. He also said he thought the projections were "very questionable."[130] The house negotiators had the solid backing of their caucus for "leaving a healthy surplus for the 1977 session."[131]

Majority Leader Coleman, who had been "straining all session long to hold a bickering 38-member majority [senate] caucus together," had a much less unified group. At one point Coleman received "an almost unprecedented slap in the face," when he was not even able to get the support of his caucus for a usually automatic procedural motion to adjourn. Coleman was clearly frustrated, and he pulled out of the stadium negotiations.[132]

The lead senate negotiator in this process was now Assistant Majority Leader George Conzemius, a large man who was not shy about pushing his views. The senate argued that taxing people more than is necessary to run state government was "immoral." Kelly, Sabo, and the other house negotiators did not buy that argument for a minute and alleged the real reason for their DFL colleagues' position was that the senate had to face reelection that fall and wanted to be able to tell voters they had passed a tax cut. As the clock ticked down to adjournment, public and private allegations of "cheap shots," "stupid," and "absurd" went back and forth between the badly split house and senate DFL.[133]

Normally such a dispute would have meant a conference committee, but the house was so adamant and the time was so short before the end of the session that the house refused to even appoint members to a conference committee as the high-stakes game of chicken continued. At the last moment, the senate said it would agree that any tax relief measure could be contingent on there being a projected surplus of $150 million. Conzemius claimed he had been told by a Sabo aide that the concept of using $50 million from any projected surplus for tax relief was acceptable to Sabo and the house. Conzemius promptly had that idea drafted as an amendment to the bill. When the usually calm Sabo saw the wording of Conzemius's amendment, he became "flushed and angered," marched over to the senate floor, and in front of reporters told Conzemius, "No, the answer is no, very clearly . . . my prime concern is having $150 million surplus." Conzemius, "apparently shocked by Sabo's reaction," responded by saying that the senate had answered the house's objections and "now they are coming up with new ones."[134]

The anger continued without compromise, and the session ended with strong animosity between the DFLers in the house and senate. There was no agreement on a stadium or tax relief. As Coleman left the capitol at about two o'clock in the morning, he found the door locked, and frustration with his own caucus and the house got the better of him. He kicked out the glass in the capitol door.[135]

An analysis piece written by a veteran legislative reporter several days after the session adjourned was titled "Legislative residue— bitterness," and noted that "the air toward the end of the session became acrid with acid remarks." A lobbyist who sympathized with the house said, "these Senators . . . are getting exactly what they deserve for the first time in four years." The article concluded: "Emotions, pride, philosophical disagreement—all led to more than usual hostility and final deadlock."[136]

The governor indicated he would be open to a special session to deal with the stadium issue, but no one was very interested. All knew the stadium issue would be back in the 1977–78 sessions—bringing to mind another Yogi Berra saying: "It's déjà vu all over again."

Leaving the Legislature

During the 1975 session, Jim Pederson, a senior administrative assistant to Governor Anderson, and Joe Graba were at a party with a number of people from the legislature and the governor's office, when Pederson mentioned to Graba that the governor appreciated the excellent work Graba had done over the years with school aids and the implementation and enhancement of the Minnesota Miracle legislation. Graba responded that it was "always nice to hear good things from the corner office." As Graba was about to leave, Pederson went on to say that a deputy commissioner at the Department of Education was retiring in 1976 and that the governor wondered if Graba would consider joining the executive branch as a deputy commissioner. Graba was totally surprised. The legislature had become a big part of his life, and he had no exit strategy from the elected-office life. He told Pederson that he would think about it.

He did. His children ranged in age from nine to four, and he was spending more and more time at the capitol as his legislative responsibilities grew. The next weekend when he went home to Wadena, he described the discussion with Pederson to his wife, Sylvia. She had grown up in a difficult family environment and as a child had bounced around several locations. She had attended thirteen schools in twelve years. After a moment's reflection, she said, "Joe, you know moving is not a problem for me, whatever you want to do is fine." Joe was not quite sure how to respond to his wife's kind words, as his own thoughts were unclear, and merely said, "Thank you, I guess I need to keep thinking about it."

As the 1975 session went on, Graba kept thinking, and he and Pederson kept talking. With each late-night 340-mile round trip on the often slippery roads to his home and family in Wadena, Graba got more interested. He talked with Commissioner of Education Howard Casmey, who told Graba he would be thrilled to have Graba in the department.

As Graba continued to analyze the situation, it became clear that a portion of his new duties would be to help the governor's office get more control over the vocational education group in the department. The possibility of an "end run" around the chief executive is a constant issue for the executive branch when dealing with departments like vocational education with strong public support and good contacts in the legislative branch. The vocational education group had become a bit of a maverick and would employ the end run strategy on occasion. The governor hoped Graba could assist in bringing about a more united executive branch effort.[137]

Faricy inadvertently found himself in the middle of this issue. He was approached by some of the mavericks in vocational education who thought their group should be a separate department in state government. The group told Faricy he really did not need to do much, because they already had the votes lined up. Faricy agreed to carry the bill, and this led to a sharp exchange between him and Governor Anderson. At a committee hearing on the bill, Faricy accused one of the governor's top aides who was opposing the bill of "spreading misinformation" and criticized the governor for "sending his people to talk to other legislators [about the bill] but not to me." The aide did not back down and said he would urge the governor to veto the bill if it passed.[138] Faricy also did not back down, and the bill passed. The governor signed it. Faricy was never aware of the conversations between Graba and the governor's office.[139]

In early 1976, Graba and his wife decided that leaving the legislature and the rural area where Graba had spent his entire life was the right decision. Graba discussed the matter with a few people, but no public announcement was made until one evening in the middle of a quiet dinner at Berg's home with some legislative friends—and a film crew, who, with cameras running and lights glaring, were making the documentary for the National Conference of State Legislatures described earlier. They were aware that Graba was going to tell the group that he was leaving, and they wanted to film the reactions and discussion.

Berg was surprised and saddened as Graba told the group he was leaving the legislative branch. Berg had served on the School Aids Committee with Graba and had come to know and respect his hard work and thoughtful approach to governing. Graba talked about his kids growing up and said that if he were ever going to spend time with them, this was the time. Berg also had young children and increasingly felt the competing tugs of family life, a law practice, and legislating. Carl Johnson, Education Committee chair, was present and, true to form, lightened the mood with an old joke, that Graba's leaving the legislature for the Department of Education would raise the IQ level of both groups.[140]

Graba completed the 1976 session, bid the legislature and his loyal campaign supporters in Wadena a fond farewell, moved his family from rural Minnesota to the Minneapolis–St. Paul metropolitan area, and became a deputy commissioner of the Department of Education. He was sorely missed by Sabo and Kelly, who relied heavily on his fiscal expertise and political skills.

The Republicans also felt a sense of loss when one of their "most influential" members, Assistant Minority Leader Salisbury Adams, announced his retirement. Adams said the main reason he was leaving was the movement toward a full-time legislature, which he viewed as "a serious mistake." He also cited the " 'intensely partisan' approach being taken by Republicans in an attempt to increase their representation in the legislature." Adams had served in the house for twenty-three years.[141]

Presidential Politics, 1976

The decision by 27 percent of Iowa Democratic activists on a cold January night in 1976 to support a southern governor for president began a process that ended up not only interrupting eight years of Republican presidential rule but also thoroughly shaking up politics for Iowa's northern neighbor.[142] As Jimmy Carter gained momentum, Minnesota's DFL Party, well used to presidential politics after Gene McCarthy and Hubert Humphrey had played key roles in the 1964, 1968, and 1972 elections, began to warm to Carter and to think again of possible national roles for its leaders, Mondale and Anderson. And although their public statements were appropriately circumspect, these DFL leaders did nothing to dampen the speculation. Senator Mondale's name surfaced early on as a possible northern liberal running mate to balance the ticket with Carter. Governor Anderson and Lieutenant Governor Perpich watched with great interest.

Rosalynn Carter described her husband's decision to select Mondale as "difficult." She said,

> Jimmy had always felt that Mondale was too liberal for him, but changed his mind when they met. Not only did they get along very well personally, they . . . agree[ed] on a variety of domestic and foreign issues. . . . Mondale was not as liberal as his reputation suggested. He was strong on defense and reducing the budget deficit. . . . Of course there were political considerations . . . as well. Jimmy, being a Washington "outsider," needed someone who knew Washington

well . . . and Mondale as a running mate would assuage the Humphrey wing of the party. . . . Jimmy never regretted his choice.[143]

When the announcement was made, the vast majority of DFL Party faithful were elated. Speculation began at once about possible replacements for Mondale in the U.S. Senate if the national ticket won. Insiders in the governor's office, while happy for Mondale, were worried because they knew the appointment of Mondale's replacement would be a tough political decision for the governor. Appointments always left those not getting the job in an unhappy frame of mind.[144]

How to deal with this potential change in the DFL's lineup was a major issue for the party. A news report noted that "some . . . of . . . the [DFL] party's liberal faction who prefer [Congressman] Fraser or [Attorney General] Spannaus . . . are clamoring for Anderson to seek advice . . . from a reconvened DFL state convention." One Anderson supporter responded, "Wendy would be a damn fool to consult the party." The Republicans were licking their chops over a potential battle within the DFL. The Republican Party chair, Chuck Slocum, said that if the senate seat opened up, "the situation in the DFL would border on civil war."[145]

State law controls the process of selecting a replacement if a U.S. senator leaves office partway through the term.[146] In Minnesota, this led to some awkwardness for the governor, lieutenant governor, and future vice president. The law specified that the governor must name a replacement, who serves the remaining portion of the term. In Mondale's case, the term ran through 1978. Mondale's top aide, Dick Moe, hinted that Mondale probably would not resign early. Moe noted that Mondale was "one of the few senators who lives here on his salary" and thus needed his monthly paycheck in the interim.[147] If the governor wanted the Senate seat once Mondale did resign, Anderson would also have to resign as governor, and the new governor, Perpich, would have to appoint Anderson. The "deal making" involved would be sure to provide ammunition to Republicans to use in the 1978 election, when Anderson would have to seek election to the Senate and Perpich would presumably seek election to the governorship.

Perpich and Anderson had never been particularly close. Anderson selected Perpich as his lieutenant governor only after others had turned down the position. Senator Nick Coleman, who had also been a candidate for governor when Anderson won in 1970, was a close friend of Perpich, and has been credited by many for convincing Anderson to select Perpich as his running mate. To no one's surprise, Perpich told reporters that he would appoint Anderson "without question."[148]

While all this speculation was under way and attention was focused on the presidential race, all the state legislative seats were up for grabs. The Republicans initially hoped to improve their standing in the house and to regain their historical control of the senate. To distance themselves from the Watergate scandals and the national party, the Minnesota Republicans officially changed the party's name in 1975 to the "Independent-Republican Party," or IR for short. (For ease of reference, the terms *IR* and *Republican* will be used interchangeably, as will *DFL* and *Democrat*.) The DFL jumped all over this cosmetic change. The DFL Party chair, Ulric Scott, said, "An Independent-Republican is an elephant that is trying to forget."[149] *Time* magazine reported that the change in name "did not get at the real problem which is that ... a recent poll showed that only 15% ... had a positive image of Republicans."[150] By October, "the once lofty goal of Minnesota's Independent-Republican (IR) party to win back control of the state senate appears to have evaporated into more rhetoric than reality."[151] With Mondale on the national ticket and the ever-popular Humphrey running for reelection to the Senate, the DFL was confident it would do well in the legislative races.

This confidence was not misplaced. The election night party returned to the Leamington Hotel, and again the band played "Happy Days Are Here Again." Not only did Carter–Mondale defeat Ford–Dole, but the DFL maintained their 104-to-30 margin over the IRs in the house and gained 11 more seats in the senate, giving them a solid 49-to-18 margin there.[152] They would no longer need to rely on IR votes to suspend the rules. Kelly, Faricy, Berg, and Sabo were all returned to office.

Shortly after the election, Anderson held a number of meetings with key advisors to discuss his political options. Many people said Anderson should take the seat immediately, but some, including Mondale aide Mike Berman, and Tom Kelm, the governor's executive secretary, expressed strong concerns. Dave Roe, president of the Minnesota AFL-CIO, was present along with Kelm at a meeting in the governor's office as the decision was being made. Roe described the discussion as starting out with the pros and cons of arranging an immediate appointment of Anderson to the Senate, rather than Anderson appointing a caretaker senator for the two years remaining in Mondale's term, and then Anderson running for the regular six-year term in 1978. Kelm was adamant in saying the caretaker option was the right one. Anderson's approval ratings were good, and Kelm argued Anderson would have an excellent chance of winning in 1978.[153]

Anderson thought he should take the position immediately. He was told that nine other governors of various states had taken the appointment route in similar situations over the years and that eight of them had lost in the subsequent elections (Happy Chandler from Kentucky was the only one that won).[154] Nevertheless, Anderson thought that with his current high popularity and with support from labor and others, he "could pull it off." Roe told Anderson that "if it is your thought that you want to appoint yourself, that's what you should do. If you want to go with Tom Kelm and do it in two years, we'll support that. But whatever you support, we're behind you."[155]

Anderson, who had already served six years, knew that "the shelf life of a governor was a lot less than that of a U.S. senator," and he found the "bird in the hand" argument persuasive.[156] On November 10, 1976, he issued a statement saying he intended to represent Minnesota in the U.S. Senate for the next two years. He said he hoped to earn the people's support to justify his election to a full term in 1978 and that he was leaving the office of governor in "good and experienced hands." The statement concluded, "I have great confidence that Governor Perpich and the DFL Legislature will continue and enhance the Minnesota record of solid accomplishment."[157]

On December 29, 1976, Anderson resigned as governor, and Perpich was sworn in as governor. Mondale resigned as senator, and Perpich promptly appointed Anderson to the Senate seat.[158]

Perpich and Anderson were very different people. Anderson, of Swedish descent, is somewhat reserved by nature. He was a well-organized governor, and his management style was to delegate and then get out of the way. This caused some to think him aloof. Perpich was of Croatian descent and was spontaneous and colorful. He did not hesitate to jump into the details of making policy. Anderson was very aware of the fiscal implications of his policies and proud of the fact that Minnesota had a strong budget surplus when he left office. Perpich was more inclined to see the world with rose-colored glasses and usually saw the financial glass as being half full. Both were strong leaders and had committed supporters.

Perpich was Minnesota's first governor from its northern Iron Range region. He broke a long line of Scandinavian governors. English was not spoken in his home when he was a child. In fact, Perpich did not speak English when he entered kindergarten. His father was a miner, and Perpich and his three brothers were all determined to avoid the mines. Rudy and two of his brothers became dentists. They also loved politics and became state senators along with Rudy.[159] The Perpich "boys" were not at all afraid to fight with local DFL Party activists. Rudy, as he was known to all, was a big man who liked to tell stories. He shared Anderson's love for the rural areas of the state, and both men connected well with working people.

For DFL house members the change in governors meant getting to know a different staff in the governor's office and adapting to a different style of governing. Sabo and most of the house members had never worked closely with Perpich.

For many of the DFL senators who were frequently at odds with Governor Anderson, the changes meant a person they knew well was now governor. Coleman was a good friend of Perpich, and Coleman much appreciated and admired Perpich's early and consistent opposition to the Vietnam War. How all this change would play out in the legislative session scheduled to start seven days after Perpich became governor was anybody's guess and the subject of much speculation.

CHAPTER 8

It's More Complicated Than It Looks

America's future is the future of its city-states—the
314 metropolitan regions where 80 percent of us
live ... they are our cash cows.

> • Neal Peirce, *Citistates: How Urban America
> Can Prosper in a Competitive World*

B y the time the 1977 legislature started, the opening festivities
of a new session were routine for Speaker Martin Sabo, House
Majority Leader Irv Anderson, and Senate Majority Leader Nick
Coleman. But while the festivities were routine, the internal politics
within the DFL House Caucus were not. There had been continuing grumbling about Anderson's performance and style as majority leader since the end of the 1974 session, and now a serious fight
broke out for the DFL majority leader position. Anderson's gruff
and at times punitive style did not play well with many legislators.
Bill Kelly had worked closely with Anderson as the vice chair of the
Rules Committee, which Anderson chaired, but the two never saw
eye to eye on many things, including how best to build the legislature
as an institution of government, a matter of significant importance
to Kelly. Kelly, with the support of Ray Faricy, Tom Berg, and many
others, nominated Neil Haugerud to take on Anderson in a battle for
the position of majority leader.

Haugerud was a fifth-term legislator, a farmer, and a former county
sheriff. He had a good sense of humor and was generally liked and
respected by legislators of both caucuses. He also could be gruff
when the occasion called for it—usually when trying to hold down
spending as the chair of an important division of the Appropriations Committee. Legislators eventually figured out that Haugerud's
gruff negotiating style covered up a generous heart, and he became
know as "Gentle Neil." The battle for the majority leader position

definitely played out on the gruff side of the ledger for Haugerud and his supporters.

Harry Sieben thought Anderson had done a good job as majority leader and nominated Anderson for reelection to the position. Anderson was from the northern part of the state and a former union leader in the paper mill where he worked. Anderson loved politics, was a hard worker, and also had the support of many legislators, both urban and rural. Both candidates worked hard to gather votes. Anderson prevailed in a close secret ballot vote.

Republican Rod Searle, who repeatedly did battle with Anderson in the legislature, commented on the status of the situation within the DFL caucus: "[Irv] Anderson was primarily responsible for the deep split . . . within the DFL caucus during the mid 1970s." Minority Leader Henry Savelkoul said he did not know much about the internal workings of the DFL caucus but that from his perspective it appeared "Sabo ran the show," and that while he recognized that Anderson came from a part of the state where politics was really hard-nosed, Anderson apparently could be "unnecessarily mean." The "deep split" Searle described certainly had the potential to cause problems similar to those suffered by the Conservatives in the late 1960s and early 1970s, but Anderson, Haugerud, and the DFL factions were generally able to paper over the long-standing split and get on with the business of governing throughout the 1977–78 sessions.[1] Sabo and Coleman were easily reelected to their positions.

The smaller Senate Independent-Republican (IR) Caucus elected Robert Ashbach as its minority leader. The house IR leadership team reelected Savelkoul as its minority leader, and Rod Searle, Arne Carlson, Darrell Peterson, and Jerry Knickerbocker were named as assistant leaders.[2]

The general focus of attention, however, was not on caucus leaders but on the new and colorful governor, Rudy Perpich. Eight days after being named governor, Perpich rapidly delivered with his slight Croatian accent a vague, twenty-two-minute State of the State message. He called for a "new era in Minnesota state government," and after noting the fast pace of the 1973 through 1976 sessions, said the legislators would "no longer be judged on the number of their new proposals . . . [but on] our wisdom in making present laws work. . . . We do not need more state employees. We do need to get full value for every dollar we spend." Perpich combined the need to "put people back to work," the need to look to the future, and his concern for the natural environment with a history lesson about jobs in lumbering and commercial fishing industries in Minnesota:

> When the fish are gone, the jobs are gone. When the trees
> are gone, the jobs are gone. . . . Today we are witnessing
> the destruction of another magnificent resource—Lake
> Superior. . . . And we still have not found a way to stop
> Reserve Mining from dumping into that lake and preserve
> the jobs of three thousand human beings at the same time.[3]

After the address, as people were comparing the less-polished public speaking style of Perpich to that of former governor Anderson, a happy and smiling Faricy commented on the governor's enthusiastic and rapid delivery: "It's great to have a guy who is obviously having so much fun."[4] Perpich promised more detail in his budget address in a few weeks.

Less than a week later, the governor raised eyebrows by disappearing for a day without letting even his close aides know where he was. When he returned to the capitol that evening, he informed the aides he had quietly driven alone to the central part of the state to get a feel for a growing and potentially violent dispute then under way concerning the location and construction of a huge power line across prime farm country. He had decided to make the secret trip when it appeared that the local county officials might be asking for National Guard troops to protect power-line survey crews from angry farmers. The governor met with a number of protestors and the local sheriff and county attorney. After the trip, the sheriff said he thought Perpich's visit would "cool the farmers down."[5]

As the session got under way, the Republicans, despite their small numbers, did a good job of getting media attention. They began a steady drumbeat of reciting DFL actions they thought would not sit well with voters. For example, on a slow news day after the State of the State address, Republican Senator Jim Ulland brought a live thirty-pound turkey to the capitol and presented it, in absentia, to now Senator Wendell Anderson. Not so subtly referring to the appointment by Perpich of Anderson to the U.S. Senate, the IRs also had a grab bag of gifts, including back scratchers for both Anderson and Perpich. Perpich's back scratcher came equipped with a small shoehorn "to get into the very small shoes he had to fill." Republican National Committeeman and soon to be Senate candidate Rudy Boschwitz donated a section of redwood fence from his home remodeling supply company for "fence straddling."[6] The DFL ignored the jokes and went about their business.

The governor then delivered what he said was a combination Anderson–Perpich budget. The budget, despite the difficulty Perpich had in saying no to people and their funding requests, emphasized cutbacks in several areas.[7] The governor proudly mentioned the state's triple-A credit rating, proposed closing two state hospitals, and called for a reduction in several state taxes. Endearing himself to many legislators for sharing the political heat for a possible pay raise, he proposed a salary increase for all top state officials and legislators. Reflecting a strong interest of his wife, Lola, Perpich also proposed more funding for arts activities throughout the state. He again mentioned the need to resolve the power-line dispute and to stop the dumping of mining waste into Lake Superior by Reserve Mining Company.[8]

Despite the proposed cutbacks, the IR leaders kept up their message of too much spending and said the budget was "less than frugal." They claimed that with all the bonding requests, Minnesota could end up as "another New York City," referring to the then near bankruptcy of New York City.[9]

For the next two months, the legislature proceeded at a slow and deliberate pace. The DFL leadership had agreed among themselves that this session would not be about new initiatives, since they did not want to raise taxes and they knew money would be very tight.[10] After almost two months of the session, not one major bill had been passed. Coleman said that the session was "thoughtful and exploratory" and, referring to the fact that many legislators held other jobs, that the "citizen legislature was being brought back." The two minority leaders were happy with the slower pace but continued to criticize the DFL. Savelkoul predicted another end of session logjam, and Ashbach quipped that "we've passed so many bills in the past three or four years that we're spending most of our time correcting them."[11]

As Perpich climbed the governorship learning curve, he continued to garner news coverage with impulsive actions. He temporarily ordered state crews to stop picking up highway litter for ninety days, arguing that the stoppage would highlight the problem of litter and save money. He also thought the delay would improve support for legislation then pending to require bottle and can deposits. Two days later, he disappeared again without letting his staff know where he was going. Instead of proceeding to Washington to a National Governors Conference as scheduled, the governor "travel[ed] around a little bit" to prepare for a meeting in Cleveland with Reserve Mining Company to discuss stopping the dumping of waste into Lake Superior. The headline in one paper describing the governor's actions read, "Oh where, oh where has our governor gone?—again."[12]

Although the governor dominated the headlines with his somewhat quirky behavior, legislative committees had in fact been methodically holding hearings and working on a variety of bills. The session picked up as these bills worked their way through the committee process.

Local–State Relations

Oversight of Local Governments

Al Hofstede, mayor of Minneapolis from 1974 to 1975, was a Democrat from Northeast Minneapolis with strong labor ties. As social and racial unrest continued after the Vietnam War, he lost his job to Charles Stenvig, a conservative police officer and "law and order" candidate whom Hofstede had defeated two years earlier. As he contemplated a rematch with Stenvig, Hofstede thought about the lessons learned in his first term and in his electoral loss.

Hofstede believed that local government was more than just "law and order," but even with that limited goal, he knew a city could not achieve it and keep the electorate satisfied without such additional things as good schools, jobs, and housing. Police power alone could not get the job done. He also realized these essentials could not be achieved and sustained under the current financial conditions in his city. Despite large amounts of state aid, the city still had high property taxes, and "more money was going out than coming in . . . something had to be done about its finances," he said.[13]

Hofstede's concern matched that of Sabo's, who had been watching core city spending and taxing trends for years and realized something was amiss. Many suburban and rural legislators were claiming that the higher costs in the core cities of Minneapolis and St. Paul were the result of overspending by careless city officials. The city officials responded that it was national and state policies that increased the concentration of people living near the poverty level in central cities that led to the higher costs. "Municipal overburden" was the catchphrase often used to describe the reasons for the higher costs in the central cities.[14]

By summer 1976, Sabo, along with Senate Majority Leader Coleman, who had also heard the complaints from his colleagues about spending in St. Paul, decided to cut through the political and policy rhetoric and get some facts to address the issue. With the concurrence of the governor, they asked the State Planning Agency to "conduct an intensive study of local governance in Minneapolis and St. Paul" to determine whether the high costs were caused by decisions of city officials or because of problems beyond the cities' control.[15]

In November 1977, Hofstede regained his old job by defeating Stenvig.[16] Mayor Hofstede quickly began to focus on many of the problems that were the subject of the State Planning Agency study and appointed a fiscal expert, Jay Kiedrowski, as director of a new budget department.[17]

The legislature had made it clear that it was not the objective of the study to embarrass the cities, but many Minneapolis City Council members thought the mere existence of the study reflected badly on them. They were mad at the legislature and at Hofstede for supporting the study but eventually "came around" and began to cooperate fully with the mayor and study researchers. All knew the results of the study would likely have significant impact on legislative decisions on the amount of state-supplied local government aid (LGA) and on the city's governing structure.[18] As the study progressed, detailed reports were issued on such things as pensions, fringe benefits, and other topics about which allegations were often made that the city costs were out of line.

The conclusions were carefully worded but did not sugarcoat the situation, and they left no doubt there were problems ahead for the two cities if steps were not taken soon to better manage infrastructure, debt, and spending. The conclusions noted that both cities relied very heavily on LGA. Both cities were also losing population, and if LGA were to be cut, both cities would need to raise property taxes even higher or cut "essential services." The high cost of pensions for municipal workers was detailed, and, in a thirty-four-year-old precursor to the 2011 debate on public employee pensions, the touchy subject of union influence at city hall was addressed:

> In the past City officials have been willing to ignore the cost problems with pensions rather than risk the loss of political support from the City's employee organizations. . . .
>   A . . . test of the City's commitment to controlling costs would be the wage negotiations, pension deliberations, and the Council's willingness to cooperate with the Mayor's proposals to reduce the City mill (tax) rate.[19]

The study also addressed the current governmental structure in the two cities and its impact on fiscal management. The study concluded that St. Paul had a strong-mayor form of government, which helped control costs, but it spoke more harshly of the structure in Minneapolis: "the current structure of Minneapolis City government is poorly equipped to deal with these financial issues. The [Minneapolis] system is very fragmented and complex."[20]

As a result of the study, Hofstede, working with Kiedrowski and others, proposed major changes in state legislation to tighten up the funding of pension plans for city employees. They also used new powers that Hofstede received from a change in the Minneapolis City Charter and implemented internal changes to the structure of city government including performance-based budgeting. Hofstede and his colleagues "caught holy hell from the city unions" for proposing the pension changes. However, no one effectively challenged the data or the analysis from the State Planning Agency study that were used to support the proposed changes. Backed by data from the study, Hofstede and the legislature stood up to the pressure from their usual political allies, and improvements in pension funding, budgeting, and fiscal management were made that helped Minneapolis move toward a more sustainable finance system.[21] While pension funding continues to cause fiscal problems for the city, the study stands as a good example of staff work that changed governmental policy for the better.[22]

Thirty-four years later, after listening to state politicians talk about "belt tightening," "cutting out the fat," and other political euphemisms used to avoid describing the services being cut, as well as seeing the effects of sharply reduced state aid to cities and schools,

Hofstede thinks a new objective study of state revenue sharing is needed. He wants the study to analyze the role and impact of LGA on the state's economy with an emphasis on the importance of the state's core cities. He believes legislators would learn a great deal about the importance of revenue sharing by the state and of investing in the core cities as economic engines for the state's economy.[23]

As part of an effort to systematically analyze how and why local government functioned as it did, a much shorter study was also completed and presented during the 1977–78 session. This was an analysis of the demographics of local government officials across the state. Berg, as chair of the Local and Urban Affairs Committee, had requested the analysis from the "small university" at House Research. He was concerned that local officials often govern beneath the radar screen of many voters, and he hoped the study of county, city, state, and federal legislators would generate publicity about local government and the people who ran it. He also hoped the publicity would spur more women to run for these posts. Berg was particularly concerned about county government and county commissioners, which he thought were not very responsive to new ideas.

The study was completed by Gary Currie of House Research and showed that only 3 percent of county commissioners, 11 percent of city council members, and 4 percent of legislators were women. County commissioners were the oldest of the local government officials, with an average age of fifty-five, and had the lowest levels of education, at thirteen years. State legislators and city council members all had average ages in the midforties and had an average of more than sixteen years of education.[24]

In 2010, county government continued to lag in terms of women in elected positions. The number of county commissioners that were women had only advanced to 12 percent, while women city council members were up to 27.3 percent, and the number of women state legislators was 35 percent. Over half the counties in Minnesota in 2010 had no women commissioners.[25]

Power and Structure of City Government

The Speaker of the house does not usually act as the chief author of legislation. Disregarding that tradition, Sabo did so for a bill in 1977 that, like the Minneapolis–St. Paul fiscal study described above, was designed to send a serious signal to the state's largest city to pay attention to its finances and its unique governmental structure.[26] The structure of city government in Minneapolis provided for several independent boards to operate such things as schools, parks, and libraries, with the directors of each board being elected by the voters. Sabo's bill was based on the state's sovereign power, and it called for the abolishment of those boards and the consolidation of city powers under a larger Minneapolis City Council. In explaining the unusual and controversial move, Sabo said, "I think there should be one elected body that makes all the basic legislative decisions for the city." He also said he drafted the bill out of frustration with the lack of coordination between the independent boards and their failure to cooperate in planning, building, and using facilities such as hockey rinks, gymnasiums, and other buildings that could have multiple uses and users.[27]

Sabo did not push for a hearing on the bill but said he hoped people would "think seriously about it." The message was received. In an example of the use of legislative power other than through the actual passage of legislation, the independent boards, with one eye on the pending legislation, began to talk seriously to each other. Without any hearing ever being held, several joint projects, including gymnasiums and park facilities, were built by the school and park boards. The result was a more efficient use of public funds to provide needed facilities.[28]

Funding Social Services

In another effort to improve the use of state funds, enable counties to better serve their citizens, and hopefully get more women interested in running for county board positions, Sabo convened a group of legislators and top staff, including Ed Dirkswager, Kevin Kenny, and Eileen Baumgartner from House Research and Cal Herbert from the Appropriations Committee, and asked them to develop a proposal to change the method of payment for social services. The proposal they developed provided more flexibility for the counties (which had the responsibilities for delivering many of the services) by eliminating specific state-set "categorical-aid programs" (such as mental health counseling for students on a free and reduced lunch program in high school) and instead using the more general "block grants" (such as mental health assistance). The use of block grants would give the county commissioners the flexibility to tailor programs to the specific needs in their county. Government services covered by the proposed legislation included such things as mental health, foster care, child care, chemical dependency, and community health. Rural counties in particular would receive more state and federal money for these services than under the existing categorical-aid method of state payment.

The bill was the first bill to be introduced in the 1977 session, and House File 1 caused angst in the inner circles of many social service provider organizations.[29] These providers often had long-standing categorical grants for their programs, and the providers did not want any change. Some argued that county commissioners were too conservative and would not adequately fund their programs. Representative Paul McCarron, one of the legislators who helped draft the proposal and who was now its chief author, addressed these concerns. He pointed out that under the bill there was actually an increase in total state money available for the various programs and noted that the bill prohibited county boards from reducing existing financing of any program during the first two years of the bill's operation. McCarron argued that this provision would ensure adequate time for existing programs to make their case to the relevant elected officials. He said the block grants were designed to simplify and clarify the state's funding and to make sure that elected county officials made the major funding decisions.[30]

At the first hearing on House File 1, advocates for day-care providers did not accept McCarron's arguments and attempted to exclude day care from the block grant approach. After a vigorous debate on the previously esoteric topic of the merits of block grants and categorical grants, the day-care providers lost on a close vote. The bill then progressed through two more committees and passed the full house.[31] But the bill's supporters could not convince the slower-moving senate, and the senate did not act on House File 1. Thus, the effort by Sabo and McCarron and their supporters to move the decision of how much state money should be allocated to a particular type program to local elected officials failed in its first effort. Categorical grants set by the state continued to fund social services. But much like the supporters of the handgun control bill, McCarron and supporters of block grants persevered. They were successful in the very next session when a slightly revised bill for block grants became law, passing both the house and senate with strong bipartisan support.[32]

Regional Development Commissions

Another long-simmering dispute concerning the power of the state also came to a head in the 1977–78 sessions. As mentioned in chapter 2, the 1969 legislature with the strong support of then governor Harold LeVander had passed a bill known as the Regional Development Act (RDA). This was an outgrowth of earlier joint-powers legislation that was designed to give local governments more flexibility. The RDA provided authority for the governor to establish commissions in planning regions around the state as a vehicle for local units of government to plan and work together in a cost-effective manner. The act generated little controversy at the time, and Governor LeVander promptly designated ten planning regions and named the first chair of each commission. Polling data showed that 71 percent of all adults supported the regional development commissions.[33]

Despite this support, a few years later an ultraconservative group based in Colorado, the Committee to Restore the Constitution, began to work against the act in Minnesota with speeches by Arch Roberts, a retired army colonel. Roberts said "regionalism" as exemplified in the Minnesota legislation was nothing less than a plot to abolish the states. His speeches drew several hundred people at each appearance. The Minnesota Committee to Restore the Constitution picked up Roberts's cause.[34] The committee and its supporters resurrected the line from a 1969 speech by Governor LeVander (which, as recounted in chapter 2, was never actually delivered) that said, "Some towns are going to die, should die, it should be as natural for towns to die as it is for them to be born." This statement was effectively used to fan the flames of fear about regional planning in rural Minnesota.[35]

As a result, several bills were introduced in 1977 that would allow the counties to withdraw from the commissions.[36] The bills were referred to Berg's Local and Urban Affairs Committee. Berg did not like the bills, thought they had little or no chance of passage, and was in no rush to use valuable committee time on the legislation. One day as he got off the elevator outside his office, he was surprised by hundreds of proponents of the bills waiting for him with hand-lettered antiregional government placards and TV news cameras in tow. The crowd demanded to have the bills heard. Berg reluctantly promised to hear the bills at a future date.

When the hearing was held in the interim between the 1977 and 1978 sessions, over a hundred opponents of "regionalism" showed up, including a number of local elected officials, who vented their feelings about the claimed unconstitutionality of "regionalism" and about being pressured to think about land-use planning. Berg held up a 1971 court decision upholding the constitutionality of regional government, but many in attendance remained unconvinced.[37] None of the bills passed the committee.

Federal–State Relations

The enforcement of the Federal Occupation Safety and Health Act (OSHA), as was noted earlier, provided an option for the states to enforce the act. In his 1977 budget, Governor Perpich initially refused to fund the $900,000-a-year state enforcement costs, but both business and labor asked Perpich to reconsider. Leaders of the AFL-CIO and the leading business group, the Minnesota Association of Commerce and Industry (MACI), jointly went to Perpich and said they would rather deal with Minnesota inspectors than federal inspectors. Perpich reversed himself, and the legislature agreed.[38] This local enforcement of federal policy continues to serve as an example of an option available to both federal and state legislators for making federalism work well.

In 1976 Ed Dirkswager left his position as the director of DFL Caucus Research and joined the executive branch as state budget director in the Department of Finance. When Perpich became governor a few months later, he and Dirkswager worked closely in preparing the governor's first budget. In July 1977, Perpich asked Dirkswager to become the acting commissioner of the Department of Public Welfare (now called Human Services) for the state. This was a major position, and Dirkswager eagerly accepted.[39]

His first task was to get confirmed by the state senate, and he began to make the rounds at the capitol, visiting key senators. He was taken aback when Majority Leader Coleman bluntly asked, "I know you have the brains for the job but have you got the heart?" Dirkswager blinked a couple of times and assured Coleman that

he did. He promised Coleman that he would prove it by his performance. He was confirmed that fall, and the "acting" part of his title
was removed.[40]

One of Dirkswager's more challenging assignments was one that
involved both his brains and his heart and raised serious issues for
the two sovereign governments in our federal system. Dirkswager
was to help get the state out from under a federal court order involving a class action that had been brought in 1972 against the state by
six mentally retarded persons who were residents in the state's hospitals. The named plaintiff, Patricia Welsch (by her father and natural guardian, Richard Welsch), asked the federal court for relief for
herself and other mentally retarded individuals who had been involuntarily committed to what was alleged to be an improperly staffed
state hospital system.

Involuntary commitment is an extremely serious legal proceeding, a proceeding in which an individual may lose legal rights and in
which a person may be taken out of their home and community and
placed in a locked and crowded facility with few staff. In this situation, federal courts are often seen as the only legal remedy left for
people who believe they have been wronged by their state government and its courts.

The plaintiffs in the Welsch case were represented by a team of
legal-aid lawyers led by a smart young litigator with a classic Scandinavian name, Luther Granquist. After a twelve-day trial and an unan-
nounced visit by the federal judge to one of the hospitals, Granquist
and the residents convinced Judge Earl Larson that the resident's
federal constitutional rights under the Fourteenth Amendment
were being violated by the state. Judge Larson found that under the
federal Constitution, "due process requires that civil commitment
for reason of mental retardation be accompanied by minimally adequate treatment" and that those committed should be placed in the
least restrictive practicable setting. In essence, the judge was saying
more staff were needed and mandatory hospitalization should only
be used as a last resort.[41]

In discussing the shortage of staffing, the judge noted that "appropriations decisions by the legislature also are at the root of the reduction and apparent shortage of staff." He mentioned the impact of
"much needed and apparently valuable help from volunteers, mainly
high school age children," and that fifty adults had participated in

the Foster Grandparent Program to provide care for inmates at the hospital. The judge then acknowledged a difficulty inherent in our federal system, saying he was "mindful of the practical limits of [the court's] abilities to resolve what is essentially a question of conflicting legislative priorities." He said he would wait until he had more information before ordering specific remedies by the state to cure the constitutional violations.[42]

As the case went on, Judge Larson issued more specific orders, including one affecting the financing of care in Cambridge State Hospital. This order not only had a significant impact for many individuals, it had major state budget implications. This order and several others were promptly appealed by the state and led to unique interactions between the executive and legislative branches of state government and the judicial branch of the federal government.[43]

The language and actions of the officials involved reflected the emotions and seriousness of the issues involved in the appeal. Judge Larson in his twenty-seven-page decision of April 15, 1976, made it clear what was needed and why. He first noted that the adverse findings in his decision were not attributable to the present staff, who, he said, "deserve the commendation and thanks of this court and of the people of Minnesota," but to a shortage of staff at the hospital. He then described some of the testimony supporting his decision to continue the case and to require improved conditions and additional staff:

> For many of the profoundly or severely retarded persons meals and the pleasure associated with eating may be one of the few happy occasions in their other wise drab lives. . . . many handicapped residents must be fed slowly, due to difficulty in swallowing. Yet, due to inadequate staffing, Dr. Clements observed many residents being rushed through the feeding process so quickly (often in a matter of five or six minutes), that the effects of indigestion were visible in the gas bubbles escaping from the residents mouths. The visible and audible choking and coughing demonstrated that what should have been a time of pleasure was just one more occasion for suffering.

After several pages of such factual description, Judge Larson concluded that

Nothing less than full compliance with . . . this Order is demanded if the constitutional rights of the mentally retarded are to be respected. . . . only full compliance can remove the public shame of years of neglect and inadequate care suffered by those of our children who have been involuntarily ordered to spend their days at Cambridge State Hospital.[44]

This matter was also an emotional issue for Perpich, and he directed Dirkswager to address the issues immediately and to keep Perpich informed. Perpich even took the unusual step of writing a letter to the federal appellate court judges saying:

As the new governor of the State . . . I want to express to you my plans and aspirations regarding care for our retarded citizens. It is my fond hope that, given sufficient time . . . , we can render unnecessary further involvement of federal courts in the funding and management of our state hospitals . . . without the trauma of a constitutional confrontation between this State and the federal courts.[45]

The state legislature was also worried about the constitutional implications of the federal district court's order, and it filed a brief in the appeal proceedings. The legislature framed the issue before the appellate court as a "usurpation of the state legislative functions." The legislature argued:

An elected legislature is charged with establishing the order of priorities for expenditures. A judge, concentrating on a single social problem, cannot possibly make the determination of allocation to the many programs that call on a State for solution. . . .
The District Court's attempt to substitute itself as the appropriating authority for the effectuation of a state program of social welfare contradicts the most fundamental concepts of the constitutional system.[46]

The appellate court weighed all these factors and upheld three of Judge Larson's orders and vacated one dealing with financing, but the court also directly addressed the governor and the legislature:

"We desire to make it clear to the present governor and the current Legislature that the requirement of the [orders the court upheld] are positive, constitutional requirements and cannot be ignored." The court noted that the question was one of what priority the legislature would give to funding, and said the legislature should have the chance to address that issue before the end of the current session.[47]

Shortly after the case was presented to the appellate court, Perpich asked for and got a meeting with both Granquist and the state's lawyers. Perpich made it clear to the lawyers he wanted the case settled. Several months later Dirkswager was able to obtain a settlement concerning the issues at Cambridge State Hospital. One reason the state had the financial flexibility to settle the lawsuit was that the legislature agreed to close another state hospital, which both Governors Anderson and Perpich had supported in earlier budget messages.[48] The settlement was approved by the plaintiffs and Judge Larson.[49] Other issues at other hospitals continued, and eventually this case involved all of the state's hospitals. The court retained jurisdiction for seventeen years, which included the terms of five different commissioners, before finally dismissing the case.[50]

The Welsch case well illustrates the type of cases referred to in the previous chapter where federal courts found that some states were not providing adequate protection to individual liberties in some of the states' institutions. Those cases involved serious and difficult questions concerning the role of the state legislatures, the federal courts, and the meaning of our Constitution. The Welsch case, brought by a few mentally retarded plaintiffs supported by loving parents with representation by legal-aid lawyers, which ultimately involved several governors, the state legislature, and numerous federal judges, vividly demonstrates both the intricacy and the capacity of federalism to deal with the day-to-day problems of citizens from all parts of society. It also shows that simple slogans in political discussions, such as "activist judges" or "separation of powers," do not do justice to the complexities and human factors involved in ascertaining the meaning of critical constitutional phrases such as "equal protection" and "due process of law" in real life settings.

As these matters were being addressed, Perpich continued in his unique ways to try to bring about change in the culture of governing. In March he announced he was pulling the plug from the coffeepot in the governor's office "to protest the sharp rise in coffee prices." He also carried his own luggage, cut back on entertaining at the governor's residence, held meetings late into the night, and often began staff meetings at 6:30 a.m.[51] It got so that key staff people, craving a full night's sleep, whispered among themselves that they hoped the governor's popular wife, Lola, would spend less time in her home in the Iron Range region and more time in St. Paul so that the governor would "get a life."

Perpich also began to promote bocce ball, an Italian lawn game that was a favorite of his and popular on Minnesota's Iron Range. Bocce ball soon became known throughout the state. When the legislature raised the governor's pay in 1977, he announced he was donating the raise to interested communities for the purchase of bocce balls.[52]

In responding to critics of his unconventional style, Perpich pointed out he was one of those people who only need about "four or five hours of sleep. . . . If I went to bed at 10 I'd be up at 2:30 in the morning." He then disarmed many of his critics by simply stating he works late because "I love this job—I'm like a teenager in love."[53] He also opened a window to his innermost thoughts as he expressed a deep-seated and personal fear: "I would like to get in six years as Governor—I really would. . . . But I feel it might not happen."[54]

Although somewhat quirky, Perpich's candid statements and unorthodox style were catching on with the voters. The Republicans sensed this and tried to "shift public attention from Perpich's unpredictable, freewheeling style to his performance." IR party chair Chuck Slocum said, "Our non-elected governor has been long on rhetoric, but extremely short on performance."[55] Such comments only made Perpich work harder.

Persistent Problems

Crime

True to his word, Attorney General Spannaus began a campaign to expand the 1975 handgun control bill to include some of the provisions that had been knocked out by the senate in the 1975 debate. The two key provisions sought were for a police background check on potential gun owners and up to a fourteen-day waiting period before a person could obtain a handgun. Bill McCutcheon, a St. Paul police officer, was the senate chief author this session, and Berg continued as the chief author in the house. With twenty-one new senators, the proponents had hopes they could pick up the needed senate votes. The opponents of the legislation announced they would "fight them every step of the way."[56]

After many more hours of committee hearings, Berg had the house bill on the floor. After another four-hour debate and thirty attempts to amend the bill, some of which Berg accepted in order to pick up votes, the vote for preliminary passage was taken. Berg thought passage would be easier this time, but the bill just squeaked by, sixty-four to sixty-three.[57] This led to another anxious night of arm-twisting, cajoling, and hand-holding as Berg, Spannaus, and Bob Hentges from Spannaus's staff found the four additional votes needed for final passage. Two legislators who had not voted on the preliminary passage vote agreed to vote yes, and two legislators switched from no to yes. After the bill passed, John Spanish, a legislator from the Iron Range region of Minnesota, said the bill was a "creeping paralysis like a cancerous type of thing, coming closer and closer to gun registration." With a sigh, Berg repeated that if the senate approved the bill, neither he nor Spannaus would seek further handgun controls.[58] Once again all eyes turned to the senate.

About two weeks later, the full senate again proved obstinate and voted thirty-eight to twenty-seven against the bill. But at the last minute chief author McCutcheon voted against his own bill. This parliamentary procedure allowed him to move to reconsider the matter at a later date. Eight days later he did just that. This time the senate passed the bill by the narrowest possible margin, thirty-four to thirty-one. Berg, noting that the bill had only the minimum votes for passage, agreed to the slightly weaker senate provisions. The final bill was quickly repassed by the house and sent to Governor Perpich, who readily signed it.[59]

The final legislation added to the 1975 act a seven-day waiting period and police background checks for persons buying handguns from dealers. After thanking Spannaus and Governor Perpich, who had helped round up votes, Berg said he was retiring from carrying any more handgun control bills, since "I'm just tired. I've been working on it so long. . . . It's hard to keep coming back and coming back."[60]

A Pay Raise

After the 1974 last-minute pay raise fiasco and veto by Governor Anderson, the legislature was nervous about its pay but thought a raise was long overdue. It decided in 1977 to again deal with the politically dangerous subject. A bill was introduced to raise legislative salaries and the salaries of other top-level state officials, including judges, commissioners, and the governor, after the next election. (The state constitution prevents the legislature from raising its own pay, and thus an intervening election must take place before any pay raise goes into effect.)[61] The bill called for increasing annual legislative salaries from the existing $8,400 to $16,500 in 1979, a 96 percent increase, and to $18,500 in 1980, another 12 percent increase.[62] The governor's salary would increase 40 percent, from $41,500 to $58,000, and commissioners' and judges' salaries also were raised.

A two-hour hearing was set to allow citizens to speak their mind on the issue. The hearing was well covered by the media and was described as follows:

> Fifty members of the Minnesota House and Senate arranged themselves around a semicircular table at the capitol to await a possible public outcry. . . . After two hours the only people not connected with the bill who showed up were two state representatives (not on the committee), a lobbyist for a farm organization who was happy that the Commissioner of Agriculture . . . was getting a raise, and a . . . judge who was unhappy that district judges were to get the same pay as county judges.[63]

Harry Sieben, chair of the committee that would hear the bill and the author of the pay increase bill in the house, said he thought the fact the no one showed up meant this was not a volatile political issue. Ed Gearty, the senate author of the bill, cautioned Sieben and others about reading too much into the lack of interest when he said, "The rank-and-file citizen normally doesn't come to such hearings."[64]

About a month later, the bill came up for a vote in the senate and passed, forty-one to twenty-five.[65] The house then took up the bill. As had happened in 1974, the bill failed, although this time by only two votes. Nevertheless, "The voting was seen as a severe blow to DFL leaders of the house who outnumbered the Republicans 103 to 31." Majority Leader Anderson was "stunned by the outcome," and Sabo was "surprised." "We have got to visit with some folks yet," Sabo said.[66] The next day, after Sabo and Anderson had done some "visiting" and after some hectic "wheeling and dealing, arm-twisting and just talking reason," the bill passed seventy to sixty-one.[67] This time the governor promptly signed the bill, and the raise went into effect.[68]

In the following year, but before the next election, the legislature tackled a related and equally politically dangerous subject: pensions. This time benefits were cut. The legislature raised the age at which a legislator could begin to receive a pension from sixty to sixty-two, raised the portion of a legislator's pension that must be contributed by the legislator, and reduced the number of years of legislative service required to be eligible to receive a pension (the vesting period) from eight to six years. The net result was lower total costs to the state but a reduced vesting period for legislative pensions.[69] Even though the total cost was reduced, the cutback in required years of service would provide campaign fodder in the next campaign for many Republicans who voted against the bill.

Instant Replay: The Stadium

A few days after becoming governor, Perpich met with Sabo, Coleman, and State Planning Agency director Peter Vanderpoel to figure out how to handle the seemingly never-ending and pervasive stadium controversy. The Twins and the Vikings continued to talk about taking their baseballs and footballs and going to other cities. Bloomington, home of the Metropolitan Stadium, where the teams then played, Minneapolis, and the northern suburb Coon Rapids were each preparing legislation that would call for a new stadium in their municipality.

The politicians decided this was a good time for a punt. They developed the concept of having a neutral commission appointed by the governor do the heavy lifting of selecting the site and overseeing the design and building of a new stadium. Two young legislators were asked to carry the legislation authorizing the new commission and a stadium.[70]

Sabo talked with Al Patton, a third-term house member from outside the Twin Cities metropolitan area who had done a good job of carrying the controversial gas tax bill in 1975. Patton had never even been to a Vikings game and after the fact told reporters, "If you think I might have been more interested in the challenge of getting [the bill] through than a stadium itself, you may be right." He agreed to prepare and carry the bill. Coleman asked one of his "bright young men," Steve Keefe from Minneapolis, to steer the bill through the senate.[71]

In addition to what became known as the "no-site bill," authored by Patton and Keefe, other stadium-related bills, one for each of the competing cities, were introduced. All the bills in the house were sent to the Local and Urban Affairs Committee.[72] At the hearing on the bills, Patton showed his unique, quiet, and effective style. As he explained his bill to committee members, he used no fancy colored maps or overlays, which had been the norm in 1975. Patton simply brought out a map of the metropolitan area and placed it on an easel so all could see. He then picked up an ashtray and explained that the ashtray represented the stadium. Without further discussion, he moved the ashtray around on the map and said the commission created in the bill could locate the stadium anywhere in the metropolitan area. He then turned the ashtray upside down, again moved it around the map, and said the commission could also make it a domed stadium if it wished.[73]

Patton thought everybody knew the issues well and was tired of hearing more of the same arguments. He politely but firmly told the Twins owner, Clark Griffith, and the Vikings general manager, Mike Lynn, to not show up at the capitol. Patton explained his strategy: "Toward the end [of the 1975 session] a different bill was being resurrected every time you turned around and it turned into a circus. One thing I've learned in my three terms around here is that pressure on legislators usually gets the opposite result of what you want." Patton's no-frills presentation carried the day, and the no-site bill progressed to the Tax Committee, which also passed it and sent it to the house floor.[74]

On May 10 the house passed the no-site stadium legislation by a vote of seventy to sixty-one. The senate passed it a day later by a vote of thirty-nine to twenty-seven. The governor promptly signed it. The final legislation provided for a seven-member commission to be named by the governor to make the key selections of site and design. The stadium was to be financed with revenue bonds issued by the Metropolitan Council. The bonds would be paid off with stadium revenues, primarily from the Vikings, the Twins, and the Minnesota professional soccer team, the Kicks.[75]

The commission could spend up to $55 million from revenue bonds for a sixty-five-thousand seat multipurpose stadium if it were domed, and up to $42 million if it were not. The commission could also decide to remodel the existing Metropolitan Stadium. There was a 2 percent on-sale liquor "backup tax," to make sure no property tax revenues would be used to fund the stadium. The legislation spelled out rather detailed requirements to make sure the teams signed leases for at least as long as it took to pay off the bonds, and to ensure that games would generally be televised. Labor contracts to build the stadium had to have no-strike clauses, and permits had to be approved or denied by state agencies within tight time deadlines.[76]

Governor Perpich promptly appointed the seven members and named Dan Brutger, a building contractor from outside the Minneapolis–St. Paul area, as the chair. Brutger said he had no preconceived ideas about the site.[77] After eighteen months of work and much lobbying of commission members, the commission decided by a vote of four to three to build what would become the Hubert H. Humphrey Metrodome in downtown Minneapolis. The legislature breathed a sigh of relief as the politically volatile issue was resolved, although subsequent sessions would continue to tinker with the authorizing legislation.[78]

A thing of beauty it was not, but the new stadium was built on time and under budget, and all bond holders were paid off early. The roof was inflated on October 2, 1981, and then partially deflated forty-eight days later as a result of a heavy Minnesota snowstorm. The dome actually deflated four other times during its tenure before its spectacular collapse in December 2010 after a huge snowfall just seven days before the Vikings were to play the New York Giants.[79]

All debt from the existing Metropolitan Stadium in Bloomington was paid off in a timely manner. This is in contrast to stadiums in New Jersey, Seattle, Indianapolis, Philadelphia, Houston, Kansas City, Missouri, Memphis, and Pittsburgh, where residents continue to pay off debt for stadiums and arenas that have been abandoned for bigger and better places.[80]

In addition to the debt being paid off, the Metrodome has not required any public subsidy since 1984. Its supporters note that it hosted the Super Bowl, Major League Baseball's All-Star Game, two

World Series, and two NCAA Men's Final Four Division I basketball championships.[81]

The related arts effort, pushed by Berg and others as a price for their stadium support, also fared better in 1977. An almost threefold increase in arts funding was appropriated using the regional distribution mechanism drafted by Berg and Kelly in their 1975 effort to get some state funds for arts organizations.[82]

Environment

In 1977, the country was in the midst of a major energy shortage. President Carter addressed the nation on April 18 and noted that the "1973 gas lines are gone . . . but our energy problem is worse tonight than it was in 1973." He called for a new effort to conserve and change energy usage habits and said the new effort on energy will be the "moral equivalent of war." As part of his plan he called for a new department of energy and, while wearing a sweater, urged everyone to turn down their thermostats. The Minnesota Legislature joined in the effort by going to a four-day work week and turning the capitol's thermostats to fifty degrees on the off day. Earlier in 1977, Perpich said he would propose the "most comprehensive energy-saving program ever considered by any state." Critics questioned whether his actual proposals met this lofty standard, and the legislature only passed modest energy-saving legislation that year.[83]

The power-line dispute also proved to be intractable despite the governor's and the legislature's many efforts. The Minnesota Supreme Court ruled that construction of the line could proceed, and protests continued with sporadic violence.[84] The legislature did pass legislation to improve the siting procedures and compensation for new power lines. Perpich, always looking at the glass as half full, said that legislation would "save us a lot of grief in the future."[85]

The courts did solve one of the other major environmental issues then facing the state, which had consumed a substantial amount of the governor's time. The federal district court's decision requiring on-land disposal of the mining waste from Reserve Mining's operation was affirmed on appeal and reluctantly accepted by the key parties.[86] The final decision to dump the waste at a site known as "mile post seven" helped preserve Lake Superior as the cleanest of the Great Lakes.

The legislature addressed another environmental problem that had been building for several years. Named after the country of the scientist that first discovered the disease, Dutch elm disease was devastating millions of elm trees throughout the Midwest. That disease, along with oak wilt, was hitting Minnesota hard and denuding urban forests in cities across the state. Berg had successfully authored legislation to help combat the diseases in the 1975 session, but the funding was limited.[87] In the 1977 session, working with foresters at the University of Minnesota and some large cities, Berg was able to convince "Gentle Neil" Haugerud, who chaired a key division of the Appropriations Committee, that these diseases were a serious statewide problem and to loosen up the purse strings. Berg asked Senator Hubert H. Humphrey III (Skip) to carry the legislation in the senate.[88] Both the house and the senate eventually passed slightly different versions of the bill, and the differences were resolved in a conference committee. When the committee finished its work, the legislation appropriated over $28 million to carry on the fight and to commence a significant replanting program for Minnesota's urban forests. A drive today down the tree-lined streets of cities throughout Minnesota shows the results of that effort.[89]

Taxes and Revenue Distribution

Governor Perpich and House Tax Committee Chair Kelly had different ideas about the state's fiscal position and what to do about it. As part of the normal legislative process, Kelly and other house and senate legislators involved in finance issues met with Perpich from time to time to discuss state finances and the questions "who pays and how much?" Kelly reflected the cautious nature of the house on fiscal issues, and often had to tell the governor that the house would "probably not go along with" some of the governor's ideas and programs. The governor did not like to hear that message, and he and Kelly were never close. In November 1977, Perpich and Kelly even had a full page in the state's largest newspaper of dueling pro and con op-ed pieces about tax issues.[90]

In early 1977, Perpich proposed to reduce revenues by $100 million in an effort to simplify the state tax code. Kelly liked the idea of simplification but opposed the plan due to the loss of revenue resulting from the changes necessary to accomplish the simplification.

Kelly and his colleagues prevailed, and the simplification provisions did not pass.[91] The governor and Kelly did agree on the need for higher taxes on iron ore, despite strong opposition from DFL legislators from the governor's home Iron Range region on how the proceeds would be used. Kelly appreciated the governor's willingness to disagree publicly with many of his strongest supporters.[92] The governor and the legislature also agreed to begin to tax public employee pensions to bring such income in line with private pension income.[93]

Near the end of the 1977 session, the legislature passed and the governor signed legislation adding three new brackets for taxpayers in the higher end of the state's progressive income tax. The house had put the new brackets into its bill as a bargaining chip in its negotiations with the senate, which wanted more tax cuts. To the surprise of the house members, the senate readily agreed to the new higher brackets. Sabo later said the brackets "were a mistake and one of our screwups."[94]

The 1977 legislature also continued efforts to hold down the impact of property taxes with revisions and expansions to the circuit-breaker program, and reduced taxes on small businesses through higher exemptions on the business payroll tax.[95] As 1977 came to an end, projections continued to show the likelihood of a significant surplus for the budget period ending in July 1979, although the amount of the projected surplus was unclear.[96]

In December 1977, the Republicans proposed that the 1978 session implement a $234 million cut in income tax rates to take effect in 1978. Senate Minority Leader Ashbach led the Republican charge for the larger tax cut. He reminded voters of the new higher brackets and said the DFL had the "unmitigated gall" in 1977 to actually increase rates despite a projected surplus in state funds. The amount of the projected surplus then became even a greater point of dispute.[97] It was lost on no one that 1978 was an important election year and that taxes would, as usual, be an important issue.

In January 1978 Perpich laid out his position, saying his chief priority was to reduce the state's income tax. Perpich argued: "Our budget is balanced. We pay as we go. Our credit rating is triple-A. . . . It makes good sense to keep some money in reserve . . . any excess funds, beyond a prudent reserve, should be used to reduce taxes." In making his pitch for a tax cut, Perpich went on to review the fiscal history of the past decade:

In 1967, Minnesota ranked 11th highest in the nation in property taxes and . . . [by] 1976 [that ranking] dropped . . . to
24th . . . [the state] dropped in all taxes areas—from 35th to
36th in sales taxes; from 3rd to 4th in individual income taxes;
and from 4th to 6th in corporate income taxes.[98]

The veteran legislators remembered the effort that went into funding the increases in state aid to schools, which made school funding more equitable across the state, and into the increased funding
for local government aid, which resulted in a reduction in property
taxes. They also took pride in having provided a prudent surplus in
each of the budget periods. Many, including Kelly and Sabo, were
wary of undoing these changes.

But Perpich persisted and pointed out that the state had the dubious distinction of having the highest income tax rate in the country
in several brackets. Perpich then formally proposed $102 million in
income tax cuts. Coleman was "sympathetic to meaningful income
tax reduction," but Ashbach correctly predicted that the proposed
income tax reductions would run into trouble in the house. Kelly,
along with the Senate Tax Committee chair, Bill McCutcheon, publicly expressed reservations.[99] Kelly noted that legislators always
wanted to cut taxes, and few were willing to raise them. He noted
that approximately 90 percent of the tax bills referred to his committee were for some type of tax cut. He expressed concerns that
property taxes would creep back up, and he raised the possibility
that other state taxes might have to be increased in the future to balance the budget if income tax rates were cut. He argued for keeping
a surplus (rainy-day fund) of about 5 percent of what legislators call
the "general fund" in case of an economic downturn. This fund is
basically all the state revenues for the two-year budget cycle less the
revenues for highways and certain other small expenditures.[100]

Roger Moe, chair of the Senate Finance Committee, and Jerry
Christenson, the finance commissioner, also raised concerns about
the small size of any surplus if the tax cuts were implemented. Independent Republicans generally applauded the governor's proposal
and claimed the low surplus projections were not accurate.[101]

As the tax debate continued, Kelly saw the political handwrit-
ing on the wall and reluctantly agreed to a compromise of $100 mil-
lion in tax cuts. These included income tax reductions for the higher

rates, exempting residential heating fuels from the sales tax, and repeal of the payroll tax. The payroll tax, discussed earlier, had been passed in 1973 with the support of both labor and business. The vice chair of the Tax Committee, and a future Speaker of the house, Bob Vanasek, shared Kelly's concerns. When the final tax cut bill came up for passage, Vanasek let it be known he was not happy with the bill but would vote for it. He "handed out clothespins to house members with the suggestion that they might need help holding their noses while voting for the measure." With or without clothespins, the votes were found, and the tax cuts were passed and signed by a happy governor.[102]

In reviewing the session and looking forward to the fall's election, many felt that "Perpich came out of the 1978 session the winner on the tax front.... He pushed and jabbed, and went directly to the public, and in the end he saw a tax bill passed." People also noticed that "part of the DFL governor's support came from an unusual source—(IR) Minority Leader Robert Ashbach.... Without prodding by the unusual duo of Perpich and Ashbach, the tax cut might never have materialized."[103]

This bipartisan effort and the resulting political implications were analyzed by many for the crucial upcoming election. One veteran reporter wrote:

Independent IR legislators supported Perpich's proposed tax cuts saying they should be even larger, and they did their best to embarrass the reluctant DFL leaders.

As the session proceeded, a tax cut began to sound like a good idea to some DFL legislators, particularly some house members who anticipate a tough election....

Nicholas Coleman who said in January he [may] run for the U.S. Senate became more enthusiastic....

Sabo, a congressional candidate, said he did not like the tax-cut bill, but was silent in the tax committee and voted for it.[104]

The projected surplus was the problem that concerned many legislators. According to the finance commissioner, after the tax reductions were figured in, the surplus would be only $23 million, or less than 1 percent of the state's $6.4 billion budget.[105] In fact, the surplus on June 30, 1979, turned out to be $234 million, or 3.6 percent of the general fund.[106] This was slightly under the amount Kelly wanted and Ashbach had predicted would exist.

It is interesting to note that at the same time these tax-and-spending arguments were being resolved by the votes of elected legislators in Minnesota, the entire electorate of California was debating and ultimately adopting Proposition 13, an amendment to California's constitution that sharply limited property taxes and made it extremely difficult to raise any taxes. The amendment, officially named the "People's Initiative to Limit Property Taxation," required a two-thirds vote by the state legislature to raise taxes.[107] The amendment helped keep the issue of taxation in the forefront of voters' minds across the country. Many argue the movement behind Proposition 13 was also part of a national movement that elected Ronald Reagan to the presidency over Carter–Mondale in 1980 and has "remained a staple of campaigns ever since."[108] This use of initiatives like Proposition 13, which present complicated issues directly to voters instead of allowing legislators to thrash out the issues, has been called "direct democracy." It has also been said to be a major reason why the country's largest state has been called "dysfunctional," "ungovernable," and even "failed."[109]

At a minimum, the experiences of California and Minnesota in 1978 and their aftermath show the importance of thoughtful discussion of "who pays and how much?" to politics and to the ability of a state to pay its bills and provide government services. The experiences also show the dangers of putting constitutional restrictions on the legislative branch, such as supermajority requirements on tax and budget issues. While legislatures and governors in Minnesota have in recent years struggled mightily over fiscal matters (see chapter 7), they have been able to reach tax and budget solutions with a simple majority vote of legislators and without having to amend the state constitution. In an effort to help solve the fiscal problems caused by the supermajority requirements in its constitution, in 2010 California voters adopted Proposition 25 and ended the requirement of a two-thirds vote to adopt the state's budget. Proposition 25 passed with over 55 percent of the vote.[110]

Performance Audits

The first evaluations of government programs as a result of the 1973 LEAP recommendations, discussed earlier, were completed during the 1977–78 sessions. The 1973 law established a newly created legislative auditor position and a legislative commission to oversee the legislative auditor. That 1973 statute was significant because it took the function of auditing state government agencies away from the executive branch and put it into the legislative branch. The statute also provided that the legislative auditor could "evaluate projects or programs requested by the commission."[111] In 1975, the legislature built on this and established a separate division to do nothing but "program evaluations" of various selected programs. The legislative auditor was to determine whether the goals and objectives of the selected state and local programs worked and whether the state received good value for the money it spent.[112] The first evaluation involved the effect of state regulation on such things as group homes for juveniles or mentally retarded persons, foster care, and community correction facilities. The second report was an evaluation of the Minnesota Housing Finance Agency. A steady stream of similar reports on a variety of topics has continued to the present day.[113]

These dull-sounding but objective and thorough reports have proven to be anything but dull in their impact. They helped in 1978 and continue to help legislators and governors ensure the state is getting good value for the expenditures of public funds. The creation of the position of legislative auditor and the use of performance evaluations are good examples of a legislature properly performing its oversight function and also of winning a battle in the ongoing tug-of-war that exists between the legislative and executive branches of government throughout the country.

A Legislature Reformed

The 1977 session was said to have been "productive" and "unusually well organized," and the last day was referred to as "a relaxed finale to a relaxed session."[114] Three tough and volatile issues—the stadium, a legislative pay raise, and handgun control—had apparently been put to bed without too much political damage to anyone. Taxes had been cut, and no legislative logjam had developed. The DFL was feeling good about the session. Both the IR and the DFL Parties were gearing up for a big election year in 1978.

The *Minneapolis Tribune,* the state's largest paper, decided to look back at the past ten years of legislative performance and analyze the many changes and reforms that had taken place. The lengthy five-part series by two experienced reporters described the major changes, the source of many of the recommendations, and the cost in dollars to implement the changes. Some of the benefits of the changes were discussed. The introduction noted that since 1967, the legislature had

> gone from biennial to annual sessions, nearly doubled the size of legislative salaries and more than doubled legislative per diem payments, provided every legislator with a private office, more than doubled the number of legislative staff members and required that the public's business be transacted in full public view.
>
> In most cases the Legislature followed the recommendations of . . . "good government groups" . . .
>
> And the public has paid the price. The total cost of the legislature's operations has risen from $6.2 million in the 1967–68 biennium to $33.9 million in the 1977–78 biennium.[115]

The articles noted that some of the changes had started under Conservative Caucus control and had been accelerated by the large influx of new and younger DFL members in the 1970s. The significant changes to open the process to public scrutiny were reviewed favorably. The dollar costs were discussed, and it was argued by some that the costs were relatively insignificant when compared to the state's $6.4 billion budget and to the improved approach to governing. Others argued the costs and changes were excessive.

There was much discussion of the increased time commitment for legislators and the fact that more legislators were making the job a full-time occupation. It was argued by some that the makeup of the legislature changed as a result of the greater time commitment. For example, in the house, the number of lawyers decreased from thirty-three to thirteen, and the number of small-business people decreased from twenty-three to twelve. Teachers increased from five to twenty. Roughly similar changes occurred in the senate.

The role of the increased staff was noted with generally supportive comments about the increased research capabilities but with concern about paid staff doing political work. The series concluded by noting that lobbyists continued to play a big role in legislating, but that as a result of the more open process and disclosure requirements, citizens could now see where and how the money flowed. It was further noted that many more public-interest-group lobbyists were present.[116]

The changes in the legislative process in the decade from 1967 to 1977 summarized above as well as other changes in legislation described in this and earlier chapters provide a good perspective from which to examine the turbulence in the state's political climate that began with the 1976 presidential election and gained momentum in 1977 as it became known that Senator Hubert Humphrey was dying of cancer. That turbulence led to political climate change on a surprising election night, November 8, 1978.

CHAPTER 9

The Minnesota Massacre, 1978 Version

We have met the enemy and he is us.

▪ Pogo, 1971

T he election of Carter–Mondale in November 1976 started a course of events within Minnesota politics that had a loose resemblance to the reaction that detonates an atomic bomb. Physicists tell us the reaction begins with one neutron striking a fertile substance such as uranium-235. This causes a portion of the uranium to split and release two more neutrons. These two loose neutrons proceed to bounce around, striking more uranium and releasing still more neutrons. This process continues exponentially until the heat, energy, and pressure become so great that the whole thing blows up.

The Players

In 1976, the opening of Mondale's Senate seat struck the political uranium-235 and caused Governor Wendell Anderson and Lieutenant Governor Rudy Perpich to break free from their existing positions. These changes caused more politicians to contemplate leaving their present positions. Before long, liberal Minneapolis congressman Don Fraser began to think seriously about running against the more moderate Wendell Anderson for the DFL endorsement for Mondale's Senate seat.[1] As word spread about Fraser's thoughts, Speaker Martin Sabo, several of his state legislative colleagues, the chair of the board of the state's largest county, and others began to imagine practicing their legislative and political skills from Fraser's soon-to-be abandoned office in Washington, D.C.[2] As we will see, by mid-1977, the Republicans had already sensed the potential explosion could be helpful to their cause, and they added significantly to the chain reaction.

When Hubert Humphrey passed away on January 13, 1978, at age sixty-six, the chain reaction stopped momentarily, as the state and nation mourned a leader President Carter called "the most beloved of all Americans."[3] Tributes came from far and wide to the memorial services at the capitols in Washington and St. Paul. Thousands of people waited in line in subzero temperatures outside the state capitol rotunda to pass by the flag-draped coffin.[4] The former mayor, vice president, and five-term U.S. senator had set the bar high for what politics and legislative service should be. His decades of outstanding service to the country had a profound and meaningful impact on many, legislators and common citizens alike.

Under state law, the governor had to appoint a person to fill Humphrey's Senate seat until the next statewide general election, then about ten months away. The Republicans pushed for an early special election. They had won four of the five special elections in legislative races and gained one congressional seat in special elections held in 1977, and thought they would do better in a special election.[5] The DFL legislators ignored the Republican requests and passed legislation making minor modification to existing law. They made it clear that the election would remain the next statewide general election.[6] The person who won that election would serve the remaining four years of that term. Thus the very rare situation was present where two U.S. Senate seats would be up for election in one year. A big issue for Perpich was whether he should appoint a "caretaker," or someone who would get a head start as an incumbent in the November election.

Before Perpich made his decision, the chain reaction sprang back to life. Ten days after Humphrey's death, Fraser announced he had decided not to challenge fellow DFLer Anderson but to seek DFL Party endorsement for the Senate seat formerly held by Humphrey. Fraser said that regardless of the outcome, he would not run for reelection for his seat in Congress. This was reported to be "a friendly warning to Perpich and other DFLers that [Fraser] will be a candidate . . . even if the governor decides on an interim appointee who would try to hang onto it."[7]

Sabo then moved quickly to stake out his claim on the seat in Congress vacated by Fraser. Two days after Fraser's announcement,

Sabo held a press conference in his home with his wife, kids, and a few neighbors, saying he was running for Fraser's seat in Congress. Several legislators plus Arvonne Fraser, an official with the U.S. Agency for International Development and Don Fraser's spouse, and Secretary of State Joan Growe—all of whom had been rumored to be interested in running—promptly indicated they would not run.[8]

On the same day as Sabo's press conference, Perpich announced his appointment of Muriel Humphrey, Hubert's popular widow, to the U.S. Senate. Many thought Perpich was appointing Muriel Humphrey as a "caretaker," but she was far from clear about whether she would merely be a "caretaker." In fact, when asked about running that fall for the remaining four years of the term, she responded, "That's too far ahead for anyone to be thinking about right now. . . . If I do a good job that's my goal."[9] Muriel Humphrey was sworn in by Vice President Mondale on February 6, 1978, and Minnesota gained its first woman U.S. senator.[10]

All this of course caused even more speculation and some difficult moments for both Fraser and Perpich. Fraser said the appointment was "a very good appointment," but that he would continue his plans to gain the DFL endorsement.[11] The Republicans seized on the appointment and Muriel Humphrey's talk of running to highlight the "appointment-not-election" issue that would become a staple of Republican attacks against the DFL for the rest of the year. Republican Congressman Bill Frenzel, also thinking about running for the Senate, said Perpich had "double-crossed the people of Minnesota," and noted that "three Minnesota senators—Mondale, Wendell Anderson, and Mrs. Humphrey—were appointed and that the last two had been appointed by an unelected governor."[12]

Several other prominent DFL players quickly announced they were interested in running for the Senate seat, but only if Muriel Humphrey decided not to run for the remaining four years of the term. These included Senate Majority Leader Nick Coleman and a member of Congress from the northern part of the state, Jim Oberstar. Abortion was a big issue in all this jockeying for position as the antiabortion "forces [had] gained considerable political strength within the state and they do not want to see Fraser advance to the Senate."[13]

A "flamboyant Minneapolis entrepreneur," Bob Short, who in 1966 had unsuccessfully run for lieutenant governor with gubernatorial candidate Karl Rolvaag, soon began to think seriously about running against the more liberal Fraser. Short announced his interest in the Senate race in early February, but only if Muriel Humphrey did not run. He said he would "probably" skip the DFL endorsing convention and go directly to the primary election. Marion Menning, a DFL legislator and one of the "most vocal opponents of abortion and gay rights," also announced he was going to seek the Humphrey seat. Several state senators, including Hubert Humphrey's son, Skip, announced that they were running or interested in running for Congress from various districts in Minnesota.[14]

The Republicans were well into the chain reaction by this time as David Durenberger, a Minneapolis lawyer and former chief of staff to Governor Harold LeVander, had announced his campaign for the governor's job in June 1977. In August, a longtime congressman and dairy farmer from the southern part of the state, Al Quie, announced for the same position. Quie, an evangelical Christian and a former Navy pilot, had served a term in the state senate before going to Congress. Arne Carlson, an assistant minority leader in the house, also began his rise as a statewide candidate with an announcement in August that he was going to run for state auditor.[15]

In October, Republican National Committeeman Rudy Boschwitz, a "wealthy and colorful businessman," announced he was running for the U.S. Senate seat held by Anderson. Two other Republicans, state senator Howard Knutson and representative Bob Johnson, would also soon become candidates for governor.[16]

The chain reaction picked up even more energy as Congress progressed on legislation creating additional federal judgeships across the country, including two for Minnesota. Attorney General Warren Spannaus, a close friend of Vice President Mondale, began to think seriously about life as a federal judge. Soon Representatives Tom Berg, Ray Faricy, Harry Sieben, and Senator Winston Borden added to the reaction as they began to "explore" the possibility of succeeding Spannaus if he were to be appointed by Carter to the new judgeship. Skip Humphrey then jumped from the congressional race to the exploratory attorney general's race. All the candidates were confident that the federal legislation would pass and that the popular Spannaus would be named a judge. About this time, Republican Knutson announced he was shifting to the race for attorney general and would not be a candidate for governor.[17]

As we saw in the previous chapter, the legislature tried to stay focused on its business of legislating on taxes, stadiums, and the like, but the heat generated from the rapidly expanding political chain reaction was clearly a distraction. By one count, at least twenty-four members of the legislature were running or were mentioned as considering running for one of the several open seats.[18]

The Sorting Process

Minnesota is one of several states that uses neighborhood political party caucuses held in late winter of election years to help select their party's candidates. The caucuses are neighborhood affairs frequently held in schools or church basements. They are open to all eligible voters.[19] In practice, the caucuses are usually dominated by political or special-interest-group activists. These caucuses elect delegates to a series of conventions culminating in the party's state endorsing convention. Each party sets its own rules for electing delegates and determining convention procedures. The state conventions are usually held in early summer and endorse candidates for various statewide offices.

The state also holds primary elections in the early fall, where the candidate endorsed by the party's convention may face candidates of the same party who have lost at the party's convention and wish to present their candidacy to a larger and more diverse electorate, or who have decided to skip the often polarized, time-consuming, and complex caucus and convention process and go directly to the primary election. The winners of the primary elections then square off in the November general election.

In 1978, the caucuses and the primary elections were a big deal. On February 28, tens of thousands of people attended caucuses in the state's four-thousand-plus precincts. The Republican caucuses elected 10,250 delegates to the next level of conventions, and the DFL caucuses elected 38,500 delegates. There is no reliable mechanism for knowing exactly how this first round of voting went, but it appeared to most observers that Quie led Durenberger and Johnson in the contested IR race for governor. On the DFL side, Fraser led both Short and Coleman. Perpich was not seriously challenged, and Anderson and Boschwitz were the clear front runners in their respective parties for Anderson's Senate seat.[20] In the congressional race for Fraser's old seat, Sabo would face an ongoing challenge from several lesser known candidates at his congressional-district endorsing convention.[21]

Senator Muriel Humphrey simplified things a bit on the DFL side in April, when she announced at a major DFL fund-raising dinner with Fraser and other interested candidates present that she would not run for election for the remaining four years of her term. Fraser breathed a sigh of relief and continued with new vigor in his quest for the DFL endorsement.[22]

In May, the number of statewide candidates dropped sharply as Spannaus announced he would wait no longer for the Congress to pass the federal judgeship bill and would instead run for reelection. The five would-be candidates, who all had campaigns in full swing, had indicated they would support Spannaus if he decided to run for reelection. They all did just that.[23] This meant it was time for a final decision by Berg, Faricy, and Sieben as to whether to run for reelection to the legislature. The two senators who were also "exploring" the attorney general's race, Borden and Humphrey, were in the middle of their four-year terms, so they continued on in the legislature.

Berg and his wife had been working hard on the attorney general's race and had not talked much about the possibility that Congress might not act in a timely manner or that Spannaus might not be appointed. Berg enjoyed the legislative process and felt public service was a meaningful and important part of his life. But, like Joe Graba two years earlier, Berg felt the tug of family and realized the opportunity to spend time with two young sons was fleeting. He also enjoyed his law practice and knew that two demanding career commitments were not sustainable over the long run. Twelve days after Spannaus's announcement, Berg announced, "with a tear in my eye," that he was not going to seek a fifth term in the legislature.[24] Faricy and Sieben continued their legislative careers for a few more years before they too returned to private life and legal careers.

Nine months earlier, Minority Leader Henry Savelkoul had also announced he was not going to seek reelection, and was returning to full-time law practice. Savelkoul was "totally burned out" and wanted to spend more time with his family. Assistant Minority Leader Arne Carlson also announced he would not seek reelection to the house but would run statewide for the position of state auditor.[25]

As the legislation session ended, there were a number of bipartisan tributes to Sabo, as he was about to leave his last session as Speaker for what all were certain would be a successful campaign for Congress. Sabo had served in the legislature for eighteen years, and legislating and politics were his life. As the tributes were made and jokes were told, he choked back tears, thanked his 133 colleagues for their long and heartfelt standing ovation, and banged down the gavel for the last time.[26]

The party endorsement process ground on, and it became clear that Quie would be endorsed as the Republican candidate for governor. Durenberger saw what was happening in both his race against Quie and in the increasingly bitter contest in the DFL Party between Fraser and Short. On April 22, Durenberger announced that he was dropping his bid to become governor and shifting his sights to the Senate seat being fought over by Fraser and Short.[27] In the congressional district convention in Fraser's old district, Sabo received the necessary 60 percent vote over several candidates who split the vote, and he moved on to an easy primary election.[28]

At the Republican state convention, Quie, Boschwitz, and Durenberger were easily endorsed in their respective races.[29] At the DFL convention, problems developed. Perpich, Anderson, and the other DFL candidates were endorsed without too much problem, but Fraser ran into big difficulties. He faced angry delegates as the contentious issues of abortion, gun control, and preservation of a huge part of northern Minnesota known as the Boundary Waters Canoe Area (BWCA) as a federal wilderness area took center stage.

Fraser was pro-choice, supported gun controls, and supported legislation to enhance protection of the BWCA from mining and from snowmobiles, outboard motors, and other motorized vehicles popular in northern Minnesota.[30] Just a week before the convention, a popular state senator, Doug Johnson, a teacher and fishing guide from the pro-life, anti–gun control Iron Range region of the state, announced his "favorite son" candidacy for the endorsement being sought by Fraser. Bus loads of people from the Iron Range region came to the convention to stop the Fraser candidacy. Many of these visitors brought whistles with them—the noisy kind that are sometimes used by people who are lost in the wilderness to lead searchers to their location. When Fraser tried to address the convention, the whistles were put to work, and there was no way Fraser could make himself heard. Finally, Jim Oberstar, Fraser's colleague in Congress who represented the Iron Range region, took the podium and asked the delegates and visitors to quiet down and let Fraser speak.[31] After much noise and fury, Fraser got to speak. His delegates finally prevailed on the third ballot, and he was endorsed.[32]

As the primary battles got under way, the candidates also had to deal with national concerns about such things as runaway inflation, the real possibility of the return of oil and gas shortages, and international competition—all of which Mondale and Carter from their White House perspective said led to a "skepticism and distrust that had taken root among Americans in the late 1960s and early 1970s."[33] To deal with these local and national issues, Short spent heavily from his personal funds and made "slashing attacks and put Fraser on the defensive." Short's strategy was to "stitch together what's been called a 'coalition of disaffection'—single-issue groups hostile to Fraser because of his stands on abortion, the Boundary Waters Canoe Area, gun control, and other emotional issues."[34] But the issue "getting most of the attention involve[d] taxes and spending." Short dealt with that by saying he wanted to "cut federal spending by $100 billion, using $50 billion for a tax cut and the other $50 billion to balance the federal budget." A frustrated Fraser responded that this was "unrealistic and would cause economic chaos." He also unsuccessfully challenged Short to be specific about where he would cut.[35]

The voters would decide how these issues would play out when they selected the candidates to proceed to the fall election. The greatest interest was in the DFL side because the results would

> be the first test . . . of the troubled DFL party, . . . of the
> depth of the so-called taxpayer's revolt, and the strength
> of a wave of conservatism that is said to be sweeping the
> country . . . [and] the strength of the party's endorsement
> system.[36]

Nearly one million voters were expected to have their say on which of the primary candidates should proceed to the general election.[37]

For the Republicans, the primary was essentially a nonevent. A potential problem for the Republicans did not materialize, since Malcolm Moos, a former speechwriter for Dwight Eisenhower and president of the University of Minnesota, decided in June not to seek the Republican endorsement and not to be a Republican "spoiler."

He continued his primary campaign against Durenberger but did not mount a major campaign.[38] As expected, Durenberger, Boschwitz, and Quie easily won their primary contests.[39]

While Perpich and Anderson won their primary races, primary election night turned into an all-nighter as a result of the Fraser–Short battle. Shortly after midnight, Fraser held a 30,000 vote lead. But as the sun was rising and the morning papers were being delivered saying Fraser had won, the votes from the heavy-voting Iron Range districts were pouring in. By midmorning, it was known that Short had in fact won by 3,451 votes out of the over 500,000 votes cast.[40]

The Short victory was a surprising blow to much of the liberal DFL Party establishment. Fraser had the support of leaders Muriel Humphrey and Walter Mondale and had received the endorsement of the Minnesota AFL-CIO—although Short had gained "support among union locals."[41] Short had campaigned vigorously and used his own money to finance the bulk of his campaign. To those who accused Short of buying the election, he offered no apologies about using his own money: "I didn't steal it. I didn't marry it and I didn't inherit it. I earned it myself with hard work."[42]

Fraser admits he did not run a good campaign and says there was "a general sentiment against the more liberal progressive politics."[43] Regardless of the reasons, it was clear that healing the bitter split within the DFL Party exacerbated by the bitter endorsement fight and primary campaign would be an extremely difficult task.

In the legislative races, there had been concern that the "throw the rascals out" argument being used by the Republicans would reach into the DFL primary, but only three of the twenty-two incumbents who faced challenges lost their jobs, and their losses were because "voters felt they weren't doing enough for their home districts, not because they were too liberal."[44] Sabo easily won his primary and continued the old-fashioned process of knocking on doors and passing out pamphlets throughout the congressional district. He estimates he knocked on over thirty thousand doors that summer and fall.[45]

With this badly split party, the DFL limped into the general election facing an increasingly confident group of Republican candidates. Perpich continued to campaign in his unorthodox style. He frequently traveled to small towns and cultivated a "just folks" image. He ignored problems with party leaders, who complained, "he's unpredictable and too much of a loner."[46] He did, however, do some orthodox things, and he joined Mondale, President Carter, and Rosalynn Carter when they all made separate trips to assist Perpich and the DFL Party.[47]

Quie was coming across to voters as "just an honest, stoic Norwegian dairy farmer," with a campaign "about as exciting as watching an automobile rust." His strong religious beliefs were made known at prayer breakfasts, where he said he prayed for all peoples in their struggles, including Perpich. He and Republican legislative candidates kept up a steady refrain about the need for tax cuts.[48]

On October 1, a leading poll showed the DFL hanging on, with Perpich ahead of Quie 51 percent to 42 percent, and Short leading Durenberger 46 percent to 39 percent. The only major Republican candidate in the lead was Boschwitz, over Anderson, 48 percent to 44 percent.[49]

During October, Quie began to attack Perpich more vigorously while trying to maintain his nice-guy image. Perpich noted the change and that Quie was engaging in "gutter politics" as the campaign entered the final days.[50] The tougher campaign was at least partially explained by Quie having told his volunteers to "do what you believe . . . just go for it. You don't have to check with . . . [the campaign] or anyone else." Quie's biographer writes about this "bureaucratic liberation" and a nasty incident on the Sunday before the election:

> One quite unattractive initiative some people in the campaign pursued was putting fliers on the windshields of cars parked near Catholic churches on the Sunday morning before Election Day that falsely claimed that the Pro-Life Rudy Perpich was pro-choice on abortion. Rather than being outright malicious, it's possible the campaign workers really did think that Perpich endorsed abortion rights, confusing him with his brother who in fact did. . . . [This] prompted Perpich's wife, Lola, to charge angrily that Quie carried a Bible in one hand and a bucket of mud in the other. Quie continues to lament the incident.[51]

The Short–Durenberger race was also getting into emotional and questionable charges. Allegations that Durenberger was responsible for "obscene and threatening telephone calls and letters to [Short's] home, and vandalism to his property" were made by Short. Short also attacked a group of liberal DFLers calling themselves "Minnesotans for Honesty in Politics," who had launched a "Stop Short" movement. Durenberger's campaign chair, Paul Overgaard, responded by saying Short has "got to be kidding. . . . Anyone who has been watching this campaign and the kind of tactics used by Short would have to find that allegation kind of sick." He went on to accuse Short and his campaign of "last minute smear tactics."[52]

Anderson and Boschwitz were in a longer-term slugfest. Boschwitz was using his wealth and outspending Anderson significantly, as both candidates made extensive use of television. Boschwitz started his commercials over a year before the election, and Anderson about a month later.[53]

Allegations of cronyism and "dubious financial practices" in connection with a state commission dealing with the Great Lakes while Anderson was governor were continuously raised by Boschwitz and Quie. When Perpich became governor, he requested an audit by the legislative auditor of the use of the Great Lakes funds. The report was completed and released in spring 1978, but the DFL members of the audit commission refused to allow release of the detailed working papers of the auditors. This refusal raised the curiosity of all and kept the matter in the news. The Republican members of the audit commission leaked some of the papers to the press. A major St. Paul paper then filed a lawsuit to have all the work papers released. A district court ruled in favor of the newspapers, but the DFL-dominated audit commission appealed the decision. All this stonewalling by the DFL provided good fodder for continuous attacks by Quie and Boschwitz. Perpich called for the release of the papers on September 1, but the DFL commission members, led by Senator Bill McCutcheon, still refused, claiming that the audit process and the individuals who gave information should be protected from public disclosure.[54] Anderson also requested the release of the papers without success, which led to Republican questions about the sincerity of the requests by both Anderson and Perpich.[55]

After still more of the working papers were leaked, the DFL members of the commission relented. On October 29, less than two weeks before the election, the commission released all the work papers. At a press conference announcing the release, commission chair McCutcheon resigned from the commission, saying he felt strongly that the work papers should not be released. He and Coleman tried unsuccessfully to turn the issue around by criticizing the Republicans for leaking the documents.[56]

Quie said this failure to release the papers for so long was the turning point in his campaign: "You just have to thank them [the DFL] for doing it that way. If they had let all the information out right away, the issue would have been over immediately. But they didn't, so I benefited."[57] And so did Boschwitz, as the suspicions were that Anderson, when he was governor, had allowed the misuse or sloppy handling of some of the funds.

More important than the specific issues for Anderson was the general image he was projecting to the voters. Anderson is a naturally somewhat shy man and, as his close friend David Lebedoff put it, a "kind and gentle person and . . . highly intelligent." But just days before the election, even Lebedoff acknowledged this was not Anderson's image with the voters. In a front-page story in the *Minneapolis Tribune* on the Sunday before the election, Anderson was described as having become "cold, distant, and nearly humorless" and one who takes press criticism "very personally and [is] unforgiving."[58] In a bad sign for a candidate, Anderson and his staff also began to openly feud with members of the media. During a screening session by the editorial board of a major paper, Anderson lost his temper. Showing a bit of pique themselves, the editors at the paper endorsed Boschwitz, even though they "agreed with Anderson on the issues."[59]

Boschwitz, on the other hand, was able to portray an image of a businessman who "watched the bucks . . . and enjoys campaigning." Boschwitz finessed his wealth by tactfully acknowledging, "I like to live comfortably . . . but I'm not much . . . for very fancy things." He also got in a subtle dig at Anderson by telling his audiences that Rudy Boschwitz "won't change . . . in Washington."[60]

The same polling firm that took the poll in early October polled the electorate again on the weekend before the election. The results showed a very close race in two of the top three races: Perpich's lead over Quie had shrunk to only four points, Boschwitz and Anderson were virtually tied, and Durenberger had pulled into the lead by fourteen points over Short. The pollsters and their believers were soon to be in for a big surprise.[61]

In the legislative races, Savelkoul voiced increasing confidence as the campaign wore on, saying the Republicans "expect to pick up about 20 (seats)."[62] In one of those races in the rural Red River Valley, Republican farmer Tony Stadum was working at trying to beat House Tax Committee Chair Bill Kelly. The campaign was generally uneventful as both candidates knocked on doors and attended the usual campaign events.[63]

Results

On election night, the explosion that had been building since late 1976 ignited with a sound and impact heard and felt far and wide. In the first race to be decided, Boschwitz beat Anderson for the six-year Senate term. The outcome was not a surprise, but the margin of victory was. Boschwitz won big, 56.6 percent to 34.6 percent. In the other Senate race, Durenberger also won, with an even bigger 61.5 percent to 34.6 percent win over Short.[64]

In the race for governor, Quie soundly defeated Perpich, 52.3 percent to 45.7 percent, as the state returned to its tradition of Scandinavian governors. Quie was "dumfounded," and Perpich said losing felt like "falling off a cliff."[65] In the other statewide races, Carlson won the contest to become the state auditor over incumbent Bob Mattson. Thus, the Republicans had surprisingly won four statewide races. The other three statewide offices were retained by the DFL. Spannaus, despite his pro–gun control stance, was reelected easily with 56 percent of the vote, and Joan Growe was returned as secretary of state with 52 percent of the vote. Jim Lord, a state senator and son of well-known federal judge Miles Lord, was reelected as the state treasurer.[66]

As the surprising statewide returns continued to flow onto the flickering TV screens at the DFL election-night party at the Minneapolis Holiday Inn, party activists and people hoping for patronage jobs began to notice a queasy feeling in their stomachs. They began to pay close attention as the 134 individual house legislative district returns scrolled across the bottom of the screens. Losses began to show up in districts where incumbents were thought to be in safe seats. Legislators like Wes Skoglund and John Brandl in Minneapolis, Walter Hanson and Dick Cohen in St. Paul, and Pete Petrafeso in St. Louis Park all lost. On the positive side for the DFL, Ray Faricy won his bid for reelection, and Dee Long won her first race in the district Berg had represented for eight years.[67] As the election-night party wound down and the people drifted out of the hotel, there was apprehension over the still unreported races, primarily from the rural areas of the state, like Kelly's.

Sabo was successful in his effort to succeed Fraser, as the solid DFL district gave Sabo 62 percent of the vote.[68] But the congressman-elect's excitement was dampened by the statewide losses happening around him and by a growing concern about the fate of his soon-to-be-former legislative colleagues. He felt sad and a bit guilty as he went to bed that election night, knowing that several of his good friends had suffered defeats they had not seen coming—and there were still legislative races that had yet to be reported.

At Republican headquarters, jubilation reigned as these same returns were seen through a different lens. The two soon-to-be U.S. senators, the new governor-elect, and their campaign staff members smiled, clapped, and congratulated each other over and over. People looked at Carlson with anticipation in their eyes. This group did suffer one surprising defeat, as Gary Flakne lost his bid for reelection as county attorney in the state's largest county to Tom Johnson, a Minneapolis DFL city council member.[69]

Eyes soon began to focus on the house as it became apparent that significant Republican gains were under way. Savelkoul knew the ninety-nine to thirty-five vote margin enjoyed by the DFL going into election night was going to shrink, but "we couldn't believe the actual numbers when they started to come in. . . . We won seats that I didn't think we had a chance to win."[70] It was a night of little sleep for the excited Republicans.

The next morning about eleven o'clock, the results of all races had been counted. In a historic first, the house was split evenly between sixty-seven Republicans and sixty-seven Democrats.[71] Stunned and amazed, the pundits and politicians began to analyze the returns and their meaning.

Causes

Kelly was one of the many DFL candidates who had been knocked down by the force of the electoral explosion. He had not seen his loss coming, and he was disappointed and angry—angry at himself for not doing more to ensure that his supporters actually got out and voted. As he looked at the returns, he quickly realized he had violated what for many is a basic rule of politics: start and end your campaign by playing to your strength. Kelly had followed the first part of the rule, starting his campaign by knocking on doors in his hometown of East Grand Forks and getting a good reception, but he had ended the campaign trying to expand his political base in less friendly territory. He lost by only 255 votes.[72]

In addition to the efforts involved in campaigns and in tax policy, Kelly had devoted endless hours of his life over the past eight years to making the legislature a well-functioning institution. In the process, the legislature had become a major part of his life and identity, which he realized was now gone. He knew it was time to move on, but that realization did not make that election morning any easier.[73]

On a statewide basis, there was no shortage of opinions as to what caused the surprising results. The most common, and the most accurate, was that it was a combination of factors that led to the Republican victory. First and foremost were the multiple appointments to high office. Voters have a gut-level belief that elections, for all their noise and rancor, are a fundamental building block of democratic government. If voters sense that the structure of that building block is being altered or, in the case of appointments, totally taken away, red flags pop up across the entire spectrum of the electorate. Second, the Republican claims of too much pay and lucrative pensions for legislators based on state legislation passed in the 1977–78 sessions fed a common perception that legislators often feather their nests with pay and pensions. Third, the ever-present concern over taxes, which was fueled by national news stories about a "tax revolt," provided ammunition for Republican attacks.

National problems such as those mentioned earlier (inflation, taxes, energy shortages, world competition) also played a part in the defeat. Mondale later described these challenges as viewed from the White House at the start of 1978: "These challenges would dominate America's economic discussion for the next 20 years, and . . . the Democrats needed answers."[74] It was clear that the answers provided by the Democrats in November 1978 were not the ones the voters were looking for.

Across the country, Republicans gained control over seven more state legislative chambers in 1978. They still only controlled eleven state legislatures, but the trend was clearly in their favor.[75] The Republicans also picked up three seats in the U.S. Senate and fifteen seats in Congress. New Republican congressmen starting their national careers that year included Dick Cheney and Newt Gingrich. George W. Bush also ran for Congress and lost.[76]

Don Fraser noted similarities in the mood of the electorate in 1978 and in the 2010 general election, where Republicans took control of both houses in the Minnesota Legislature, ten other legislatures around the country, and the House of Representatives in Washington, D.C.[77]

The 1978 Republicans had done a good job of exploiting the DFL weaknesses. They coordinated their campaigns, found attractive candidates, and pounded on common themes. Quie also successfully played to "Fundamental Christians and New Right conservatives from diverse backgrounds—many of them former DFLers."[78] State employees, mad at Perpich and the DFL legislators for starting to tax their pensions, were also thought to have supported Quie and Republican candidates in greater numbers than is usually the case.[79]

Kelly and others blamed Perpich for much of the problem: "Yes, I think House members do blame him. . . . He has a responsibility as a governor to be the leader of the party . . . and as such I think that the election reflects on all of us and him."[80] Perpich had in fact not run a good campaign. His campaign manager admitted that the campaign was "slow in getting started," and others noted the lack of coordination with DFL legislative candidates.[81] Perpich was outspent by an almost two to one margin by Quie, who did not take public financing and thus could spend as much as he could raise.[82] The DFL's failure to release the audit work papers in a timely manner not only hurt Perpich and Anderson, it also contributed to the feeling that it was time for a change.

Analysts further pointed out the problem of getting out the vote in nonpresidential years, which hurt Kelly and others. The DFL Party faithful were not as enthused in 1978 as the Republicans. The residue of the Short–Fraser primary battle left a bitter and divided party, which contributed to the get-out-the-vote problem. There were over 354,000 fewer votes (22 percent) cast in the 1978 election than in the 1976 presidential-year election.[83]

Assistant Minority Leader Rod Searle, writing several years later about the governmental problems caused by the sixty-seven to sixty-seven split in the legislature, gave the traditional Republican Party explanation for the 1978 election:

> Frustrated by our lack of impact on the legislative process and the mounting arrogance of DFL leaders, we could only hope [in 1978] that their actions—questionable government appointments, failure to control taxes and to limit state spending—would lead to voter dissatisfaction. It took a few years, but a record of political mistakes—little and big— gradually accumulated.
> Taxation and spending are always a major concern. . . . Under the DFL, state spending nearly doubled, and Legislative salaries and other payments (per diem) to legislators more than doubled. . . . The refusal by the DFL-controlled tax committee to index income-tax brackets resulted in a substantial yearly windfall for the state. . . . The DFL dismissed our claims and went blithely on with their program of tax and spend.[84]

Assistant Minority Leader Jerry Knickerbocker, an important member of the election effort for the House Republican Caucus, gave reasons that were less policy oriented and more grounded in reality:

> I am not so naïve to believe Republicans got elected necessarily because they were the best candidates. . . . I think it was strictly a matter of timing. We caught the Democrats sleeping; we caught them fat, dumb and happy. They had been elected by big margins over the years, and they thought people were happy with what they'd done.[85]

Knickerbocker's comments fit with those of DFL legislator Jim Casserly, who managed to survive the election: "Incumbency became a liability. . . . the idea was to throw the 'bums' out and we were the 'bums' who were in."[86] Sabo also acknowledged that "a number of our candidates simply didn't work as hard as they should have."[87]

Sabo and his DFL colleagues strongly disagree with the accuracy of Searle's claims of lack of impact and arrogance. They point out the record of bipartisanship on many bills and believe Searle, like many people in politics, confuses the alleged "lack of impact" with "not being agreed with." These are two very different things, and they do not necessarily reflect arrogance. Savelkoul noted that while Sabo and the DFL "called the shots, it wasn't like we weren't given an opportunity to be involved."[88]

The DFL legislators also disagree with the tax-and-spend analysis, although they concede the Republican attacks on these issues had some political effect. The DFLers point out that the state was in good financial condition in 1978. There was money in the bank for a prudent reserve (at the end of the fiscal year on June 30, 1979, there was a $234 million surplus),[89] the state had a triple-A credit rating, and schools were funded in a manner that provided an equal opportunity for children from all districts, rich and poor. A progressive tax system was in place that was, in their opinion, properly balanced between property, sales, and income taxes. This tax system would provide sustainable income for the state to provide a fair and appropriate level of government services for the future. They do agree, however, that the income tax bracket changes in 1977 were politically ill-advised. They also point out that taxes of any type, in any amount, at any time are a tough political sell for any political party—even though necessary to both provide the services wanted by the public and balance the budget.

The Aftermath

In 1979, Quie successfully pushed his campaign promises with some DFL support through the divided legislature, and reversed some of the previous DFL-enacted fiscal policies: "Quie was able to win legislative approval for a tax-indexing plan, which protected Minnesota taxpayers from being pushed into higher brackets as a result of the inflationary spiral spinning through the U.S. economy." However, the very high inflation rate (11.3 percent in 1979, and 13 percent in 1980) continued to raise the cost of delivering services.[90] Thus, the indexing "had the result of reducing state revenues by nearly $800 million and exacerbating the deficits that would continue to plague Quie during the remainder of his four-year term."[91] By December 1981, "revenue estimates revealed a new $768 million deficit." Quie had to call the legislature into a lengthy special session in 1981, which resulted in a "temporary income-tax surtax, spending cuts and some spending shifts into the next biennium." Who pays and how much?

continued to be a key and contentious legislative topic. Quie decided not to seek reelection in 1982.[92]

The Minnesota Massacre, as the 1978 election came to be known, was a stunning but short-lived defeat for the DFL in the legislature. In 1980, as the country made a political right turn, Carter–Mondale were soundly defeated by Reagan–Bush, but in Minnesota the DFL staged a comeback. The senate remained in DFL hands, and the DFL regained control of the house, seventy to sixty-four. Harry Sieben was elected Speaker of the house.[93]

End of an Era

Whatever the causes, the 1978 election marked the end of a historic era, an era in which the sovereign state government began to re-spond to the legitimate concerns of the majority of people of the state and not just to the concerns of a handful of powerful special-interest groups. The 1968–78 decade saw significant changes made in the institution of the legislative branch of state government and the election process. These changes made it possible in turn to change the substantive law in almost every area of legislation. The state con-stitution was amended to allow time to analyze issues, listen to vot-ers, and reach compromises. Money was appropriated to provide modern tools so that legislators could properly do their jobs. Sig-nificant attention was paid to making government at both the state and local levels work well, and to be accountable when it did not. Voters were given more and timely information about the legislative process and about political campaigns and how they were financed. Steps were taken to address issues especially important to women and gays. There was an emphasis on fair funding for schools all across the state, and on fair treatment of taxpayers by careful analysis of the questions, who pays and how much? Much of this was done with bipartisan support and by people who put the public good high on their priority list.

This approach slowly began to change in the 1979 session and be-yond, as the focus of attention moved in bits and spurts back to the single and narrower fiscal issue, How much? As discussed in the next chapter, this one issue now dominates the legislative process to an extent that is detrimental to the country's historic culture and values.

Many of the legislators in their midthirties and forties who were very instrumental in making the positive changes did not return for the 1979 legislative session. Some, like Martin Sabo and Arne Carlson, moved on to other elected positions. Some, like Henry Savelkoul and Tom Berg, retired from the legislature and returned to private life. Wendell Anderson, Don Fraser, Bill Kelly, and Gary Flakne were involuntarily retired. But regardless of the reasons for leaving, all these legislators fall within Ernie Lindstrom's apt phrase "volunteers for democracy." These people, the staff who helped them, and many others across the country who have made the legislative process a part of their lives are extremely proud of their legislative service. They also fervently hope that the lessons they learned and the best aspects of their work will continue to be put to good use—in forming a more perfect Union.

CHAPTER 10

Where Do We Go from Here?

Sail, sail thy best, ship of Democracy
Of value is thy freight, 'tis not the present only
The Past is also stored in thee.

> ▪ Walt Whitman, "Thou Mother with
> Thy Equal Brood," *Leaves of Grass*

Since 1980, the pace of change in the country has quickened, and the economy has continued its ups and downs. The nation has also suffered through September 11, 2001, fought two wars, cut taxes, and continued to have environmental and energy concerns. The federal government has gone from a budget surplus of $86.4 billion in 2000 to an estimated deficit of $1.4 trillion in fiscal year 2011.[1] In seeking to meet these evolving challenges at the federal level, voters have tried both major political parties and elected three Republicans (Ronald Reagan, George Bush, and George W. Bush) and two Democrats (Bill Clinton and Barack Obama).

At the state level, Minnesota voters have also lurched back and forth, and even sideways, during this period, as they selected governors from three different party affiliations. The state returned to the DFL Party (Rudy Perpich) in 1983–90, then to the Republican Party (Arne Carlson) in 1991–98, jumped sideways to the Reform Party (Jesse Ventura) in 1999–2002, then again tried the Republican Party (Tim Pawlenty) in 2003–10, and returned to the DFL Party (Mark Dayton) in 2011–14. The Democrats controlled the state senate throughout the period, while the house went back and forth between DFL and Republican control until the Republicans gained control of both the house and the senate in a surprising 2010 election win.[2]

While these political changes were taking place, the constant constitutional pressure requiring the states to balance their budgets kept fiscal problems in the forefront of state government discussion throughout the country. The Minnesota budget reserve fund has gone up and down as the national economy has gone through its cycles. Legislators have used it to help handle shortfalls and have also provided for its increase. The state's budget discussions have ranged from what to do with surpluses to how do we eliminate the shortfalls. At times taxes have been raised, and at times cut, and politically popular rebates have been issued to taxpayers. One thing is clear from all this: the failure to consistently face fiscal reality in a timely way, coupled with inflation in the cost of providing government services such as health care, and the increase in population in the state requiring more local government and state services have increasingly resulted in budget shortfalls, higher local property taxes, and reduced government services.[3]

Compounding the fiscal problems for the local, state, and federal governments has been the rise of a new political ethic in large segments of the Republican Party and in the conservative Tea Party: the refusal to even consider raising taxes, and a total unwillingness to compromise on the subject. Veteran Republican Senator Olympia Snowe in explaining her 2012 decision not to seek reelection described this new ethic as "political domination as opposed to governance."[4]

Non-officeholders like Grover Norquist and his Americans for Tax Reform, with its no new taxes pledge, and Rush Limbaugh, with his no-compromise attitude, have been effective. They have convinced the people who have actually faced the electorate and won an election to change the discussion from how to compromise on taxes and spending to how to cut spending and how to shrink the role of government. Limbaugh expressed the view this way right after the 2010 midterm elections, in which the Republicans made big gains: "Compromise is off the table. They didn't compromise with us and we have no business compromising with them. They lost. Losers compromise. We don't. We've got nothing to compromise."[5]

A detailed analysis of the reasons behind this new ethic are beyond the scope of this book, but any such analysis should include David Brooks's "maybe it's part of living in a postmaterialist economy, but nearly every practical question becomes a values question," Walter Mondale's "I can't say that I know for sure . . . but I believe it has something to do with the success of the right wing in using religion as a weapon," and Matt Miller's "For me the story starts with America's loss of unrivaled economic supremacy, and the strains the middle class faces as nations such as India and China rise."[6]

Whatever the reasons, it is clear there is an antigovernment frame of mind in portions of the electorate that cannot be ignored. This antigovernment group has power beyond their numbers in those situations and legislatures where supermajority requirements exist, such as in California, where a constitutional provision requires more than a 50 percent vote to pass certain tax legislation, and in the U.S. Senate, where the "hold" (allowing any one senator to hold up an appointment) and the filibuster procedures exist.

The fiscal and political problems this frame of mind has caused came to a head in Minnesota in 2011 and led to the shutdown of state government for three long weeks. Unfortunately, many other states and the federal government were having similar problems, and several states, such as New York, California, and New Jersey, as well as the federal government, were also discussing shutting down.[7]

At the same time, some local units of government actually did default on obligations, and cities such as Harrisburg, Pennsylvania; Central Falls, Rhode Island; Vallejo, California; and Pritchard, Alabama, filed for bankruptcy.[8] A large part of the problem in these cities and in some states is unfunded pension obligations, similar to the problems discussed in chapter 8. Most of the pensions are modest. For example, in the Pritchard case, "the average pension was only about $15,000 a year ... the highest pension was $36,000 annually for a fire chief who had nearly four decades of service to the city."[9] These failures to meet the contractual obligations of low and moderately paid government workers should not happen in a well-functioning system of federal, state, and local governments.

These fundamental breakdowns in the workings of our governments in several parts of the country make it clear that changes must be made, and made soon. Just waiting for one party or the other to gain complete control and then implement its policies while ignoring the minority party is not the way to run our governments. Discussion and compromise have been a part of our history since the Constitution was adopted, and they should remain so.

History Teaches

In determining the necessary changes and how to implement them, it makes sense to consider policies that have successfully addressed similar problems in the past. Many of the examples of local, federal, and Minnesota state government actions described in the previous chapters are just that. The times were in some ways similar to today: a difficult economy, high energy prices, the fighting of a protracted and expensive war, social unrest, serious environmental problems, and growing international economic competition. The complexities faced then also have many similarities. The expanding role of women, the necessity to make our evolving cities function with decent transit and housing, health insurance coverage, concerns about education and equal learning possibilities for students from both rich and poor districts, environmental concerns, and a political system too heavily influenced by money from special interests—all these issues were addressed, and with bipartisan support. Many other states and local governments also functioned well during this period with timely and balanced budgets.[10]

As noted previously, partisanship was very present as Republicans and Democrats argued and fought bitterly with each other and among themselves, but they also elected leaders who saw to it that the job of governing on behalf of the people who elected them got done. Republican governors Harold LeVander and Al Quie, DFLers Wendell Anderson and Rudy Perpich, and legislators of both parties managed to find compromises that improved life for the vast majority of the state's citizens. The common purpose of improving the quality of life in the state frequently ranked above partisan concerns.

The country needs to continue to implement thoughtful change, and voters and officeholders should get about the task. Governments must use their significant mental and physical resources better. They must work smarter. The first step is to admit that there is no quick fix, silver bullet, or other simple answer. While there may be no simple answers, there are answers. Paying attention to the culture and the Constitution, and adding the correct dose of enlightened politics can, in the words of Garrison Keillor, get the country "recombobulated."[11] The citizenry needs to stop wasting energy on fist waving and hand-wringing and together make positive change happen.

As voters decide who to elect or reelect to various offices, they should focus on candidates who will bring an open mind to the governmental problems they will encounter during their several years in office. A political philosophy is one thing, rigid ideology is another. With an open mind and a thoughtful application of the lessons and actions described below, voters and officeholders can move our three levels of government so that federalism will function as the country's founders envisioned.

Lessons Learned

With twenty-twenty hindsight, these three lessons from one of Justice Louis Brandeis's laboratories of democracy stand out.

Understand Culture and Values

Understanding the fundamental culture and values of citizens is a critical first step in making government work. This basic understanding of people and their values and culture has always been the key starting point in developing a workable government in America. Thomas Jefferson's eloquent eighteenth-century Declaration of Independence begins by referring to the fundamental "Laws of Nature and of Nature's God" and goes on to describe certain "unalienable rights" that came from that foundation. Only then does the Declaration describe the purpose of the government (to secure these rights) and the long list of problems caused by the English king. Similarly, most major legislative changes in the intervening 220-plus years, such as ending slavery, universal suffrage, social security, Medicare, and insuring voting rights for all, reflected an accurate understanding of the basic culture and values of the majority of citizens at the time.

It is not just understanding the current and local culture and values that leads to sound changes in government policy, it is also understanding the historic culture and values of the country—and then figuring out how to merge the two. This is where the art of politics comes into play. For example, how do you meld the need to curb a current culture of urban handgun violence with historic values supporting hunting and possession of weapons in the home, as we saw being done in Minnesota in the mid-1970s? Or how do you meld a historic culture of "local control" in a largely agrarian society with a new culture of urbanization and the need for a regional approach to delivering transit and other services?

These types of questions arise in many different contexts, and each context needs careful analysis based on hard facts. Jumping to conclusions and analysis based on simplistic slogans are only good for generating controversy (and ratings that sell advertising) on Internet blogs and TV and radio talk shows. Too often the analysis is merely designed to put a favorable spin on the legislation to make the proposing party look good.

The "small university" described earlier was a critical part of performing a proper nonpartisan analysis and gathering the hard facts. Actual practice at solving tough political problems shows that at least three things are essential to finding a workable solution to such problems: (1) a well-defined statement of the problem, (2) an understanding of the culture and values of the people involved on all sides of the controversy that led to the problem, and (3) knowledge of the hard facts involved in the issue. Such a complete understanding can then usually lead to compromises, and those compromises can fit with current values, 220-plus years of history, and the Constitution. Thus, the starting point, once a problem has been identified and defined, is to look at what is included in our current culture and value system.

Who pays and how much? are still relevant questions to ask in defining our culture. Fiscal prudence has clearly moved up the priority list of values for many after the Great Recession. But despite much of the current political discussion and commentary, these are not the only questions, and taxes is not the only topic that defines current culture and values. In addition to values such as equal rights, an educated workforce, and a safe and sustainable relationship with nature, the majority of Americans also value such things as energy independence, affordable health care, a strong economy that generates good-paying jobs, and a political system that is not so dominated by paid lobbyists.

How we achieve these values is often appropriately a controversial part of the political process. In discussing values and government programs, it is important that we not confuse political controversies over proposed solutions with support for the values underlying those solutions. This confusion frequently causes much gnashing of teeth on all sides, without generating the kind of understanding that can lead to a workable compromise on the method of implementing the value. For example, the Minnesota Miracle legislation finally passed and was signed into law when legislators and the governor came to agreement on the need to implement the underlying values of equal educational opportunity for children from rich and poor districts and lower property taxes. The legislators and governor then compromised on the more-controversial implementation features of income and sales tax rates and limits on property tax increases. Focusing first on understanding the underlying purpose of a legislative proposal and then letting staff offer suggestions as to how to implement, as Senator Stanley Holmquist did with the Minnesota Miracle negotiations, are often effective legislative techniques. It should be used more in Congress and in the state legislatures.

We should also remember that over time, some values change and become less important to our culture. Simplicity is one. Many of us are not comfortable with the complicated nature of today's world—but we better get over it. The changes over the past two centuries in population, living patterns, lifestyles, geography, business practices, and technology, to say nothing about our growth from a collection of thirteen colonies to a world power, require a more complicated system of government.

While most agree complexity in and of itself is not a good thing, most also agree it is frequently a necessary part of modern life and government. Simplicity was not high on the list of values the Founding Fathers sought to preserve. They adopted the Declaration of Independence, scrapped the Articles of Confederation, and replaced them with the Constitution not to preserve simplicity and avoid complexity, but to create a government where people could pursue happiness and compete in the international world, while having their property rights, individual liberty, and freedom protected.

Instead of fighting change and anguishing over the loss of the good old days, as some do, the current political culture should recognize the inevitability of change and make efforts to shape it. The actions of government can, to a significant degree, change culture. The late senator Daniel Patrick Moynihan accurately described the relationship between politics and culture this way: "The central conservative truth is that it is culture, not politics, that determines the success of a society. The central liberal truth is that politics can change a culture and save it from itself."[12]

A similar point was made by the French political scientist Alexis de

Tocqueville in his writings about American federalism in the 1830s. In analyzing the power of patriotism to move citizens toward a common goal, he noted, "It is within the power of the law to awaken and guide the vague patriotic instinct that dwells permanently in the heart of man and, by linking that instinct to everyday thought, passions, and habits, to turn it into a conscious and durable emotion." He went on to remind legislators that it is never too late to try to bring about such change: "nations do not grow old in the same way as men. Each new generation . . . is fresh material for the lawmaker to mold."[13]

The discussion of changing values and culture and their implications for government could go on endlessly, and in some circles, probably will. But in the real world of governing, the country needs to act. As President Kennedy said, "We [elected officials] are not permitted the luxury of irresolution. Others may confine themselves to debate, discussion, and that ultimate luxury—free advice. Our responsibility is one of decision—for to govern is to choose."[14]

There are many values the majority of citizens agree with, and those should be the basis for action. In addition to those mentioned above, transparency (or "sunshine in government"), competency in implementing programs, prudence in fiscal matters, and responsiveness to current problems (such as immigration, energy usage, and the delivery of health care) are values most people support. Free enterprise and equal opportunity are generally accepted values that also serve as tools to achieve other goals. With these chosen values and the goals and safeguards provided in the Constitution in mind, we turn to lesson learned number two, in our effort to get our current system of three levels of government in sync with the people it governs.

Think in Three Dimensions

Legislators need to think about government in a more realistic way—the way the government works in practice, and the way constituents view and interact with government every day. The United States has three levels of government, and yet the elected officials and policy makers in state capitals and in Washington spend most of their time viewing the world through glasses that filter out the critical third dimension of local government. The importance of understanding and working to improve local governments is the second lesson learned.

Former Speaker of the House Tip O'Neill famously said, "all politics is local."[15] The second lesson learned about the art of governing leads to a corollary to the Speaker's insightful expression. That corollary, "All government ends up local," is based on a hard look at what causes the long-term success of virtually all domestic governmental programs. Local government may be an unglamorous workhorse to many, and caring for the workhorse does not have the political sex appeal of several of the suggestions described below, but it is critical to getting the government system functioning in a proper manner.

The corollary is true even if the program is primarily federal or state in scope and regardless of which level of government pays most of the bill. For example, in educating children, whether the money comes from Washington, D.C., the state capital, or the local school district, the interaction between the local teacher, parents, and children is crucial. Similarly, whether it is enforcing a criminal law passed by Congress or a state legislature or enforcing a county or city ordinance, an important part of the process almost always comes down to a police officer or deputy sheriff talking to a citizen and gathering facts for the prosecutor or another law enforcement agency, often from another level of government. In delivering mass transit, local questions such as where to run the bus or rail line or locate the stops can make or break the programs. Federal or state standards play a role, and often an important role, but experience shows that unless "the locals" are brought into the process or figure out on their own how to have a say in the critical details, the program does not work as well as it should, or maybe not at all.

A few more examples are in order to make this important point. Building housing or industrial parks often involves state tax incentives, but local zoning codes and their interpretation can cause the projects to succeed or fail. Similarly, in deciding whether to issue building permits for wind turbines, or determining where to locate the power lines from a proposed wind farm funded in part with state and federal energy tax credits, the local government employees should be able to explain to the local opponents of the wind farm and power lines that a federal or state energy policy requires that the new facilities be built. So it is with other new programs: to prevent such programs from being brushed aside as too complex, languishing in bureaucratic "in baskets" for a variety of possible reasons, or even facing subtle sabotage, local support is vital. It is in everyone's best interest to "get the locals on board" early in the process.

Analyzing issues from a realistic (which often means regional) perspective is important, as "citizens in metropolitan areas expect . . . to travel easily to and from places of work, commerce and recreation. They understand intuitively . . . problems are not confined to local and government boundaries."[16] Responding to this intuition is an area where states, with their power to allow or mandate cooperation among multiple local units of government and share revenues, can be creative and helpful. Local governments for their part should not fight this perspective, as it "can also mean local government with greater potential to fulfill its purely local role."[17] As shown by the many examples described throughout this book, local governments, when given the proper mix of authority, financial assistance, and oversight, can be a creative part of federalism.

All who have dealt with local governments know that they can, however, be parochial, suffer from a lack of will to raise their own taxes, and lack perspective as to what is needed to properly address a problem. It is a part of human nature—or at least political nature—to think of funding from another level of government as "free money." Thus, some form of matching funding, ongoing reporting, and performance audits is appropriate. Where funding is to be shared, the challenge is to get the percentages of revenue that each level must contribute to be fair and efficient.

The sovereign states, with their life-or-death power over the existence of local government and its boundaries, and the federal government, with its revenue-raising and distribution powers, have ample ability to force, persuade, or otherwise get local governments to collaborate. Examples of the use of these capabilities to achieve federal goals are the financial incentives employed in some highway funding programs and in the "race to the top" education initiative. If push comes to shove, additional tools include loss of political power (making an end run around the unit of government), adverse publicity (the power of the bully pulpit), and even jail time (criminal sanctions for failing to follow a law).

Each of these tools presents its own set of political and bureaucratic problems. The best method is to use the sovereign authority sparingly and develop policies in cooperation with the local officials so they enthusiastically believe the policies should be implemented. Federal and state officials should remember, as John Gardner noted,

"It is hard to feel individually responsible with regard to the invisible processes of a huge and distant government."[18]

It is unfortunate but true that local and state governments have at times had to be brought to the national interest kicking and screaming. Racial integration, fair housing, and basic civil and voting rights are examples of situations where the federal courts and the executive and legislative branches of the federal government have had to push, and at times force, the national interest on the states. While this has been appropriate in these examples, all should understand that just because there is a national problem, one national solution is not necessarily the best answer.

Our federal system often provides other possible and better solutions via the states. For example, the increasing tendency to make local actions federal crimes—requiring the FBI or other federal law enforcement agencies to investigate and prosecute—instead of letting the states handle the issues is often inefficient and confusing and has a "corrosive impact on the local, state, and indeed, federal governments."[19] Such things as carjackings, arson, and drive-by shootings would be better off left to the states, which regularly deal with such matters and already have extensive law enforcement, prosecution, and judicial infrastructures.[20]

If a state or local unit of government takes an action that is in conflict with a properly defined national interest, our history, culture, and values as a nation require that the local actions give way to that national interest. Congress with its preemption power, and the federal courts with their powers to enforce the Constitution can and should enforce the national interest. The national interest is a trump card that should be carefully played but nevertheless played when needed.

There is no simple formula for how the sovereign states and the sovereign federal government should deal with each other and with local units of government. Deciding whether to preempt or mandate or to provide financial incentives, matching grants, or some other device requires good judgment, common sense, and consideration of the values and culture of the nation, state, and locality. All these factors need to be considered in the context of the problem being addressed. Thoughtful people, with the Constitution to guide them and a culture of coming together for a common purpose, can overcome parochialism and uncompromising partisanship in a variety of contexts.

Much more time and thought about implementing this active three-dimensional approach are needed than are available in these pages. Some of the topics argued about during the 2010 midterm elections and still being argued about today (such as the workings of the Tenth Amendment) deal with these three-dimensional questions, but campaign rhetoric is typically too general to adequately address the topic. The concepts involved and their implications are fundamental and need to be well understood, not just by academics but also by those in elected or appointed office, those who write news stories, columns, and blogs, and those who appear on Sunday-morning talk shows. There are reasons why the country has the three-level system and why that system has survived 220-plus years. If it is concluded that significant change is needed, the changes should be based on well-thought-out and generally understood reasons, and not merely on campaign slogans about "looking to the future" or "taking back the country."

Consideration should be given to establishing a multilevel group, such as the Advisory Commission on Intergovernmental Relations (ACIR), to help coordinate thinking on these issues. Think tanks should help develop the needed details and cost analysis for various programs. State legislatures, various governmental organizations including the National Governors Association, the National Conference of State Legislatures, the Council of State Governments, the National League of Cities, the United States Conference of Mayors, and the National Association of Counties should spend time and resources working together to make this happen—not just to relieve their own financial burdens but to produce a well-functioning system of governments.

Leaders Matter

This third lesson is even more tricky than the somewhat abstract notions involved with the previous two. This lesson often involves strong personalities and political ideologues, some of whom believe compromise and pragmatism to be contaminated concepts. Both political parties and an increasingly polarized media often feature such persons. Some of these people are jerks, and some quite charming, but regardless of their personality, legislators, partisans, and general voters must be wary of strident ideologues who refuse to even listen seriously to opposing views. Legislative leaders must be selected who have a thorough understanding of American history, a broad sense of the common good, and an ability to develop an atmosphere where legislators and committees can, at least at times, reach accord across party lines. Ideally, this atmosphere should itself become part of the culture of the legislative institution.

James Madison in the Federalist Papers discussed the founders' grave concerns about "factions" (political parties) and pointed out that human nature supports the rise of political parties. He was so worried about them he said, "The regulation of these . . . forms the principal task of modern legislation."[21] Similarly, after two terms as president, George Washington gave the nation a farewell address and described his concerns about what he called "the spirit of party." He advised the young nation that "the common and continual mis-chiefs of the spirit of party are sufficient to make it the interest and duty of a wise people to discourage and restrain it."[22]

Fast-forwarding to the twenty-first century, we see that the con-cern about partisanship is even greater:

The two parties are more ideologically opposed today than they have been for the past few decades . . . there is also a line—difficult to draw, but far too easy to cross—beyond which party spirit must not be permitted to go without seri-ously damaging the very conception of Congress as an "insti-tution of American Constitutional democracy."[23]

The seriousness of this was echoed in a U.S. Senate debate in 2009: "We have crossed the line with over 100 filibusters and acts of ob-struction in less than one year. . . . Never since the founding of the Republic, not even in the bitter sentiments preceding Civil War, was such a thing ever seen in this body."[24] A quick look at the political blogs, news shows, or the editorial pages of conservative or liberal papers readily shows the sharp partisanship across the country and across the levels of government.

Political scientists have attempted to devise labels for the culture or spirit necessary to restrain this "spirit of party" and yet recognize the human nature involved. "Comity," "bipartisan cooperation," and "consensualist democracy" have all been used to describe the emotions and thoughts necessary to achieve at least some significant bipartisan action.[25] Whatever the label, the proper conditions were present in Minnesota during the 1970s to reasonably restrain the "spirit of party." There was a belief by the legislators that compromise would lead to at least slightly better government for their constituents and that both parties could convince the voters of that fact during the next election.

Leadership played an important role in creating the atmosphere where discussions led to compromises that led to bipartisan action. Speakers Aubrey Dirlam and Martin Sabo and Minority Leader Henry Savelkoul were all tough partisans, but even during heated discussions, they were always civil with each other (Savelkoul said he could always tell when Sabo was getting angry, as he "looked straight at you and really squinted his eyes").[26] These leaders did not make every issue a partisan battle nor put political spin on every piece of legislative action. Their leadership style gave members and committees time and space to work on a bipartisan basis.

While human nature may give rise to factions and political parties, it also allows friendships and commonality to grow and foster some level of goodwill and cooperation. Savelkoul and Sabo both always stressed the importance of "visiting and listening to other legislators, to learn about them as people, and not just politicians."[27] Savelkoul noted that it is "so easy to be strident if you don't have to be there and make decisions," and he repeatedly stressed the importance of legislators knowing on a personal level some of the people and values behind opposing views. Almost forty years later, he fondly remembers having a discussion of legislative issues over a beer with his frequent political opponent Sabo, and laughing as Sabo told him, "Henry, one way to tell the difference between Republicans and Democrats is that Republicans drink their beer out of a glass, and Democrats drink it out of the bottle."[28]

When bipartisan social events, often hosted by lobbyists, were permissible, members would not only drink beer out of glasses and bottles, they would talk and come to realize that beneath their partisan labels, they were all human beings with families, problems, emotions, and dreams. Such an understanding helped make compromise possible. Legislators and government watchdog groups should consider that an unintended consequence of some of the ethics laws passed in the intervening years may be an impediment to such understanding.

The current oppressive climate of partisanship, frequently imposed by caucus and party leaders, and the isolation of members from people with different political views all too often result in the failure to share across party lines the personal joys and sorrows of the human experience. Since many issues are not partisan at their core, legislators should ask their caucus leaders and themselves why an issue is being made a partisan one. Applying partisanship spin to everything that comes along is unhelpful and makes legislators look petty and foolish to all but their most partisan supporters. The 1857 Minnesota constitutional convention, where the parties would not even meet in the same room, shows how ridiculous such actions can become.

Legislative leaders should create an environment where members can exercise party discipline on votes and actions that reflect genuine and important partisan differences, but also where legislators can work together and compromise based on a common humanity and common values. Leaders' conduct should reflect their responsibility to their caucus members and to the legislative institution. Creating such an environment should be a part of every legislative leader's job description.

Voters, campaign workers, and financial donors also bear part of the blame for the current excess of partisanship. Instead of demanding more partisanship from candidates, as occurred at the out-of-control 1972 DFL convention, voters, campaign contributors, and even party leaders should consider favorably a candidate's willingness to talk, listen, and compromise for the common good. Party activists as well as legislators should remember that good government involves compromise, and good government also usually makes for good politics.

The past few decades in America have shown that partisanship readily leads to a downward spiral of retaliation, with even more partisanship from the opposing party. Former congressman Dan Rostenkowski, who served thirty-six years in Congress before losing in 1994 as a result of a corruption scandal, described the role of politics in the process: "We looked at politics as compromise.... We were going to get something done. We were Democrats and Republicans but we were also legislators. Politics is war today. Everybody wants to fight. Nobody wants to give in."[29]

Voters, thoughtful legislators, and political commentators need to work to slow down the accelerating downward spiral of the country's partisan political water. If it accelerates much more, it may suck in more good political leaders of both parties and take them all down the drain. The country cannot afford to let that happen—we need every good leader we can find.

Based on these three lessons, which were learned and relearned many times, here are some changes to help mold the three levels of government in our evolved federalism into an efficient system that fits within the accepted culture and values of most citizens.

Changes Needed at the Federal Level

As the preamble to the Constitution explains, the purpose of government in the United States is to "establish justice, insure domestic tranquility, provide for the common defense, promote the general welfare and secure the blessings of liberty to ourselves and our posterity." Accomplishing these tasks takes money and local implementation. Since the federal level of our three-level system of government can raise funds in a more efficient manner than the other two and brings a national perspective to the local implementation, the federal role is a good starting point for discussing how best to achieve the objectives spelled out in the preamble.

Form Active Partnerships with State and Local Governments

More clearly defined partnerships among the three levels of government should be developed. A sound fiscal relationship must be a key part of these partnerships. The fiscal relationship among the partners may involve a number of forms: categorical grants, block grants, incentive payments, local government aid formulas, or revenue sharing, as described in chapter 7 and discussed further below. But before these fiscal relationships and partnerships can be made to work properly, the vital federal fiscal system must be put in better working order.

Taxes are not something people like to pay, or something legislators like to vote for. But as was shown in earlier chapters, if the taxes are seen as fair and if good value is understood as being received for the tax dollars spent, taxes will get paid, and legislators who vote for those taxes and spending decisions can get elected and reelected. In regard to perceptions of fairness and value, all levels of government have work to do. Legislators, the president, and governors need to focus on developing programs that work and honest answers to the questions of who pays, how much, and what benefits are received for the tax dollars spent. When an interstate freeway bridge over the Mississippi River falls down, as happened in Minneapolis in 2007, or an oil well blows out in the Gulf of Mexico and the government looks helpless, as happened in 2010, taxpayers understandably wonder what is going on. When the number of special provisions and loopholes in the tax laws have grown so complex that millions of dollars must be spent every year for tax preparation advice, support for all government programs declines, and general voter anger rises. The entire governmental system and in turn the citizenry suffer as a result. Detailed solutions to the fiscal issues are varied, complex, and beyond this book, but they do exist, and they need to be implemented.[30]

Implement Revenue Sharing

As we implement these solutions and begin to take steps to regain our fiscal balance, the federal government should recognize the importance of revenue sharing between the federal government and state and local governments. The federal government should consider implementing some form of the Nixon–Kennedy–Johnson revenue sharing, grant making, and A-95 review processes. Because of its broader geographical base, the federal government has broad revenue-raising capabilities not available to the states or local units of government. As a general rule, the smaller the unit of government, the more difficult it is to raise revenue.[31] Thus, revenue sharing in some form by the federal government is important to the fair delivery of services by local governments with varying fiscal capabilities.

For some people, the relative difficulty of raising revenue that state and local governments have is reason enough to be a strong proponent of local government and an opponent of revenue raising by the larger state and national governments. These people tend to believe that state or federal action means their overall tax burden will be higher. In the short term, they may be right. A more thorough look, however, shows the long-term costs of such things as poor public transportation, poorly educated workers, and poor public health lead to higher overall costs and a country less able to compete in the international market.

There needs to be some type of coordinating mechanism to achieve efficient use of the federal, state, and local funds. An updated A-95 review system, with significant local input, should be implemented. Martin Sabo, after his many years as a state legislator and a member of Congress, described the A-95 review process as "a prime example of how the federal government can get states and local governments to think."[32] While this review will inevitably involve some bureaucracy and complexity, it will also help ensure efficiency, fairness between geographic areas, accountability, and transparency— all values our culture holds high.

Change Legislative Procedures

Legislative procedures can seem arcane, but, as shown earlier, they are critical to achieving sound legislation in a timely manner. The procedures currently in use in Congress and in the Senate in particular no longer fit with the country's culture, pace of change, or sense of fairness. The power granted senators, whether to put holds on Senate actions or to threaten a filibuster, needs to be modified. This existing individual power allows for an irresponsible blockage of majority views by one person under the guise of a claim for "deliberation." A procedure to ensure more responsible use of these powers is needed. As Senator Mike Mansfield stated in an earlier, successful fight to modify Senate rules, "We cannot allow a member or a small group of members to grab the Senate by the throat and hold it there."[33]

In the House, at times a "closed rule" procedure is adopted. Under this procedure, no amendments to a bill are allowed even to be offered.[34] While some controls are obviously needed on amendments in the 435-member House, excessive use of this closed rule procedure stifles debate and frustrates the minority party.

If these and other outdated procedures continue, our federal legislative institutions run the risk of losing even more support from a society that needs to compete in a timely manner in a fast-paced world. As new and younger state legislators changed their rules in the 1970s to provide more fair and open legislative processes, so should new and younger members of the Congress help jump-start the efforts to modernize its rules. Being bound by tradition is not necessarily a good thing.

While a more detailed discussion of federal government procedural reform is beyond the scope of this book, Thomas Mann and Norman Ornstein's *The Broken Branch*, discussed earlier, and *It's Even Worse Than It Looks*, and *The Legislative Branch*, a collection of essays by top political scientists, are recommended for a more thorough understanding and developing of many needed procedural changes.[35]

Changes Needed at the State Level

State legislatures, including Minnesota's, also need to change. Generally speaking, good offices, computers, and related office equipment are now present in most state legislatures. Tough ethics laws have been passed in the past decades to reduce improper conduct and provide transparency for voters. But in many states, the laboratories of democracy are still not producing much in the way of innovation in government. *Time* magazine, instead of touting "A State That Works" on its cover, as it did in 1973, headlined "The Broken States" on its June 28, 2010, cover. The Great Recession is part of the problem, but an honest look at the states requires an admission that there are other causes as well for their problems.

Here is a summary of eight actions that states should take that would help improve not only the states but all three of our intertwined governmental systems. Several states are doing a number of these things in bits and pieces, but all levels and units of government would benefit from a comprehensive review of their existing programs in each of these areas.

Build a Partnership with Local Government

This takes time and hard work. It involves building trust and a spirit of cooperation. One party to the partnership, the state, is a sovereign power and thus has more "power" under our system of federalism. In essence, there is a symbiotic relationship between the state and local governments. The state needs the local government to carry out its programs, and the local government needs authority and resources from the state. Depending on the scope of the issues being addressed, these partnerships can be a part of the three-dimensional partnerships discussed above, or they can be two party. Regardless of the issue, it is in everyone's best interest to make sure the levels of government work well together.

The Minnesota Legislature in the 1970s used its sovereign power wisely to modify, and at times override, local action with the Minnesota Miracle and fiscal disparities legislation. But Minnesota and most other states have not always used this sovereign power as carefully. For example, in legislation known as Maintenance of Effort (MOE) legislation, the Minnesota Legislature required that counties maintain spending levels on various mandated mental health and library programs.[36] The counties tactfully protested that there are "wiser and more cost efficient" ways to deliver the services than via the mandated programs. Since this involves hundreds of millions of dollars of local property tax dollars raised by the counties, the county commissioners are clearly not happy with their legislator partners.[37] The need for better communication and problem solving is obvious.

Forcing local governments to spend in a certain manner, as in the previous example, or shifting the payment date for state aid by a few days so that payment occurs in the next fiscal year, as is often done by states, may allow a state budget to be balanced but is not sustainable. This game playing by the sovereign power is not fair to the local government partner, who must meet the payroll on a regular basis. It also confuses the local taxpayers. In the long term, such actions cause more distrust of both the state and local government officials.

State legislatures should adopt a formal mechanism to meet and discuss such problems regularly with elected representatives from various local governments. For their part, local officials should not cry wolf at every turn and should not blame all their ills on the state. Hennepin County's taking the lead and working with the Metropolitan Council to build light-rail transit in 2001 in the Minneapolis–St. Paul metropolitan area and the building of the Northstar commuter line are examples of how the state–local partnership, together with financial help from the federal government, can solve problems.

Create and Use a "Small University"

Knowledge is power, and most state legislatures now have a research staff with access to sufficient amounts of information so the legislature can hold its own in that area in dealing with outside interests or the executive branch. The information problem today usually involves determining which bits of information are important and relevant, and how to present such information in a useful manner.

The role of the small university needs to be defined. To ensure credibility, to reduce partisanship, and to attract top researchers, the staff should be nonpartisan and work on nonpartisan issues. The staff should also be available to all members, regardless of political party.

A separate partisan staff is a necessary accommodation to the realities of politics. Unfortunately, in the partisan atmosphere that currently exists, legislators too often view everything as partisan and exclusively use the partisan staff. This practice adds to the political spin, which gets applied to more and more things and furthers gridlock.

The partisan staff should work on the limited number of issues that are truly partisan. This will help insulate the nonpartisan staff from being asked to serve partisan purposes and will improve their credibility with the public and the credibility of any resulting legislation. In the staffing example discussed in chapter 6, there was an understanding of these respective roles and mutual respect among the people involved. In developing a sound working relationship with both partisan and nonpartisan staff, the key is to hire smart, intellectually honest, and savvy people who care about their legislature and state.

Having such a staff is only part of the solution. Legislators have to use it. Big egos, "I'm too busy" (often with fund-raising and political matters), and "I'll get to it later" all get in the way of a well-functioning staff–legislator relationship. Good legislators know that the staff is critical to the legislator's long-term political success, and good staff members know it is wise to leave the media appearances to the elected officials. Legislators need continuing education, just like other professionals. The nonpartisan staff can be a key provider of this education, with such programs as the Minnesota Horizons and retreats, as discussed below.

Legislators have been elected in large part because of their knowledge of and perspective on local culture and values. They should use that knowledge and perspective to challenge and analyze the information presented by their own staff as well as outsiders. Legislators should not allow staff to get by with sloppy buzzwords, jargon, and imprecise phrases such as "the community," "public policy," "reforming the system," and terms of art that mean something to experts in a particular field but are lost on the general public. Clear communication is a big part of good governing.

Watch the Time and Money

Will Rogers said it well in 1931: "Politics has gotten so expensive that it takes lots of money to even get beat with."[38] This bit of wit and wisdom continues to highlight a major problem. Recent Supreme Court decisions interpreting the constitutional guaranty of free speech as including spending money on campaigns, including that spent by individuals, corporations, labor unions, and other groups, make regulating the influence of money on politics complicated at best.[39] Trying to mesh that constitutional guaranty with the democratic value that all should have an equal say in determining who is elected is difficult. But the fact that the problem is difficult does not mean it can be ignored.

Significant campaign contributions do give valuable access and influence to those who are able and choose to make such contributions. It is easier for wealthy individuals to contribute, advertise for votes, hire top campaign staffs, and flood the Internet with campaign materials than it is for people struggling to provide basic necessities for their families. If that wealth was inherited, it adds insult to injury since the cultural concept of meritocracy is also eroded.

One often-overlooked cost related to political fund-raising is the time it takes to raise the money. The thousands of hours talking on the phone and attending events to raise campaign money have reached a stage where they now occupy the majority of time for some elected officials. In a revealing brief filed in 2005 in a campaign finance case before the U.S. Supreme Court, Senators Bill Bradley (Democrat) and Alan Simpson (Republican) quoted from their colleagues and described the huge amounts of time devoted to fund-raising and the resulting harm to democracy. The brief quotes Senator Fritz Hollings saying, "We have been transformed from a body of lawmakers into a body of full-time fundraisers," and Senator Dennis DeConcini describing his feelings:

> The worst thing about it is that members have to spend so much time in the pursuit of campaign finances that . . . their ability to do really their best as legislators is jeopardized. . . . When I was running, I was spending about two hours a day on the phone raising money. Minimum. Six days a week. That

takes away from your ability to represent your constituents, or do your legislative work.[40]

In some circles, expectations have changed so much that donors will not contribute at all without a personal call or special event with the candidate present. As a result, candidates spend hours listening to only one perspective. If a candidate hears only from wealthy people, leaders of labor unions, or corporate executives, the candidate's perspective on a problem quickly becomes skewed.

This is not how democracy should work. The majority of such fund-raising time would be much better spent listening to a broader range of constituents, evaluating programs, developing legislation, and trying to find compromise solutions to the many seemingly intractable problems—in short, governing.

Some form of partial public funding for campaigns and complete disclosure of major contributions in a prompt manner are still the best solutions to the problem of money and politics. Such legislation results in some leveling of the playing field, gives voters information to decide the seriousness of the inherent conflicts of interest that may develop between a donor and an elected official, and allows the officeholders time to do their jobs. The downside is that it takes tax revenue. Preserving fairness and confidence in our electoral system is well worth the price.

Talk to Each Other

The leaders of an organization that annually spends billions of dollars, builds complicated transportation systems, educates millions of children, and ensures public order need to spend some time thinking, planning, and coordinating their long-term activities. As directors from businesses, labor organizations, and nonprofit organizations get away from day-to-day problems to hold strategic planning sessions and retreats, so too should state legislators. The general goals of such sessions and retreats are to build better communication and trust and a sense of camaraderie among legislators of different parties, and to ensure a serious discussion of the proper role of government and its procedures. Other techniques exist to do this, but the experience of the private sector shows that retreats work well.

Legislators will inevitably get criticized for attending retreats, but if the retreats are handled properly, the criticism will not be well founded and can be endured. The benefits of a two-day legislative retreat every few years at a reasonable location with reasonable costs will far outweigh any criticism.

Such an event will not happen unless it is scheduled well in advance at a convenient location away from the capitol. Caucus leaders must join in and strongly encourage caucus members to attend. The leadership of Republican Assistant Minority Leader Arne Carlson and DFL Speaker Martin Sabo made the Minnesota experiment described earlier work well. In that experiment, only legislators and a handful of staff necessary to run the event were present. No media or lobbyists were allowed, and all discussions were "off the record."

Some of the topics discussed were general and designed to have participants think about big-picture problems. The intent was to elicit a variety of views in a nonthreatening environment on such questions as Why did you become a legislator? Where does the legislature fit into the country's system of three levels of government? and What do voters have a right to expect from their state's legislature? Newsman Phil Jones's question is even tougher, and it is worth repeating: "Is your legislature what people have died for on many a battlefield?"

New York Times columnist David Brooks has written about the critical need for people in politics to "step back and think about the weakness in [one's] own thinking and what should be done to compensate." He concluded that the ability to do this is rare and that "the rigors of [political] combat discourage it. Of the problems that afflict the country, this is the underlying one."[41] The Minnesota retreat was an effort to spend at least a few hours reflecting on such matters. The report of the event prepared shortly afterwards said:

> The theme was [legislative] introspection and the
> location, . . . St. John's [University] was the ideal place. . . .
> From the minute we arrived everyone seemed overtaken
> with eagerness and enthusiasm. . . . Members of both
> caucuses remarked throughout the 24 hour program that
> they were struck by the cooperation and interest of the
> participants.[42]

Legislating is serious business, and serious and bipartisan thought and discussion should be a part of the process.

Ask for Help

Our society consistently produces some of the world's best minds in business, sociology, religion, government, and science. Our society does not consistently use these minds to improve the public good.

The Loaned Executive Action Program (LEAP) initiative of Governor Wendell Anderson was one of the best innovations to come out of that innovative administration. It led to long-lasting structural and operational changes that made government work better for less money.

There are two main reasons LEAP worked so well: the governor was solidly behind it, and the business executives really "got into it." These executives studied, analyzed, and developed solid recommendations. Too often such "blue ribbon panels," "study commissions," and "panels of experts" are merely window dressing or are designed to provide political cover for actions politicians have already decided to take. LEAP, however, was the real deal. The executives developed the ideas on their own and testified before the legislature to help sell their finished products.

Legislatures should regularly ask various organizations, such as Catholic Charities, Lutheran Social Services, and the Salvation Army, about programs to help the homeless. Ethnic groups can offer good ideas on a variety of problems facing recent arrivals to the state. Academic sociologists should be asked to climb down from their ivory towers and discuss trends and specific ideas regarding the ever-shifting mix and age of our population. Accurate scientific data and opinions put into understandable form are always needed in a variety of areas, and most universities have experts ready and willing to help if asked. Business leaders are constantly having to innovate and meet changing market conditions, and their knowledge of organizational dynamics should be put to good use by state governments trying to keep up with a rapidly changing world.

Most leaders outside of government are flattered to be asked to help the government solve problems, and if they have an assurance their work will be seriously considered by the legislature and governor, they are more than willing to help. Given the complexities faced by the states, asking for help should be high on the legislature's priority list.

Evaluate Performance

Legislators and governors are evaluated at the end of every term. Whether that is two, four, or six years, elected officials face voters, the media, watchdog groups, and frequently an opponent, all asking tough questions about performance in office. For the vast majority of government programs, however, the only evaluation of their performance is that done by the agency itself—an agency that has a vested interest in a positive report.

While financial audits are routinely done by persons outside of the agency, these audits usually are limited to ascertaining that funds were spent in accordance with the legislation. The tougher questions as to whether the funds brought about the desired results and whether taxpayers received good value for their money are not answered. This is where independent performance audits come into play.

There are various ways this can be done. The use of independent inspectors general and hiring nongovernmental evaluators and legislative auditors are all options. Whatever the mechanism, the performance audit process needs to be nonpartisan. Selecting the programs to audit should be nonpartisan and not designed to embarrass any individual, political party, or program. These audits should be performed on both local and state programs. The final results should be published, and corrective steps taken to deal with any problems uncovered. Trying to sweep a known problem under the rug is a recipe for a political disaster.

If thorough and accurate performance evaluations are not performed by government, the media or various bloggers will perform the function—often without much thought. The results may properly highlight performance issues that need correction, but the suggested remedies will too often be draconian and reported with an emphasis on the spectacular. Such reporting may result in corrections but also in erosion of voter support for related programs that are well run. To gain respect and confidence of voters, legislatures should be methodical, vigorous, and honest in evaluating performance of all governmental programs.

Reapportion with a Commission

The constitutional requirement that legislative and congressional district boundaries be redrawn every ten years has played a critical role in integrating diverse cultural and regional values into our political system. The one person, one vote concept has brought a continuing sense of fairness to the political system as the country's ethnic mix has changed and as people continue to move from one city, state, or region to another.

The mapmaking that takes place after every census has also led to changes in how the new district lines are determined. Political consultants using sophisticated computer programs now assist political parties in figuring out how best to satisfy the one person, one vote legal requirement while keeping legislators in "safe districts" (without significant opposition from an opposing party). Using polling data and computer-generated analyses of past voting records, reapportionment cartographers can get a good idea of the likely political makeup of each proposed district. Move a few precincts from one district to the next, and you can change the likely outcome of many local and state legislative elections.[43] As a result, the number of "safe seats" has risen dramatically both in Congress and in the state legislatures.[44]

Given the existence of partisanship, the work, stress, and high costs involved in campaigns, and the human tendency to seek the easiest path through a political thicket, incumbent legislators want safe districts for themselves and their party—and "swing districts" (those districts that have an approximately equal number of voters from each party and thus could "swing" either way) for the opposing party. Some combination of these factors explains why Martin Sabo, Lyall Schwarzkopf, and their colleagues in the state senate did not successfully redistrict the legislature and why Joe Graba almost did not run for reelection in 1972.

One result of more "safe districts" is that the performance evaluation of legislators is often less rigorous. The toughest questions and evaluations usually come from those of another political party. If the districts are primarily safe for one party, the competition is effectively limited to intraparty competition. While such competition may be fine with party activists and can result in incumbents losing elections, it has the effect of limiting the choice of independent voters. While there are good legislators from both safe and swing districts, the theory that competition means better performance leads to the conclusion by many that more "swing districts" are better.[45]

The "bare-knuckle politics" inherent in reapportionment that Sabo talked about (see chapter 4) is a reason to keep the courts out of the process, at least in the initial line-drawing stage. The courts are much better at resolving issues once the parties have defined the nature and parameters of a dispute. General public support for the judicial system is critical to keeping the government running well, and getting heavily involved in the initial stages of the inherently political nature of reapportionment will weaken that support.

In addition to partisan politics and competitiveness, other factors further complicate the tough job of reapportioning a legislative body. The racial and ethnic background of voters is a factor in reapportionment decisions as our diverse society considers the appropriate mix of persons to reflect the various cultures and values in its legislative bodies. In addition, existing boundaries of counties and cities have a bearing on where district lines should be drawn, since it often is more efficient and easier for voters to understand redistricting if existing boundaries are followed. Courts have continued to wrestle with all these concepts as they apply the one person, one vote standard.[46]

An alternative approach to legislators drawing their own boundaries or to having the courts draw the boundaries is to have an independent commission draw the new district lines. Approximately twelve states now use this method for drawing state legislative boundaries, and six use it for drawing federal congressional boundaries.[47] There are many difficult questions with this approach: Who should appoint the commission? How many members should it have? Can the commission use political information in drawing the lines (Arizona says it cannot)? Should competition be a factor? Should drawing congressional district boundaries be handled differently?

In 1980 a commission approach was proposed in Minnesota, and the legislature agreed to put the necessary constitutional amendment on the general election ballot. The voters gave the amendment a majority of votes, but that number was 3,125 votes short of the "extraordinary majority" required for a constitutional amendment.[48] A bipartisan commission, including Democrat Walter Mondale and former Republican governors Al Quie and Arne Carlson, studied these and other issues and in 2008 again proposed a commission approach.[49]

It is clear that having the legislature draw the lines does not work well and that courts are not equipped to draw the lines. Some form of a reapportionment commission should be adopted. But whether it is a commission, the legislature, or the courts, voters, watchdog groups, and the media need to vigorously monitor reapportionment map drawing to determine the fairness, the level of competition, the impact on diversity, and the respect for existing local government boundaries that are likely in the newly defined districts.

Build and Teach Twenty-First-Century Civics

Retired Supreme Court Justice David Souter, noting that a recent survey showed "two thirds of U.S. citizens cannot name all three branches of government," said, "We have to take on the job of making American civics education real again." His colleague, retired Supreme Court Justice Sandra Day O'Connor, picked up the cause of keeping civic education current, because "you don't inherit that knowledge through the gene pool."[50]

Making civics real and current requires reflection on what is meant by civic education. Many aspects of "civics" as it used to be taught should not be brought back (we do not need to memorize the names of cabinet officers or even presidents in a boring junior high school class). It may even be helpful to get rid of the word *civics* and start with a broader and more current word or phrase that better captures what society wishes to convey about our country, its history, its government, and why people become engaged in activities that help the common good. The problem with the civics of old is that while focusing on the abstract political principles found in the Declaration of Independence and the Constitution is of interest to some, for most people it leaves a dry taste. Put in a more eloquent fashion,

> People are not likely to find in political principles the deep
> emotional content and meaning provided by kith and kin,
> blood and belonging, culture and nationality. . . . A nation
> is defined by the common tradition, culture, heroes and vil-
> lains, victories and defeats, enshrined in its mystic chords of
> memory.[51]

This is not to say that civic education should not include a healthy dose of historical facts, political principles, and dates, but it should also include a discussion of modern factors. The concept of non-political civic engagement must be a part of twenty-first-century civics. For example, it ought to include a discussion of why today's students might be motivated to serve or work in government, the military, AmeriCorps, or the Peace Corps. Helping in a local school or in a business-related service, such as those involved in the LEAP program did, or participating in groups like the Citizens League or the League of Women Voters should be discussed as important vehicles for helping provide for the general welfare.

Civic education must also explain the context and concepts behind the political science and history, and the explanation must be understandable to people of diverse backgrounds and ages. This is easy to say but tough to do; even members of Congress may not know the basics. *The Economist* magazine pointed out that Congresswoman Michele Bachmann from Minnesota did not understand a basic point when she spoke in 2010 at a rally in the nation's capital. She spoke to cheers and applause in support of the position that the framers of the Constitution wanted to check the central government and protect the rights of the states. The article pointed out that the Constitution was designed to do exactly the opposite, to "bolster" the federal government and "weaken the power of the states."[52] As this example vividly shows, civic education must be more than memorizing dates and reading words without knowing the historical context.

Schoolchildren are a special audience that needs to be reached. As we teach the three Rs, we also need to build a curriculum around things that will grab and keep the attention of students. A lively course with music, film, and text built around three dates, 1776, 1865, and September 11, 2001, could hold students attention and effectively teach a great deal of American culture, government, geography, and history. Good teachers will be able to develop the curriculum, give it a name, and connect it with their students.

Legislators have unique knowledge and skills about how our governmental system works. It should be a part of the job description of every legislator to help educate constituents about the workings of all levels of government and the need for good people to serve in the many local units of government. This should not just be done in campaign season, when lessons become almost exclusively political, but year-round. Speaking and writing opportunities abound for legislators, and they should take some time to assist with civic education.

Many groups are currently working on these topics, including the Center for Civic Education, iCivics, the National Conference of State Legislatures, and the American Bar Association, but with fiscal pressures and strong efforts pushing solely a core reading, writing, and arithmetic curriculum, it is tough going.[53] Ironic as it may be, education about American government has in some cases fallen victim to the "bring back the basics" school reform movement.

If we hope to have Americans living another 220-plus years under our Constitution, we better get on with teaching the next generation what the Declaration of Independence and the Constitution say, and why they say it. As Robert Maynard Hutchins noted, "the death of democracy is not likely to be an assignation from ambush; it will be a slow extinction from apathy, indifference and undernourishment."[54]

Forming a More Perfect Union

The preamble to the Constitution teaches us that our Union of states and one federal government was formed to do five things: (1) establish justice, (2) insure domestic tranquility, (3) provide for the common defense, (4) promote the general welfare, and (5) secure the blessings of liberty to ourselves and our posterity. These goals have inspired many and have proved elusive, but they have also endured as a sound statement of the purposes of government. Ever since the preamble and the seven articles that follow it were adopted, the country has strived to achieve these goals, although even the strongest believers must admit that at times the country has gone sideways and a few times actually moved backward in its efforts.

As the country struggled with slavery and the role of its states, it fought a civil war and determined that our complicated system of sovereign states and a sovereign federal government would endure as one Union. As the country expanded westward and the population grew from almost four million people to over three hundred million people, the roles of the states and the federal government have continued to evolve. Local implementation has become more important as the complexity of delivering services has increased. As we continue into the twenty-first century with an increasingly diverse population, understanding the culture and values of different peoples and merging those values into the values embodied in our Constitution become even more complex, at the same time as they become more essential. A strong partnership among the federal, state, and local governments is required. America's unique federalism, with its dual sovereignty, its multiple levels of government, and its frustrating checks and balances, continues to be the best way for the country to merge the cultural values and achieve the preamble's goals.

Numerous poets, artists, writers, composers, and performers have described the efforts to implement the nation's goals and the results of these efforts in a manner that reaches far deeper than the legal structure explained in these pages. These creative people have reached into the heart and soul of the nation and found a proud but frustrated people. Whether that pride is manifested by Aaron Copeland's music of Appalachia in the spring, raucous baseball fans singing that they are "proud to be an American," or young, newly elected politicians in a hockey arena singing "America the Beautiful," there can be no doubt that millions of Americans feel that their country is a special place with a special form of government. Few would change places with citizens from other countries, not because this country has the perfect mix between levels and branches of government, or because our economy and tax structure are ideal, or because the issue of the day is being handled well, but because of a belief that our federal system has moved us forward better and faster than any other country and that it will continue to do so. A belief that with thought, focus, and shared sacrifice the states and federal government in partnerships with local governments will be able to form a more perfect Union with each other—and with the people of the United States.

Acknowledgments

Research for this book included interviews with state representatives and senators; legislative, state, and local government staff; a governor; executive branch personnel; campaign and political party staff; and a vice president of the United States. The people interviewed were generous with their time and candid about their thoughts and experiences. Their stories and insights make this history come alive, and the interviews were both informative and enjoyable. For this I thank Wendell Anderson, Eileen Baumgartner, Ed Burdick, Edward Dirkswager, Raymond Faricy, Gary Flakne, Donald Fraser, Warren Gahloon, Joseph Graba, Carl Johnson, William Kelly, Kevin Kenny, David Lebedoff, Ernest Lindstrom, William McGrann, Walter Mondale, Thomas Newcome, James Nobles, James Pederson, David Roe, Martin Sabo, Henry Savelkoul, Lyall Schwarzkopf, Rodney Searle, Harry Sieben, James Solem, and Robert Tennessen.

Telephone interviews were conducted with many interested persons, including John Boland, Keith Carlson, Jack Davies, David Durenberger, John Finnegan, Don Gemberling, Luther Granquist, John Haynes, Al Hofstede, Josie Johnson, Jay Kiedrowski, Jean LeVander King, Andy Kozak, Lisa Larson, Robert Latz, John Lindstrom, Bill Marx, Al Mathiowetz, Paul McCarron, Richard Moe, Patrick Murphy, Al Patton, Arturo Perez, Wes Skoglund, and Tom Todd.

In addition to the formal interviews, many persons outside the governmental and political processes were consulted. Professors Alan Rosenthal from Rutgers University and Tom Scott from the University of Minnesota stuck with me through four years of writing, researching, and editing with helpful encouragement. Bill Pound, Karl Kurtz, and Arturo Perez from the National Conference of State Legislatures (NCSL) also were consistently helpful with information and positive comments. The Minnesota Legislative Reference Library, and particularly its director, Robbie LaFleur, and librarians Betsy Haugen, Jess Hopeman, Elizabeth Lincoln, Lacey Mamak, and Paul VanCura, provided invaluable assistance in digging out clippings, reports, and citations that confirmed personal memories and documented important history. Lars Johnson provided advice on social media, and Patrick Coleman and his colleagues at the Minnesota Historical Society were always willing to look further to help me find elusive documents.

Early readers of all or portions of the manuscript—John and Sheila Mohr, Tom Barrett, Jim Hale, David and Karen Minge, Fred Morrison, Don Ostrom, Dick Niemic, John Bretzke, and my wife, Margit, and sons, Erik and Jeff—helped to keep the manuscript focused and accurate. Professor Kathryn Pearson and reporter Bill Salisbury also provided excellent and specific suggestions as did copy editor Mary Keirstead. As the publication process began, the people at the University of Minnesota Press consistently gave me sound suggestions that improved the book.

The Sabo Center at Augsburg College provided top-quality research assistance led by students Anna Boyle and Jacob Quarstad. Their advisor, Professor Gary Hesser, attended numerous meetings of the group of eight who collaborated on this book, and contributed many cogent comments on form and style. Thank you also to Carol Thompson, Patricia Aberman, and Julieann Lane for transcribing interviews and helping preserve important history and to Denise Carlson for excellent work on the index.

Specific credits for photographs in the book are given in captions, but Minnesota House and Senate photographers Tom Olmscheid and David Oakes went beyond their job descriptions to help me find a pictorial record of much of what happened during the time period covered. Sandra Date from the *Star Tribune* photo library cheerfully helped locate marvelous photographs of the people involved in the process of making government work.

The manuscript for *Minnesota's Miracle* would never have seen the light of day without the assistance over several years from staff members at my law firm of Hinshaw and Culbertson. A special thanks to Linda Swanson, Tim Brown, Lynne Wagner, Patti Walsh, and librarian Dana Herman for prompt and professional service.

Finally, one more thank you to Martin Sabo, whose leadership was crucial to the project and to the decade of government that led to this book, and to the seven people who met regularly, read every word, and offered encouragement and thoughtful comments. You are wonderful people.

Selected Significant Legislation Enacted in Minnesota, 1967–78

1967

Established Metropolitan Council

1969

Regional Development Act

1971

Fiscal Disparities Act
Flexible session constitutional amendment
Established Housing Finance Agency
Established Loaned Executive Action Program (LEAP)
Minnesota Miracle—Omnibus Tax Act
State Building Code

1973–74

Critical Areas Act
Established Commission on the Future
Established Departments of Finance and Personnel
Environmental Policy Act
Ethics and campaign finance regulations
Established Environmental Quality Council
Equal Rights Amendment ratification
Data Privacy Law
Increased mass transit funding
Metropolitan Reorganization Act
Increased minimum wage
No-fault auto insurance

Open Meeting Law
Party designation for legislators
Public employees bargaining
Same-day voter registration
School aids equalization
Uniform Probate Code
Wild and Scenic Rivers Act
Working-poor tax changes

1975–76

Community Health Services Act
Catastrophic health insurance
Certificate of Need
Community mental health centers pilot program
Clean Indoor Air Act
Handgun Control Act
Family Farm Security Act
Administrative Procedures Act
Established Department of Transportation
Metropolitan Land Planning Act
Established equal opportunity in athletics
Established Council on the Economic Status of Women
Circuit-breaker tax changes
Increased taconite production tax

1977–78

Metrodome stadium authorization
Energy conservation
Power-line siting regulation
Handgun Control Act amendments
Court Reorganization Act
Expanded shade tree disease control

Members and Committee Chairs of Minnesota Legislature, 1973–74

The 1972 election was a nonpartisan election, and the major political affiliation caucuses were Conservative and Liberal. In 1972 the election law was changed, and after the 1974 election the Conservative Caucus became known as the Republican Caucus, and the Liberal Caucus became known as the Democratic-Farmer-Labor Caucus.

C = member of Conservative Caucus
L = member of Liberal Caucus

Members of the House

Art Braun – L	Greenbush
Andrew Skaar – C	Thief River Falls
William Nelson Kelly – L	East Grand Forks
Willis Eken – L	Twin Valley
Irvin N. Anderson – L	International Falls
Norman Prahl – L	Keewatin
Doug St. Onge – L	Bemidji
Glen Sherwood – L	Pine River
Peter X. Fugina – L	Virginia
John J. Spanish – L	Hibbing
William R. Ojala – L	Aurora
Douglas J. Johnson – L	Cook
Willard M. Munger – L	Duluth
Mike Jaros – L	Duluth
Jack H. LaVoy – L	Duluth
James Ulland – C	Duluth
Neil Wohlwend – C	Moorhead
Arian Stangeland – C	Barnesville
Frank H. DeGroat – C	Lake Park

Joe Graba – L	Wadena
Calvin R. Larson – C	Fergus Falls
David Fjoslien – C	Brandon
Melvin J. Miller – L	Randall
Stephen G. Wenzel – L	Little Falls
Don Samuelson – L	Brainerd
Howard E. Smith – L	Crosby
Douglas W. Carlson – C	Sandstone
Bernard Carlson – L	Cloquet
Delbert F. Anderson – C	Starbuck
Glen Anderson – L	Odessa
Joe Niehaus – C	Sauk Centre
B. J. Brinkman – L	Richmond
Al Patton – L	Sartell
James Pehler – L	St. Cloud
Lynn H. Becklin – C	Cambridge
Bob McEachern – L	St. Michael
Michas M. Ohnstad – C	Stacy
Charles R. Weaver – C	Anoka
Harry Peterson – L	Madison
Russell P. Stanton – L	Marshall
John C. Lindstrom – L	Willmar
Aubrey W. Dirlam – C	Redwood Falls
Adolph L. Kvam – C	Litchfield
Harold J. Dahl – L	Howard Lake
August Mueller – C	Arlington
Carl M. Johnson – L	St. Peter
Robert E. Vanasek – L	New Prague
Robert Culhane – L	Waterville
Walter K. Klaus – C	Farmington
Victor Schulz – L	Goodhue
Verne E. Long – C	Pipestone
Wendell O. Erickson – C	Hills
George Mann – L	Windom
Thomas M. Hagedorn – C	Truman
Gilbert Esau – C	Mountain Lake
A. J. Eckstein – L	New Ulm
David R. Cummiskey – L	Mankato
Richard Wigley – C	Crystal

Dale E. Erdahl – C	Blue Earth
Rod Searle – C	Waseca
Henry J. Savelkoul – C	Albert Lea
Helen McMillan – L	Austin
John S. Biersdorf – C	Owatonna
Darrel R. Miller – L	Pine Island
Thomas H. Resner – L	Rochester
E. W. Quirin – L	Rochester
Richard Lemke – L	Lake City
M. J. McCauley – C	Winona
Neil Haugerud – L	Preston
Leonard C. Myrah – C	Spring Grove
Ralph Jopp – C	Mayer
R. J. Menke – L	Prior Lake
Ernest A. Lindstrom – C	Richfield
James C. Swanson – L	Richfield
Dave Cleary – C	Bloomington
Joseph P. Graw – C	Bloomington
Mary Forsythe – C	Edina
Ray Pleasant – C	Bloomington
Joan R. Growe – L	Minnetonka
Gerald C. Knickerbocker – C	Minnetonka
Julian Hook – C	St. Louis Park
Robert J. McFarlin – C	St. Louis Park
Tad Jude – L	Mound
Salisbury Adams – C	Wayzata
O. J. Heinitz – C	Wayzata
Richard J. Parish – L	Golden Valley
Lyndon R. Carlson – L	Brooklyn Center
J. B. Clifford – C	New Hope
Wm. H. Schreiber – C	Brooklyn Park
Ernee M. McArthur – C	Brooklyn Center
Paul McCarron – L	Spring Lake Park
Joe Connors – L	Fridley
Joel Jacobs – L	Coon Rapids
Gordon O. Voss – L	Blaine
Richard Andersen – C	St. Paul
Robert C. Bell – C	St. Paul
Vince Lombardi – C	Lino Lakes

Tom Newcome – C	St. Paul
Jerome J. Belisle – C	St. Paul
John Boland – L	St. Paul
Gary Laidig – C	Bayport
Michael Sieben – L	Newport
Raymond Pavlak – L	South St. Paul
Harry Sieben Jr. – L	Hastings
Ray Kempe – L	West St. Paul
Bradley G. Pieper – C	Burnsville
John J. Salchert – L	Minneapolis
James I. Rice – L	Minneapolis
Stanley J. Fudro – L	Minneapolis
John J. Sarna – L	Minneapolis
James R. Casserly – L	Minneapolis
Tom Berg – L	Minneapolis
Phyllis Kahn – L	Minneapolis
Martin Olav Sabo – L	Minneapolis
John W. Johnson – C	Minneapolis
Arne Carlson – C	Minneapolis
Linda Berglin – L	Minneapolis
Ken Nelson – L	Minneapolis
James L. Adams – L	Minneapolis
Stanley A. Enebo – L	Minneapolis
Gary W. Flakne – C	Minneapolis
Ray Wolcott – C	Minneapolis
Neil Dieterich – L	St. Paul
Walter Hanson – L	St. Paul
Ray W. Faricy – L	St. Paul
Robert W. Johnson – C	St. Paul
Bob Ferderer – C	St. Paul
Roy R. Ryan – L	St. Paul
Fred Norton – L	St. Paul
Donald M. Moe – L	St. Paul
Bruce F. Vento – L	St. Paul
Tony Bennett – C	St. Paul
Robert L. Paviak – C	St. Paul
John Tomlinson – L	St. Paul

House Committee Chairs, 1973–74

Agriculture	George Mann – L
Appropriations	Fred Norton – L
City Government	Roy Ryan – L
Commerce and Economic Development	James Adams – L
Crime Prevention and Correction	Helen McMillan – L
Education	Carl Johnson – L
Environmental Preservation and National Reserves	Willard Munger – L
Financial Institutions and Insurance	Bernard Brickman – L
General Legislation and Veterans Affairs	Stanley Fudro – L
Governmental Operations	William Quirin – L
Health and Welfare	James Swanson – L
Higher Education	Peter Fugina – L
Judiciary	Richard Parish – L
Labor-Management Relations	Stanley Enebo – L
Local Government	Harry Peterson – L
Metropolitan and Urban Affairs	John Salchert – L
Rules and Legislative Administration	Irv Anderson – L
Taxes	Ray Pavlak – L
Transportation	Bernard Carlson – L

Members of the Senate

Richard W. Fitzsimons – C	Warren
Roger D. Moe – L	Ada
Norbert Arnold – L	Pengilly
Gerald Willet – L	Park Rapids
George F. Perpich – L	Chisholm
Tony Perpich – L	Eveleth
Sam George Solon – L	Duluth
Ralph R. Doty – L	Duluth
D. H. Sillers – C	Moorhead
Roger Hanson – L	Vergas
Wayne Olhoft – L	Herman

Myrton O. Wegener – L	Bertha
Winston W. Borden – L	Brainerd
Florian Chmielewski – L	Sturgeon Lake
Charles Berg – C	Chokio
Ed Schrom – L	Albany
Jack Kleinbaum – L	St. Cloud
Robert Dunn – C	Princeton
Jerald C. Anderson – L	North Branch
J. A. Josefson – C	Minneota
Alec G. Olson – L	Willmar
John Bernhagen – C	Hutchinson
Earl W. Renneke – C	Le Sueur
Clarence M. Purfeerst – L	Faribault
George Conzemius – L	Cannon Falls
John L. Olson – C	Worthington
Howard D. Olson – C	St. James
Carl A. Jensen – C	Sleepy Eye
Arnulf Ueland Jr. – C	Mankato
John Patton – C	Blue Earth
C. E. Baldy Hansen – L	Austin
Mel Frederick – C	West Concord
Harold G. Krieger – C	Rochester
Roger A. Laufenburger – L	Lewiston
Lew W. Larson – C	Mabel
Jim Lord – L	Chanhassen
W. G. Kirchner – C	Minneapolis
Jerome V. Blatz – C	Bloomington
Otto Bang – C	Edina
John Keefe – C	Hopkins
B. Robert Lewis – L	Minnetonka
George Pillsbury – C	Wayzata
Rolf Nelson – C	Robbinsdale
Hubert H. Humphrey III – L	New Hope
Al Kowalczyk – C	Brooklyn Park
David D. Schaaf – L	Fridley
Stanley N. Thorup – L	Blaine
Robert O. Ashbach – C	St. Paul
John Milton – L	North Oaks
Jerome M. Hughes – L	Maplewood

Robert J. Brown – C	Stillwater
J. Robert Stassen – C	South St. Paul
Howard A. Knutson – C	Burnsville
Edward Gearty – L	Minneapolis
Eugene Stokowski – L	Minneapolis
Robert J. Tennessen – L	Minneapolis
Allan H. Spear – L	Minneapolis
Harmon T. Ogdahl – C	Minneapolis
Stephen Keefe – L	Minneapolis
Jack Davies – L	Minneapolis
Mel Hansen – C	Minneapolis
Robert North – L	St. Paul
Joseph T. O'Neill – C	St. Paul
Edward G. Novak – L	St. Paul
Nicholas D. Coleman – L	St. Paul
John C. Chenoweth – L	St. Paul
Bill McCutcheon – C	St. Paul

Senate Committee Chairs, 1973–74

Education	Jerome M. Hughes – L
Finance	Edward G. Novak – L
Governmental Operations	Edward Gearty – L
Health, Welfare and Corrections	George Conzemius – L
Judiciary	Jack Davies – L
Labor and Commerce	C. E. Baldy Hansen – L
Local Government	Alec G. Olson – L
Metropolitan and Urban Affairs	John C. Chenoweth – L
Natural Resources and Agriculture	Norbert Arnold – L
Rules and Administration	Nicholas D. Coleman – L
Taxes and Tax Laws	Tony Perpich – L
Transportation and General Legislation	Roger A. Laufenburger – L

Minnesota Governors, 1951–2011

In 1958, the Minnesota Constitution was changed to provide four-year terms beginning in 1963.

	ASSUMED OFFICE
C. Elmer Anderson	1951
Orville L. Freeman	1955
Elmer L. Andersen	1961
Karl F. Rolvaag	1963
Harold LeVander	1967
Wendell R. Anderson	1971
Rudy Perpich	1976
Al Quie	1979
Rudy Perpich	1983
Arne Carlson	1991
Jesse Ventura	1999
Tim Pawlenty	2003
Mark Dayton	2011

Notes

Preface

1. The Democrats are known as the Democratic-Farmer-Labor Party (DFL) in Minnesota. See the beginning of chapter 1 and related endnotes for a more detailed explanation of the history of this name.

2. In 1968, the Minnesota Legislature was by state statute "non-partisan," and the majority caucuses were the Conservatives and the Liberals. The other statewide offices were "partisan," and officeholders such as the governor and attorney general were identified as Republicans or Democrats. How the change from "non-partisan" to "partisan" came about is described in chapters 1 and 6.

Introduction

1. *New State Ice Co. v. Liebmann*, 285 U.S. 262 (1932) (Brandeis, J., dissenting); Alan Rosenthal, *Engines of Democracy: Politics and Policymaking in State Legislatures* (Washington, D.C.: CQ Press, 2009).

2. Ralph Blumenthal, "Recalling New York at the Brink of Bankruptcy," *New York Times,* December 5, 2002.

1. Forming a More Perfect Union

1. *Minnesota Legislative Manual, 1971–1972* (St. Paul: Secretary of State). Three of the new house members had served in the house at some time in the past.

2. The Democrats are known as the Democratic-Farmer-Labor Party (DFL) in Minnesota as the result of a rich political history. For an excellent discussion of that history, see John Earl Haynes, *Dubious Alliance: The Making of Minnesota's DFL Party* (Minneapolis: University of Minnesota Press, 1984).

3. Understanding the workings of caucuses can be an important part of understanding the workings of a legislature. In addition to these political caucuses, there were less formal caucuses that legislators would join. These were usually formed on the basis of geography or an issue, for example, a

Rural Caucus, a Pro-Life Caucus and, in the 1950s, even a Dry Caucus. Rod Searle, interview by project members, February 6, 2009.

4. *Minnesota House Journal,* 67th Leg., Reg. Sess., 1–10 (1971); *Goodwin v. Flahaven et al.,* 182 N. W.2d 182 (1971). The fight for control of the senate and the seating of Richard Palmer after the election in 1970 is an interesting story well told in Betty Wilson, *Rudy! The People's Governor* (Minneapolis: Nodin Press, 2005), 46; and Steven Dornfeld, "Legislature's Opening Day 20 Years Ago Pretty Hard to Top for Political Chaos," *St. Paul Pioneer Press,* January 6, 1991.

5. Winston Borden, a young lawyer from Brainerd in northern Minnesota, defeated thirty-year senator Gordon Rosenmeier, and Robert Tennessen, a young lawyer from Minneapolis, defeated thirty-five-year senator Donald O. Wright. *Minnesota Legislative Manual, 1971–1972.*

6. For a detailed discussion of "A Nonpartisan Partisan Legislature," see G. Theodore Mitau, *Politics in Minnesota,* rev. ed. (Minneapolis: University of Minnesota Press, 1970), 80–97.

7. Joseph J. Ellis, *American Creation: Triumphs and Tragedies at the Founding of the Republic* (New York: Alford A. Knopf, 2007).

8. Samuel Eliot Morrison, *The Oxford History of the American People* (New York: Oxford University Press, 1965), 305–16.

9. For an excellent discussion of the relative current workings of the legislative branch at the federal level, see Thomas E. Mann and Norman J. Ornstein, *The Broken Branch: How Congress Is Failing America and How to Get It Back on Track* (New York: Oxford University Press, 2006) and Mann and Ornstein, *It's Even Worse Than It Looks* (New York: Basic Books, 2012). For an excellent discussion of the workings of the fifty state legislatures, see Rosenthal, *Engines of Democracy.*

10. *Colegrove v. Green,* 328 U.S. 549 (1946). This case involved a potential congressional reapportionment for the State of Illinois. See note 23 below for cases in which the Court changed its position on this issue.

11. For a general discussion of constitutional limits, see Edward Corwin, *The Constitution* (Princeton, N.J.: Princeton University Press, 1958); and Morrison, *The Oxford History of the American People,* 968–70.

12. *American State Legislatures,* Report of the Committee on American Legislatures of the American Political Science Association, ed. Belle Zeller (New York: Thomas Y. Crowell Co., 1954); John Kaplan, book review, *Harvard Law Review* 68: 1097–1105 (1955).

13. Jerome Ellison, "Our Quaint Political Folkways," *The Nation,* November 16, 1963, 323.

14. Walter Heller, *New Dimensions in a Political Economy* (Cambridge, Mass.: Harvard University Press, 1966).

15. Henry S. Reuss, *Revenue Sharing: Crutch or Catalyst for State and Local Governments?* (New York: Praeger Publishers, 1970).

16. President Nixon's Message to Congress, August 13, 1969.

17. Reuss, *Revenue Sharing*, xi.

18. Walter Mondale, interview by author, July 7, 2010.

19. North Dakota Legislative Council, "Fiscal Assistance to State and Local Governments Act of 1972," October 2003. There is some confusion and overlap concerning definitions of revenue sharing, block grants, categorical grants, and general support aid from the federal government to the states. For a good summary of the definitions and the amounts provided from 1968 to 1977, see "In Brief, the Intergovernmental Grant System: An Assessment and Proposed Policies," Advisory Commission on Intergovernmental Relations, Washington, D.C. (1978).

20. Office of Management and Budget Circular No. A-95, July 1, 1976.

21. Mitau, *Politics in Minnesota*, 83, 94.

22. Lyall Schwarzkopf and Gary Flakne, interview by author and project members, April 20, 2009.

23. *Baker v. Carr*, 369 U.S. 186 (1962); *Reynolds v. Sims*, 377 U.S. 533 (1964); and subsequent cases. In those cases, the Supreme Court ruled that the reapportionment of legislative districts is a proper question for the federal courts and that the equal protection clause of the U.S. Constitution required that both state legislative districts and federal congressional districts be reapportioned to reflect the one person, one vote concept. For an analysis of the impact of these decisions, see Jeffrey R. Lax and Mathew D. McCubbins, "Courts, Congress, and Public Policy, Part II: The Impact of the Reapportionment Revolution on Congress and State Legislatures," *Journal of Contemporary Legal Issues* 15 (2006): 199–218. The Supreme Court at various times has used both the phrase "one person, one vote," *Gray v. Sanders*, 372 U.S. 368 (1963); and "one man, one vote," *Moore v. Ogilvie*, 394 U.S. 814 (1969).

24. Joe Graba, interview by author, April 8, 2009.

25. *Honsey et al. v. Donovan*, 236 F. Supp. 8 (D. C. Mn. 1964). Subsequently, three separate reapportionment plans were put forth between December 1964 and May 1965, when the legislature finally passed, and the governor signed, a reapportionment act, which took effect in the 1966 election. For a more detailed discussion of the contentious battles involved in Minnesota's efforts to comply with these rulings, see Mitau, *Politics in Minnesota*, 98–99.

2. The Pendulum Begins to Swing

1. In 1962 the Minnesota House of Representatives membership increased from 131 to 135 as part of the 1959 redistricting plan. In the 1962 election, the Conservative Caucus increased to 81 members, and the Liberal Caucus dropped to 54. Ed Burdick, interview with project members, August 27, 2008; Lyall Schwarzkopf at Augsburg College Symposium, September 26, 208; and Schwarzkopf and Flakne, interview.

2. See *Regional Planning and Development in Minnesota*, Minnesota State Planning Agency, July 1969.

3. Mitau, *Politics in Minnesota*, 42–44.

4. John Herbers, "Minneapolis Area Council Is Emerging as a Pioneer in Strong Regional Government," *New York Times*, February 7, 1971.

5. Jean LeVander King, interview by author, September 23, 2011.

6. Dave Durenberger became a U.S. senator from Minnesota and served from 1978 to 1994.

7. King, interview.

8. Burdick, interview; Minnesota House of Representatives, *Session Weekly* 25, 1, February 15, 2008.

9. Burdick, interview.

10. The legislative drafting office was known as the Office of the Revisor of Statutes, first established in 1939 under the jurisdiction of the Minnesota Supreme Court. The office was removed from the court to the legislative branch in 1973. 1973 Minn. Laws. 3.304; Searle, interview; Burdick, interview.

11. *Minnesota Legislative Manual, 1971–1972.*

12. Schwarzkopf and Flakne, interview.

13. Minnesota Statutes § 299 D.03 Subd.1 (b)(10) (2007).

14. Ernie Lindstrom, interview by author and project members, January 12, 2009.

15. Searle, interview.

16. Lindstrom, interview; Searle, interview; Tom Newcome, interview by project members, June 1, 2009; Warren Gahloon, interview by author and project members, April 16, 2009; Thomas L. Pahl, "Minnesota," *Midwest Review of Public Administration* 5, 2 (August 1971).

3. Life in the Minority Caucus

1. Martin Sabo, interview by author and project members, December 19, 2008.

2. Ibid.

3. Jim Pederson, interview by author, January 12, 2009. At that time in Minneapolis, the key local DFL unit was a ward. The "ward club" was the powerful group of grassroots activists, who usually selected local candidates. For an interesting discussion of the workings of a ward club and national politics, see David Lebedoff, *Ward Number Six* (New York: Charles Scribner's Sons, 1972).

4. Martin Sabo defeated Carl Hagland, 4,307 to 3,483 in 1960. *Minnesota Legislative Manual, 1961–1962.* Tad Jude was elected in 1972 at age twenty and turned twenty-one just a few weeks before being sworn in. *Minnesota Legislative Manual, 1973–1974.*

5. In 1960 the population of a district was based on 1913 census informa-

tion and thus varied significantly from district to district. The 2010 number is based on 2010 census estimates.

6. Sabo came in second in a three-person race with the top two being elected. Sabo received 4,170 votes, and Leonard Johnson received 3,669. First place went to incumbent Representative Jim Adams, with 4,992 votes. *Minnesota Legislative Manual, 1963–1964.*

7. Julie Sabo was elected to the Minnesota Senate in 2000 and served until 2002, when she was the lieutenant governor candidate with gubernatorial candidate Roger Moe in an unsuccessful race against Jesse Ventura. *Minnesota Legislative Manual, 2003–2004.*

8. Bob Latz, interview by author, August 16, 2009.

9. The phrase "not bound by tradition" was put in a speech for Governor Anderson by Jim Peterson, then an administrative aide to Governor Anderson. Jim Pedersen, interview by author, December 10, 2008.

10. "Rep. McMillan Decides Not to Seek 7th Term," *Rochester Post Bulletin,* April 6, 1974.

11. *Minnesota House Journal,* 67th Leg., Reg. Sess., 129 (1971).

12. Discussion with Representative Charlie Weaver and author.

13. Pahl, "Minnesota." The vote was sixty-five in favor and seventy against all the amendments except for two, where there were seventy-one against and sixty-three and sixty-four in favor. *Minnesota House Journal,* 67th Leg., Reg. Sess., 46–53 (1971).

14. *Minnesota House Journal,* 67th Leg., Reg. Sess., 46–53 (1971).

15. Ernie Lindstrom, interview by author and project members, June 9, 2009.

16. "War Legality Bill Gains Support, *Minneapolis Star,* March 20, 1971.

17. "Protest," *Minneapolis Tribune,* May 14, 1972.

4. Legislating a Miracle

1. "Minnesota: A State That Works," *Time Magazine,* August 13, 1973.

2. Property Tax Reform and Relief Act, 1967 *Minnesota Laws* 2143.

3. *New Formulas for Revenue Sharing in Minnesota* (Minneapolis: Citizens League, September 1, 1970), 2.

4. "Candidates Give Views," *St. Paul Dispatch,* September 12, 1970.

5. *New Formulas for Revenue Sharing,* 2.

6. Ibid.

7. Tim L. Mazzoni Jr., "State Policy Making for the Public Schools of Minnesota," Educational Governance Project, Ohio State University, 1974. This article contains an excellent and detailed discussion of the tax issues in the 1970 campaign and the development of the 1971 Omnibus Tax Act and its effect on fiscal policy in Minnesota.

8. Ibid., 53–55.

9. Wendell Anderson, interview by author and project members, October 26, 2009.

10. Finlay Lewis, "School-Tax Proposal May Decide Governor Race," *Minneapolis Tribune,* October 11, 1970; Finlay Lewis, "Anderson, Head Resume Debate on Question of State Tax Policies," *Minneapolis Tribune,* October 16, 1970.

11. *Minnesota Legislative Manual, 1971–1972.*

12. Editorial, *Minneapolis Star,* December 30, 1971; Martin Sabo, letter to the editor, *Minneapolis Star,* January 5, 1971.

13. John Haynes, interview by author, October 11, 2011.

14. Steven Dornfeld, "The Minnesota Miracle: A Roundtable Discussion," *Minnesota History* 60 (Winter 2007–08): 313–25.

15. Ibid.

16. Eileen Baumgartner, interview by author, August 13, 2009.

17. Ibid.

18. Haynes, interview.

19. Dornfeld, "The Minnesota Miracle"; Baumgartner, interview.

20. Mazzoni, "State Policy Making," 59–60; Haynes, interview.

21. Haynes, interview.

22. Mazzoni, "State Policy Making," 65.

23. Dornfeld, "The Minnesota Miracle," 313.

24. *Minnesota Legislative Manual, 1971–1972*; Stanley Holmquist, *Memorable Reflections: Education Is the Life of Democracy* (self-published, 2001).

25. Martin Sabo, interview with author and project members, April 21, 2009.

26. Sabo, interview, April 21, 2009.

27. Dornfeld, "The Minnesota Miracle," 322; *Minnesota House Journal,* 67th Leg., Reg. Sess., 4254 (1971).

28. Dornfeld, "The Minnesota Miracle," 322; *Minnesota House Journal,* 67th Leg., Ex. Sess., 3 (1971).

29. Minnesota Constitution, art. IV § 12.

30. Schwarzkopf and Flakne, interview.

31. For the forgettable lyrics, see Steven Dornfeld, "Freshman Senator Stages 'Polka Protest' at Capitol," *Minneapolis Tribune,* June 9, 1971.

32. *Minnesota House Journal,* 67th Leg., Ex. Sess., 541 (1971); *Minnesota Senate Journal,* 67th Leg., Ex. Sess., 516 (1971).

33. *Minnesota House Journal,* 67th Leg., Ex. Sess., 460 (1971).

34. Excerpts from Governor Wendell R. Anderson's Veto Message, August 3, 1971, Minnesota Legislative Reference Library, St. Paul.

35. Dornfeld, "The Minnesota Miracle," 323.

36. Committee members were Liberals Martin Sabo, L. J. Lee, Nick Coleman, and Harold Kalina. Conservatives were Stanley Holmquist, Harmon Ogdahl, Jerome Blatz, Aubrey Dirlam, Ernie Lindstrom, and Salisbury Adams.

37. Haynes, interview.

38. Ibid.

39. Martin Sabo, interview by author and project members, July 15, 2009.

40. Ibid.

41. *Serrano v. Priest,* 487 P.2d 1241 (1971). Another important case dealing with the disparity between districts was *San Antonio Independent School District v. Rodriguez,* 337 F. Supp. 280 (W.D. Tex. 1971). For a discussion of the *Seranno* and *Rodriguez* trial court decisions and the subsequent cases (including reversals) as well as the role of litigation in school finance issues in the early 1970s, see W. Norton Grubb, "The First Round of Legislative Reforms in the Post–Serrano World," *Law and Contemporary Problems* 38, 3 (Winter-Spring 1974): 459–92.

42. *Van Dusartz v. Hatfield,* 334 F. Supp. 870 (D.C. Mn. 1971).

43. Martin Sabo, interview by author and project members, August 13, 2009.

44. Steven Dornfeld, "Legislature Ends Record 157 Day Session," *Minneapolis Tribune,* October 30, 1971.

45. Omnibus Tax Act, 1971 Minnesota Laws 2561.

46. Minnesota Constitution, art. XIII, § 1.

47. *Minnesota House Journal,* 67th Leg., Ex. Sess., 541 (1971); *Minnesota Senate Journal,* 67th Leg., Ex. Sess., 516 (1971).

48. Sabo, interview, July 15, 2009.

49. Gerald W. Christenson, *A Minnesota Citizen: Stories from the Life and Times of Jerry Christenson* (privately published, 2005), 134. Sabo served in Congress from 1979 to 2006. He was a member of the Appropriations Committee and chaired the Budget Committee from 1993 to 1994 and then served as the ranking Democrat in 1995 and 1996.

50. Advisory Commission on Intergovernmental Relations, "The Minnesota Miracle," ACIR 13th Annual Report: Federalism in 1971: The Crisis, February 1972.

51. Fiscal Disparities Act, 1971, Minnesota Laws 2286; "Study of the Metropolitan Area Fiscal Disparities Program," prepared for the Department of Revenue by TischlerBise, February 13, 2012 (revised), Minnesota Legislative Reference Library, St. Paul.

52. Minnesota Statutes § 617.18 et. seq. (1971).

53. House File 588, *Minnesota House Journal,* 67th Leg., Reg. Sess., 287 (1971).

54. House File 757, *Minnesota House Journal,* 67th Leg., Reg. Sess., 373 (1971).

55. House File 836, *Minnesota House Journal,* 67th Leg., Reg. Sess., 412 (1971).

56. House File 879, *Minnesota House Journal,* 67th Leg., Reg. Sess., 436 (1971).

57. Minutes of Health, Welfare and Corrections Committee, February 12, 1971, et. seq. Box 129.C.3.8F, Vol. 16, Minnesota State Archives, Minnesota Historical Society, St. Paul.

58. "Abortion Foes Seek Probe," *St. Paul Pioneer Press,* March 19, 1971; "Ojala Asks Probe of Antiabortion Ad," *Minneapolis Tribune,* April 17, 1971.

59. *Minneapolis Star,* March 18, 1971.

60. *Minnesota House Journal,* 67th Leg., Reg. Sess., 4263 (1971).

61. Gordon Slovut, "Chances Slim for Change in Abortion Law," *Minneapolis Star,* March 18, 1971.

62. *Roe v. Wade,* 410 U.S. 113 (1973).

63. David M. Herszenhorne, "Democrats Rally to Obama's Call for Health Vote," *New York Times,* March 21, 2010; Executive Order 13535, "Ensuring Enforcement and Implementation of Abortion Restrictions in the Patient Protection and Affordable Care Act," March 24, 2010.

64. Bernie Shellum, "Lindstrom Plans to Attack Conservative Business Ties," *Minneapolis Tribune,* April 16, 1972.

65. Bernie Shellum, "Lindstrom: Campaign Funds Being Diverted," *Minneapolis Tribune,* April 15, 1972.

66. Shellum, "Lindstrom Plans to Attack."

67. Bernie Shellum, "Lindstrom Loses Caucus Fight over Campaign Funds," *Minneapolis Tribune,* April 17, 1972.

68. Robert J. O'Keefe, "Conservatives Settle Dispute over Funds," *St. Paul Pioneer Press,* April 17, 1972.

69. *Minnesota Legislative Manual,* 1969–1970.

70. Jim Solem, interview by author and project members, May 13, 2009.

71. Ibid.

72. "Excerpts from Inaugural Talk by Anderson," *Minneapolis Star,* January 6, 1971.

73. "Minnesota's Continuing Crisis in Housing," Governor Wendell Anderson, Special Message to 67th Legislature, March 5, 1971, Minnesota Legislative Reference Library.

74. Up to five authors are allowed on house bills, and up to three authors are allowed on senate bills. The first author presents the bill and does most of the work. The coauthors are usually to provide geographical and often bipartisan support.

75. *Minnesota House Journal,* 67th Leg., Reg. Sess., 4263 (1971).

76. 1971 Minnesota Laws 1020.

77. *Minnesota House Journal,* 67th Leg., Reg. Sess., 3002 (1971).

78. Ibid., 3003–8.

79. Ibid.

80. Josie Johnson, interview by author, October 29, 2009.

81. Bill Richardson, "Hartl Dumped as Two Incumbents, Two Women Named Regents, *Minnesota Daily,* May 17, 1971; "Regent Power," editorial, *Minnesota Daily*, May 17, 1971; Joe Blade, "U Regents Know Their Jobs Are on the Line," *Minneapolis Star,* September 9, 1971.

82. Sabo, interview, October 12, 2009.

83. During her time in Denver, Josie Johnson became the chief of staff for the first African American lieutenant governor in the United States since

Reconstruction; Johnson, interview. Harold Greenwood and other officers of a failed savings and loan association were subsequently convicted of multiple counts of fraud and racketeering. Greenwood served time in a federal prison; *United States v. Greenwood et al.*, 22 F.3d 783 (1993).

84. Connor Shine, "Sviggum to Remain Regent," *Minnesota Daily*, April 4, 2011.

85. Sviggum denied any real or perceived conflicts of interest and claimed that any problems could have been handled by a "conflict-of-interest management plan," under which he would have another Republican Caucus staff member handle any direct communications about the University of Minnesota and would abstain from certain matters as a regent if the Board of Regents said he should. Jenna Ross, "Regents Will Draw Lines for Debate over Sviggum's Dual Roles," *Star Tribune*, February 10, 2012. Sviggum then claimed he had been treated unfairly and resigned his regent position and continued to work for the Republican Senate Caucus. Jenna Ross, "Embattled Sviggum Resigns as U Regent." *Star Tribune*, March 9, 2012.

86. Mitau, *Politics in Minnesota*, 3.

87. 1971 Minnesota Laws 2300.

88. *Minnesota Legislative Manual, 1973–1974.*

89. Alison Lobron, "Reawakening the Two-Party System in Mass," *Boston Globe*, February 4, 2009.

90. *Minnesota House Journal*, 67th Leg., Reg. Sess., 4273 (1971).

91. Sabo, interview, July 15, 2009.

92. Ibid.

93. "Sabo's View May Decide Redistricting Plan's Fate," *St. Paul Pioneer Press*, November 3, 1971.

94. Ibid.

95. Sabo, interview, July 15, 2009.

96. Robert J. O'Keefe, "Governor Vetoes Legislature Remap," *St. Paul Pioneer Press*, November 2, 1971.

97. Anderson, interview.

98. *Beens v. Erdahl, et al.*, 336 F. Supp. 715 (D.C. Mn. 1972). The size of the legislature had long been a contentious issue that did not follow party lines. For example, in the house, Ray Faricy and Tom Berg supported a smaller legislature, and Bill Kelly, Joe Graba, and Martin Sabo did not. The Supreme Court continues to give deference to state legislative reapportionment plans as shown by an important Texas reapportionment case under the Voting Rights Act of 1965; *Perry v. Perez,* 132 S. Ct. 934 (2012).

99. *Sixty-Seventh Minnesota State Senate v. Beens et al.,* 406 U.S. 187 (1972).

100. David Kuhn, "Shifting Districts Keep Legislators on the Move," *Minneapolis Tribune,* May 4, 1972.

101. Deborah Howell, "Redistricting May Help Both Parties," *Minneapolis Star,* June 2, 1972.

102. The final court plan also eliminated the concept of "at large" districts, which had existed in Minnesota for the cities of Minneapolis and Duluth. This meant that in those cities, house members had to run in the entire senate district. In the rest of the state, house members had a district half the size of the senate districts. For example, in the 1970 election, freshmen Ray Faricy, Joe Graba, and Bill Kelly ran in a district half the size of a senate district, and Martin Sabo and Tom Berg ran on an "at large" basis. This meant they campaigned in a full senate district, and two representatives were selected from four candidates on the ballot. Starting with the 1972 election, all house districts were half the size of a senate district. The final plan also reduced the number of house members from 135 to 134. *Beens v. Erdahl,* 349 F. Supp. 97 (D.C. Mn. 1972).

103. Memorandum from Martin Sabo to House DFL Members, June 22, 1972, personal records of author.

104. Howell, "Redistricting May Help Both Parties."

5. A Truly Historic Election

1. Richard Berke, "The 1994 Elections," *New York Times,* November 1, 1994. In the 2010 election, the Minnesota Legislature switched back to Republican control, but the DFL gained the governorship.

2. Gallup Poll, *Minneapolis Tribune,* November 6, 1972.

3. "Your Leaders Are Sexual Bigots," Gay Caucus handout, personal records of the author.

4. Robert J. O'Keefe, "Hubert Gets 7 Delegates," *St. Paul Pioneer Press,* June 12, 1972.

5. Steven Dornfeld, "G-A-Y Rights Caucus Spells Out Goals to DFL Convention Goers," *Minneapolis Tribune,* June 29, 1972.

6. Dave Roe, interview by author, May 26, 2010.

7. Allan Spear, *Crossing the Barriers: The Autobiography of Allan H. Spear* (Minneapolis: University of Minnesota Press, 2010), 238.

8. DFL news bureau, press release, June 14, 1972. For a further discussion of DFL Party problems at the time, see Wilson, *Rudy!,* 55.

9. DFL news bureau, press release, June 14, 1972.

10. Robert J. O'Keefe, "DFL Refuses Abortion Plank," *St. Paul Pioneer Press,* June 12, 1972; "Anderson Disavows Some DFL Planks," *Minneapolis Star,* June 14, 1972.

11. DFL Party Platform, 1972, personal records of the author.

12. Richard Moe, interview by author, August 17, 2009.

13. Bill McGrann, interview by author, August 16, 2009; and Memorandum from Bill McGrann to Paul Ridgeway, et al., September 26, 1972, Minnesota State Archives, Minnesota Historical Society, St. Paul. The "kids" included Paul Ridgeway, Larry Meyer, John Norton, Barry Tilly, Bill

Strusinski, Kevin Foley, Jim Smieja, Curt Lowe, Kathy Kownack, Wanda Schumaker, Pat Bauer, and Mary Ann Boch. Many of these people went on to assume important DFL and governmental positions.

14. Sabo, interview, July 15, 2009.

15. Ibid.

16. Personal records of the author. Questionnaires sent out in 1971 included those from the Committee for Effective Crime Control (gun issues), the League of Women Voters of Minnesota, Citizens for Educational Freedom (aid to private schools), National Council of Jewish Women, Task Force on Corporate Farming, Minnesota Education Association, and Minnesota Citizens Concerned for Life.

17. Richard Wolffe, *Renegade: The Making of a President* (New York: Crown Publishers, 2009), 211.

18. Americans for Tax Reform, http://www.atr.org/, accessed August 25, 2011.

19. Brian Rosenberg, "That's One Too Many Pledges of Allegiance," *Star Tribune*, August 14, 2011; Trip Gabriel, "GOP Hopefuls Navigate the Pledges," *Star Tribune*, July 17, 2011.

20. Moe, interview.

21. Ibid.

22. Peter Ackerberg, "Smoke but Not Fire, Label Pinned on DFL Secrecy Broadsides," *Minneapolis Star,* October 10, 1972; "Politics 72," *Minneapolis Tribune*, October 17, 1972.

23. DFL 1972 Sample Ballot, Minnesota State Archives.

24. Bernie Shellum, "State Mining Industry Seeks Stronger Political Stance," *Minneapolis Tribune*, July 30, 1972.

25. Peter Ackerberg, "Businessmen Act to Slow DFL State Senate Drive," *Minneapolis Star,* October 25, 1972.

26. Joe Graba, interview by author, July 15, 2009; Graba campaign brochure, 1972, personal records of Joe Graba.

27. *Minnesota Legislative Manual, 1973–1974.*

28. Ray Faricy, interview by author, July 25, 2009.

29. Ibid.

30. *Minnesota Legislative Manual, 1973–1974.*

31. House File 2228, *Minnesota House Journal,* 67th Leg., Reg. Sess., 1134 (1971); Dornfeld, "G-A-Y Rights Caucus Spells Out Goals."

32. Finlay Lewis, "House Unit Imperils Use of Studded Auto Tires," *Minneapolis Tribune,* April 28, 1971.

33. *Minnesota Legislative Manual, 1973–1974.*

34. For an inside look at the workings of a major election recount, see Jay Weiner, *This Is Not Florida: How Al Franken Won the Minnesota Senate Recount* (Minneapolis: University of Minnesota Press, 2010).

35. Bill Kelly, interview by author, July 27, 2009.

36. *Minnesota Legislative Manual, 1973–1974.*

37. Spear, *Crossing the Barriers*, 246. Spear noted that he and Sabo had clashed earlier in 1970 and 1972, but that Sabo's help was "perhaps the most important" that Spear received in his successful 1972 election.

38. "Record 6 Women Win Seats in Legislature," *Minneapolis Star*, November 8, 1972; Warren Wolfe, "Berglin to Leave Minnesota Senate," *Star Tribune*, July 26, 2011.

39. *Legislators Past and Present*, Minnesota Legislative Reference Library, St. Paul. The first African American legislator was John Francis Wheaton, who served in the 1899–1900 session of the legislature.

40. "Voting May Be Record in State," *Minneapolis Star*, November 8, 1972.

41. Peter Vaughan, "DFL Wins Senate, Is Ahead for House," *Minneapolis Star*, November 8, 1972.

42. Ibid.

43. "Legislature '73," *St. Paul Pioneer Press*, December 31, 1972.

44. Bill Riemerman, "Women, Blacks, Youth Gain Political Clout," *St. Paul Pioneer Press*, November 10, 1972. The students elected were Tad Jude, David Cummiskey, Russell Stanton, and Mike Jaros.

45. For an excellent analysis and discussion of the importance of experience, age, and other demographic factors, see Royce Hanson, with the assistance of Charles Backstrom and Patrick McCarmack, *Tribune of the People: The Minnesota Legislature and Its Leadership* (Minneapolis: University of Minnesota Press, 1989), 42–54.

46. "Reporter's Notebook," *60 Minutes*, January 22, 2006.

47. Hanson, *Tribune of the People*, 42–54.

48. *Minnesota Legislative Manual, 1973–1974*, 546–54; chapter 3, n34.

49. David Brooks, "The Tea Party Teens," *New York Times*, January 5, 2010.

50. Robert J. O'Keefe, "Rep. Sabo Says He'll Be Candidate for Speaker of House," *St. Paul Dispatch*, November 10, 1972.

51. Steven Dornfeld, "DFL Takes Legislature for 1st Time," *Minneapolis Tribune*, November 9, 1972.

52. Ibid.

6. Breakout Session

1. Steven Dornfeld, "DFL May Find No Money for '73 Programs," *Minneapolis Tribune*, November 14, 1972.

2. Ibid.

3. Gerry Nelson, "Lindstrom to Concentrate on Crusade in 1973 House," *Rochester Post Bulletin*, November 16, 1972.

4. *Minnesota House Journal*, 68th Leg., Reg. Sess., 7–45.

5. Ibid., 48–74. A few of the offered amendments that were administrative and not political in nature were adopted.

6. *Minnesota House Journal,* 68th Leg., Reg. Sess., 563.

7. Sabo, interview, October 12, 2009; *Minnesota House Journal,* 68th Leg., Reg. Sess., 12.

8. Sabo, interview, October 12, 2009.

9. Bernie Shellum, "The Legislature: Control Changes Hands," *Minneapolis Tribune,* January 28, 1973.

10. "Congress and Secrecy," editorial, *Minneapolis Star,* May 11, 1973.

11. Mark Bowdon, "The Story behind the Story," *Atlantic Monthly,* October, 2009.

12. David Carr, "Olbermann, Impartiality and MSNBC," *New York Times,* November 7, 2010.

13. "The News Industry," *Economist,* July 11, 2011.

14. *Minnesota House Journal,* 68th Leg., Reg. Sess., 179.

15. Citations to specific statutes described in this chapter may be found in "Legislative Summary 1973–74," prepared by DFL house and senate caucus staff, Minnesota Legislative Reference Library. See also the two volumes "Actions of the 1973 Minnesota Legislature" and "Actions of the 1974 Minnesota Legislature," prepared by House Research Department, Minnesota House of Representatives, October 1973 and August 1974, Minnesota Legislative Reference Library.

16. 1973 Minnesota Laws 2.

17. 1973 Minnesota Laws 785.

18. *Minnesota Legislative Manual, 1973–1974;* Robert J. O'Keefe, "Party Label Bill Planned for Offices in 3 Major Cities," *St. Paul Dispatch,* January 30, 1973.

19. 1973 Minnesota Laws 1789.

20. "At the Capitol," *Minneapolis Tribune,* April 21, 1973.

21. Dave Giel, "Election Day Registration Bill Advances," *St. Paul Pioneer Press,* May 11, 1973.

22. *Minnesota House Journal,* 68th Leg., Reg. Sess., 179; 1974 Minnesota Laws 355, § 66 (re tree diseases).

23. Mark Munger, *Mr. Environment: The Willard Munger Story* (Duluth: Cloquet River Press, 2009), 177.

24. Ibid., 57. The original water permit was issued to Reserve Mining in 1947.

25. Hank Kehborn, "It's the Limit," *St. Paul Pioneer Press,* February 2, 1974.

26. *Minnesota Legislative Manual, 1983–1984.* In 1982 Johnson was the DFL lieutenant governor candidate on the ticket with then attorney general Spannaus. They lost in a primary to Rudy Perpich and Marlene Johnson.

27. Peter Vaughan, "Education Still Is Biggest Legislature Item," *Minneapolis Star,* May 26, 1973.

28. Rod Searle, *Minnesota Standoff: The Politics of Deadlock* (Waseca: Alton Press, 1990) is an interesting history of the partisan battles over the

Speakership of the Minnesota House after Sabo was elected to Congress in 1978.

29. Vaughn, "Education Still Is Biggest Legislature Item."

30. Ray Faricy, interview by author, July 25, 2009.

31. 1974 Minnesota Laws 842.

32. Dan Wascoe Jr., "At the Capitol" *Minneapolis Tribune,* March 23, 1974.

33. Peter Vaughn, "Handgun Bill Dies with a Whimper," *Minneapolis Star,* April 28, 1973.

34. "Legislative Summary 1973–74" contains citations to the tax legislation referred to in this paragraph.

35. Betty Wilson, "State Surplus Hits $224 Million," *Minneapolis Star,* August 23, 1974; and Gary Dawson, "State Budget Surplus Denounced as DFL Artifice," *St. Paul Pioneer Press,* August 24, 1974.

36. Irv Anderson, oral history, January 31, 1973, Minnesota State Archives, Minnesota Historical Society, St. Paul.

37. Faricy, interview.

38. Dave Roe spoke at the capitol on March 5, 2011, at a gathering of legislators and friends of Nick Coleman on the thirtieth anniversary of Coleman's death.

39. 1973 Minnesota Laws 2177.

40. Sabo, interview, October 12, 2009.

41. House File 951, *Minnesota House Journal,* 68th Leg., Reg. Sess., 514 (1973).

42. 1974 Minnesota Laws 1149.

43. Robert J. O'Keefe, "Problems Keep Popping Out on Campaign Bill, *St. Paul Dispatch,* March 21, 1974"; *Minnesota House Journal,* 68th Leg., Reg. Sess., 6979; *Minnesota Senate Journal,* 68th Leg., Reg. Sess., 6054 (1974).

44. *Citizens United v. Federal Election Commission,* 558 U.S. 50 (2010); *McComish v. Bennett,* 560 U.S. Order List (2010); editorial, "Keeping Politics Safe for the Rich," *New York Times,* June 9, 2010.

45. James Solem, interview by author, January 18, 2009; 1974 Minnesota Laws 441; "State Legislature Passes $450 Million Home Loan Program," Session Scenes, Minnesota House Information Office Newsletter, April 18, 1974. Representative Bruce Vento went on to serve in the U.S. Congress from Minnesota's Fourth District for twenty-three years, from 1977 to October 10, 2000.

46. Cindi Christie, "Streaking Hits SCS, Legislators Try Regulation," *The Chronicle,* St. Cloud State College (St. Cloud, Minn.), April 2, 1974.

47. Files of Michael C. O'Donnell, 1968–73, Minnesota State Archives Notebooks, Minnesota Historical Society, 1971–73; Governor's Loaned Executive Action Program, State Archives Notebooks, Minnesota Historical Society, 1971–73; "Legislative Summary 1973–74," Minnesota Legislative Reference Library.

48. House File 2037, *Minnesota House Journal*, 68th Leg., Reg. Sess., 1373 (1973); 1973 Minnesota Laws 680.

49. Minnesota Department of Administration Advisory Opinion: 09–020; Thomas Barrett, municipal attorney, interview by author, January 13, 2010.

50. Bob Tennessen, interview by author, April 2, 2011.

51. Health, Education, and Welfare, Report of the Advisory Committee on Automated Personal Data Systems, "Records, Computers and the Rights of Citizens," 1973.

52. John Lindstrom, interview by author, May 23, 2011.

53. 1974 Minnesota Laws 1199.

54. Ibid.

55. Betty Wilson, "Privacy Law to Open Files—and Eyes," *Minneapolis Star,* June 8, 1974.

56. "Franken Grills Tech Companies on Mobile Location Data," *Star Tribune,* May 10, 2011.

57. Edward J. Dirkswager Jr., "A Commission on Minnesota's Future," master's Plan B paper submitted to the School of Public Affairs, University of Minnesota, June 8, 1973.

58. 1974 Minnesota Laws 550.

59. 1974 Minnesota Laws 1096; 1975 Minnesota Laws 604; Gary Dawson, "Go-Slow View Criticized for Performance Auditing," *St. Paul Pioneer Press,* September 15, 1974.

60. James Nobles, interview by project members, December 12, 2008.

61. Sabo, interview, October 12, 2009.

62. Peter Ackerberg, "'74 Legislators Vote Pay Boost, Then Head Home, *Minneapolis Star,* March 29, 1974.

63. "Legislative Pay-Raise Protests Thunder In," *Minneapolis Star,* March 30, 1974; Gerry Nelson, "Governor Faces Bombshell over Legislative Pay Hikes," *Brainerd Daily Dispatch,* March 30, 1974.

64. Bernie Shellum, "Anderson Decides to Veto Pay Raise," *Minneapolis Tribune,* April 4, 1974.

65. Sabo, interview, October 12, 2009.

66. *Minnesota Legislative Manual, 1975–1976*; Fred L. Morrison, "An Introduction to the Minnesota Constitution," *William Mitchell Law Review* 20 (1994): 287.

67. Morrison, "An Introduction to the Minnesota Constitution."

68. Jack Davies, interview with author, August 25, 2010.

69. Ibid.

70. 1974 Minnesota Laws 787; *Minnesota Legislative Manual, 1975–1976.* The new language is technically an amendment to the original document, and all subsequent amendments to the constitution have been tied to this 1974 amendment.

71. Nobles, interview.

72. Ibid.

73. Kevin Kenney, interview with project members, July 15, 2009.

74. Nobles, interview.

75. Ibid.

76. Ed Dirkswager, interview by author, December 8, 2009.

77. Minnesota State Planning Agency, *Pocket Data Book* (St. Paul: Minnesota State Planning Agency, 1973).

78. Dirkswager, interview

79. Bill Kelly, interview by author, July 27, 2009.

80. *State Legislatures Magazine,* "The History of Us," July/August 1999; Karl Kurtz, interview by author and project members, September 28, 2009.

81. Sabo, interview, October 12, 2009.

82. 1973 Minnesota Laws 664; *Minnesota House Journal,* 68th Leg., Reg. Sess., 3971–73 (1973).

83. Bernie Shellum, "Young Legislators Battle for Controversial Bills and Sometimes Win," *Minneapolis Tribune,* May 7, 1973.

84. Doug Growe, "Allan Spear's Legacies: Civil Rights Advocate for All, Landmark Protection for Gays," www.minnpost.com, October 13, 2008; Spear, *Crossing the Barriers.*

85. Growe, "Allan Spear's Legacies."

86. Bernie Shellum, "Legislators Plan Two-Day Retreat," *Minneapolis Tribune,* November 28, 1973.

87. Ibid.

88. Phil Jones, notes of speech in records of author.

89. "Inside the Interim," Minnesota House Information Office Newsletter, August 1973.

90. In *Hoppe v. Northern States Power Company,* 215 N. W. 2d 797 (1974), the Minnesota Supreme Court upheld the validity of these procedures.

91. Editorial, "Not All Good, Not All Bad," *The Forum,* October 15, 1973.

92. Pursuant to the legislature's Joint Rules 20 and 23(c), bills recommended by the committees were sent back to the last committee to act on it for a summary repassage or other action as the committee deemed appropriate. First Assistant Chief Clerk Patrick Murphy, interview by author, January 13, 2010.

93. Steve Alnes, "Our New Legislature: Policy and Operations," *Minneapolis Star,* February 26, 1974.

94. Steven Dornfeld, "Dirlam Confirms He Won't Seek Reelection," June 5, 1974; "Six Members Will Retire," Minnesota Legislative Information Office Newsletter, 1 no. 13, June 1974.

95. Steve Alnes, "Full-Time Legislature Viewed as a Must," *Minneapolis Star,* May 21, 1974.

96. Karl T. Kurtz, Gary Moncreif, Richard Niemi, and Lynda W. Powell, "Full-Time, Part-Time, and Real Time: Explaining State Legislators' Per-

ceptions of Time on the Job," *State Politics and Policy Quarterly* 6 (fall 2006): 322–38.

97. Numerical analysis provided by First Assistant Chief Clerk Murphy, interview.

98. Bernie Shellum, "Hard Words Define State GOP Goals," *Minneapolis Tribune*, June 30, 1974. The Republicans zeroed in on Tom Kelm and even filed a "Protest and Dissent" claiming that members of the house had been "blatantly coerced by members of the Governor's staff." This was filed and printed in the *House Journal*, pursuant to Minnesota Constitution art. IV, § 16; *Minnesota House Journal*, 68th Leg., Reg. Sess., 4191 (1973). The document was seen as political and received no publicity.

99. "Shellum, "Hard Words Define State GOP Goals."

100. "GOP Fails to File Bids for 14 Districts in House," *Minneapolis Tribune*, July 19, 1974.

101. "Except for Kelm Issue, Wendy's Campaign Serene, *St. Paul Dispatch*, November 1, 1974.

102. Wilson, "State Surplus Hits $224 million"; Dawson, "State Budget Surplus Denounced as DFL Artifice."

103. Peter Vaughn, "DFLers Win 5 out of 8 U.S. House Seats, *Minneapolis Star*, November 6, 1974.

104. *Minnesota Legislative Manual, 1975–1976.*

105. Robert Wheratt, "Win Makes Flakne a GOP Power," *St. Paul Dispatch*, November 6, 1974.

106. Jim Shoop, "State GOP Says It Caught in Down Cycle," *Minneapolis Star*, November 6, 1974.

107. Munger, *Mr. Environment*, 312.

7. Presidential Politics and Musical Chairs

1. John Beargrease was the son of a Chippewa chief, and in the winter from 1887 to 1900 he delivered mail by dogsled from Two Harbors to Grand Marais along the North Shore of Lake Superior. A sled dog race is run every year along his 411-mile mail route; John Beargrease Sled Dog Marathon, www.beargrease.com.

2. *Minnesota Legislative Manual, 1975–1976.* Henry Savelkoul, interview by author, August 26, 2011. Graven lost the congressional race to Al Quie in 1962 and, along with Nick Coleman and others, dropped out of the race for governor after Wendell Anderson received the DFL endorsement in 1970.

3. Gary Dawson and Bruce Nelson, "Legislature Opens on Harmony Note," *St. Paul Pioneer Press*, January 8, 1975.

4. Gerry Nelson, "Sabo Expects a Less Busy 1975 Legislative Session," *St. Paul Dispatch*, November 9, 1974.

5. Steven Dornfeld, "3 Young DLFers Head House Units," *Minneapolis Tribune,* December, 4, 1973.

6. Linda Charlton, "Rockefeller Sworn In as Vice President," *New York Times,* December 19, 1974.

7. Theodore H. White, *America in Search of Itself: The Making of the President, 1956–1980* (New York: Harper and Row, 1982), 152, 160.

8. Ibid., 244.

9. Wendell R. Anderson, Second Inaugural Address, January 8, 1975, Minnesota Legislative Reference Library.

10. Bernie Shellum, "Anderson's Speech Fuels Speculation That Governor Is Eying Higher Office," *Minneapolis Tribune,* January 13, 1975.

11. Christenson, *A Minnesota Citizen,* 126.

12. "Minnesota Horizons," *Minneapolis Tribune,* January 12, 1975.

13. The Minnesota Constitution gives the legislature the authority to allow cities to adopt "home rule charters" so the cities do not need to return to the legislature for changes in their structure; Minnesota Constitution, art. XII, § 3–5. The legislature has given such authority to Minneapolis and St. Paul. For a discussion of how this has worked out for these cities, see Iric Nathanson, *Minneapolis in the Twentieth Century: The Growth of an American City* (St. Paul: Minnesota Historical Society Press, 2009), 15–36. Some other states have home rule charters for certain cities written into their constitutions; for example, see Colorado Constitution, art. XX.

14. *Encyclopedia of the American Legislative System* (New York: Charles Scribner's Sons, 1994), 83–85.

15. Advisory Commission on Intergovernmental Relations, "Federal Statutory Preemption of State and Local Authority," A-121, September 1992, ch. 1, 9; Joseph Zimmerman, "The Nature and Political Significance of Preemption," American Political Science Association, symposium, July 2005.

16. 29 U.S.C.A. § 1001.

17. Advisory Commission on Intergovernmental Relations, "Federal Statutory Preemption of State and Local Authority," ch. 1, 9; Zimmerman, "The Nature and Political Significance of Preemption."

18. 20 U.S.C.A. § 6301.

19. In the 39 years from 1965 to 2004, Congress used the power 365 times, while in the previous 175 years from 1790 to 1965, Congress had only used the preemption power 522 times; Zimmerman, "The Nature and Political Significance of Preemption." There is another legal doctrine called "Abstention," which relates to situations where the federal court "stays its hands" in dealing with state issues. For a discussion of the doctrine, see Wright, Miller, Cooper, and Amar, *Federal Practice and Procedure* (Eagan, Minn.: Thomson/West, 2007), 17A §4241.

20. Sabo, interview, October 12, 2009.

21. Sam Dillon, "State Challenges Seen as Whittling Away Federal Edu-

cation Law," *New York Times,* August 15, 2011; "Majority of States Say They'll Seek Waivers under NCLB," *Education Week,* October 29, 2011; Kim McGuire, "Minnesota Freed from 'No Child Left Behind' Sanctions," *Star Tribune,* February 9, 2012. Additional waivers were granted to other states for other provisions of the act, bringing the total number of states with waivers to twenty-four. "World/National Briefs," *Star Tribune,* July 1, 2012.

22. *Arizona v. United States,* 132 S. Ct. 2492, (2012); *National Federation of Independent Business v. Sebelius,* 132 S. Ct. 2561 (2012). The National Federation opinion is a consolidation of three cases, two of which were filed in Florida.

23. *National Federation of Independent Business v. Sebelius,* 132 S. Ct. 2561 (2012).

24. Ibid.

25. *Encyclopedia of the American Legislative System,* 83–85.

26. *National Federation of Independent Business v. Sebelius,* 132 S. Ct. 2561 (2012).

27. *Brown v. Board of Education of Topeka,* 347 U.S. 483 (1954). In a related case, the court applied the due process clause of the Fifth Amendment to the public schools of the District of Columbia to reach the same conclusion. *Bolling v. Sharpe,* 347 U.S. 497 (1954).

28. In general terms, the court began in the 1930s to interpret the due process and equal protection clauses of the Constitution to include various individual liberties specified in the Bill of Rights. This has affected many state actions, including criminal procedure and statutes relating to religion. For a more detailed discussion of the legal issues, see Michael Kent Curtis, "The Bill of Rights and the States: An Overview from One Perspective," *Journal of Contemporary Legal Issues* 18, 3 (2009). Linda Greenhouse, "A Voice from the Past," *New York Times,* June 1, 2011.

29. *Brown v. Plata,* 131 S. Ct. 1910 (2011).

30. "Congress, Preemption, and Federalism," American Political Science Association, symposium, July 2005.

31. Vermont Constitution, 1793. The balanced budget provision of the Minnesota Constitution is in art. XI, § 6. The enforcement mechanism is a statewide property tax to be levied by the state auditor.

32. U.S. Constitution, Art. I § 8.

33. *Brayton vs. Pawlenty,* Minnesota Sup. Ct., May 5, 2010.

34. Pawlenty's presidential ambitions ended with a third-place showing in the Ames, Iowa, straw poll in August 2011. Minnesota Congresswoman Michele Bachmann won the poll. Kevin Diaz, "Out of Fuel, Pawlenty Exits Race," *Star Tribune,* August 15, 2011.

35. Bill Salisbury, "Victory Caps Governor-Elect's Comeback, but He Inherits a Big State Deficit and a Legislature Controlled by Rivals," *St. Paul Pioneer Press,* December 19, 2010.

36. Baird Helgeson, "Finally, a Deal," *Star Tribune*, July 15, 2011.

37. Bill Salisbury, "It's a Deal—Dayton Agrees to an Earlier Republican Offer to End the Shutdown—with Caveats," *St. Paul Pioneer Press*, July 15, 2011; "Freshman Power," *Session Weekly* 28, 20, Public Information Services, Minnesota House of Representatives, July 15, 2011; Americans for Tax Reform, www.atr.org/, accessed August 25, 2011.

38. Helgeson, "Finally, a Deal."

39. Salisbury, "It's a Deal."

40. The deal also included other provisions, including the passage of a $500 million bonding bill for various construction projects, the borrowing of $700 million from the proceeds of a legal settlement the state had previously received from large tobacco companies, the agreement by Republicans to drop a demand for a 15 percent reduction in the state workforce, and the elimination of "policy" changes the Republicans had been demanding regarding abortion, photo identification at the polls, and a ban on cloning that would limit stem cell research. "FAQ on the Deal Ending the State Government Shutdown," *MPR News*, Minnesota.publicradio. org, July 20, 2011.

41. Baird Helgeson, "Painful Deal Delays Day of Reckoning," *Star Tribune*, July 16, 2011.

42. Ibid.

43. Bernie Shellum, "$5-Billion State Budget Proposed by Anderson," *Minneapolis Tribune*, January 17, 1975.

44. *New Formulas for Revenue Sharing in Minnesota* (Minneapolis: Citizens League, September 1, 1970), 2.

45. Press release, Office of the Governor, December 15, 1971, Minnesota Legislative Reference Library. The 1973 session of the legislature extended the life of the commission and modified its charge to "study longer range tax policy." 1973 Minnesota Laws 601. subd. 4 (not coded).

46. Wendell R. Anderson, Budget Message, January 19, 1975, Minnesota Legislative Reference Library.

47. Steven Dornfeld, "Tax Plan Unworkable, DFL Legislators Claim," *Minneapolis Tribune*, March 31, 1975.

48. Steven Dornfeld, "Anderson Wants Surplus to Be Saved," *Minneapolis Tribune*, March 28, 1975.

49. Dornfeld, "Tax Plan Unworkable."

50. Anderson, Budget Message.

51. Bruce Nelson, "School Aid Bill Has Most Spending Ever," *St. Paul Pioneer Press*, May 25, 1975.

52. Bill Kelly, interview by author, June 5, 2010.

53. House File 1674, *Minnesota House Journal*, 69th Leg., Reg. Sess., 2087 (1975).

54. House File 1722, *Minnesota House Journal,* 69th Leg., Reg. Sess., 2948 (1975).

55. Gene Lahammer, "Gas Tax Rise Part of State Road Package," *Minneapolis Tribune,* May 19, 1975; 1975 Minnesota Laws 543.

56. Ralph Blumenthal, "Recalling New York at the Brink of Bankruptcy," *New York Times,* December 5, 2002.

57. "The 1975 Legislature: Hard-Working Session," editorial, *Minneapolis Tribune,* May 21, 1975.

58. The final circuit breaker mechanism provided that if property taxes exceeded a certain percentage of income (from 1 percent to 4 percent) a credit (or direct payment) from $325 to $475 would be given to the taxpayer on their income tax bill. 1975 Laws of Minnesota 1573.

59. Minutes of the Committee on Rules and Legislative Administration, Minnesota House, April 14, 2010, Minnesota State Archives, Minnesota Historical Society, St. Paul.

60. "House Leaders Agree Logjam Worst Ever," *Duluth Herald,* May 22, 1975.

61. Gary Dawson, "Frantic Rush Marks Windup of Legislature," *St. Paul Dispatch,* May 20, 1975.

62. Jim Shoop, "Final Sprint Winds DFL" *Minneapolis Star,* May 23, 1975.

63. Dawson, "Frantic Rush Marks Windup of Legislature."

64. "The 1975 Legislature," editorial.

65. "Legislature Won't Be Recalled," *The Forum,* June 3, 1975.

66. *The First Branch of Government: From Grass Roots to Law,* directed by Charles Guggenheim, film produced for the National Conference of State Legislators, 1976.

67. 1975 Minnesota Laws 385.

68. U.S. Constitution, art. 1, §10.

69. *Minnesota Legislative Manual, 1977–1978.*

70. Betty Wilson, "'For Men Only' Cafe Yields to DFL Women," *Minneapolis Star,* January 21, 1975.

71. Equal opportunity in athletics, 1975 Minnesota Laws 985; Keep name after marriage, 1975 Minnesota Laws 266; Council on the Economic Status of Women, 1976 Minnesota Laws 1343. For a discussion of the work of the commission, see Lori Sturdevant, "Women's Council Strives to Continue Record of Success," *Minneapolis Tribune,* February 5, 1979.

72. House File 679, *Minnesota House Journal,* 69th Leg., Reg. Sess., 374 (1975); Senate File 625, *Minnesota Senate Journal,* 69th Leg., Reg. Sess., 374 (1975).

73. Ibid.

74. "Minnesota Handgun Homicides/Suicides 1972–1974," Minnesota Legislative Reference Library.

75. Joe Rigert, "Guns: Out of Control?" *Minneapolis Tribune,* February 16–22, 1975.

76. Minutes of Committee on Crime Prevention and Corrections, March 4, 1975, Box 129 A. 6.2(F), vol. 95, Minnesota State Archives.

77. Ibid., March 11, 1975.

78. Ibid. A more detailed discussion of the hearings is contained in a Joint Religious Legislative Coalition (JRLC) paper in the personal records of the author.

79. Minutes of Committee on Crime Prevention and Corrections, March 18, 1975.

80. *Minnesota House Journal,* 69th Leg., Reg. Sess., 1738 (1975).

81. Ibid.

82. Minutes of the Appropriations Committee, April 9, 1975, Box 129.C.4.5B, vol. 83, Minnesota State Archives.

83. House File 679, *Minnesota House Journal,* 69th Leg., Reg. Sess., 1738 (1975).

84. *Minnesota House Journal,* 69th Leg., Reg. Sess., 1741 (1975).

85. Ibid., 1742.

86. Gerry Nelson, "House Faces Emotional Gun Bill Vote," *The Forum,* April 23, 1975; 1975 Minnesota Laws 1278.

87. Jim Shoop, "House Approves Handgun Controls," *Minneapolis Star,* July 24, 1975. On the final vote, Sieloff and Adams joined Kelly in voting yes, and Munger voted no. *Minnesota House Journal,* 69th Leg., Reg. Sess., 1843 (1975).

88. Liza Fourre and Patrick Larkin, "Amended Gun Control Bill Reaches Senate Floor," *Minnesota Daily,* April 21, 1975.

89. Ibid.

90. Bernie Shellum, "Handgun Control Bill Passed," *Minneapolis Tribune,* May 18, 1975.

91. 1975 Minnesota Laws 1278.

92. Ibid.

93. Robert J. O'Keefe, "Spannaus Still Has Sights on Tougher Handgun Bill," *St. Paul Dispatch,* May 25, 1975.

94. Bruce R. Nelson, "House Snuffs Sabo, Bans the Butt," *St. Paul Pioneer Press,* January 25, 1975.

95. 1975 Minnesota Laws 633; *Minnesota House Journal,* 69th Leg., Reg. Sess., 86.

96. Wendell R. Anderson, Second Inaugural Address, January 8, 1975, Minnesota Legislative Reference Library.

97. Sabo, interview, October 12, 2009.

98. Dirkswager, interview.

99. 1976 Minnesota Laws 1088. The final health-care bill changed CHA to MCHA.

100. Dirkswager, interview; Chen May Lee, "First Bit of Reform Offers Little to State," *Star Tribune*, August 13, 2010.

101. 1975 Minnesota Laws 810.

102. 1976 Minnesota Laws 43.

103. *Minnesota House Journal*, 69th Leg., Reg. Sess., 6398, 3417, 2922 (1975).

104. "*Transit: Redirect Priorities toward a Small-Vehicle System and Shorter Trips*" (Minneapolis: Citizens League, January 21, 1974); Statement of Wayne Olson to Senate Committee on Metropolitan Affairs, February 8, 1973, Minnesota Legislative Reference Library.

105. Olson, statement to senate committee.

106. Betty Wilson, "Berg's Peacemaker Role Faces Key Test," *Minneapolis Star*, December 5, 1973.

107. John Boland, interview with author, June 24, 2010.

108. Dan Wascoe Jr., "House Panel Asks New Transit Study," *Minneapolis Tribune*, March 15, 1974; 1974 Minnesota Laws 1424.

109. Steven Dornfeld, "MTC Head in Trouble with Leading Senators," *Minneapolis Tribune*, February 18, 1975. Kelm was not confirmed until almost a year later, when he mended his fences with the senate. With some help from his brother, he was confirmed in February 1976. "State Senate Confirms Kelm as MTC Head," *Minneapolis Tribune*, February 24, 1976.

110. Betty Wilson, "Action on New Transit System Unlikely," *Minneapolis Star*, March 17, 1975.

111. Fred Cohen, "House Committee Head Reserves Commitment to High-Cost Transit Plans," *Minnesota Daily*, February 19, 1975.

112. Metropolitan Transit, Report by Tom Berg and Pete Petrafeso, May 1975, Minnesota Legislative Reference Library.

113. Ibid.

114. "Forget Fixed-Guideway Transit," editorial, *Minneapolis Star*, May 19, 1975.

115. 1975 Minnesota Laws 543.

116. 1976 Minnesota Laws 292; 1976 Minnesota Laws 496.

117. Nathanson, *Minneapolis in the Twentieth Century*, 187–210, contains an excellent discussion of the Hiawatha Avenue issue and describes an example of the impact of federal and state governments on a city's development. Martin Sabo, interview by author, June 21, 2010.

118. Chris Havens, *Star Tribune*, May 12, 2010.

119. "The Coolest Ballpark in America," *Twin Cities Business*, March 2010, 43.

120. Baird Helgeson and Mike Kaszuba, "Dayton Gets Last Word as He Vetoes Reworked GOP Tax Cuts," *Star Tribune*, May 15, 2012. "The Numbers," *Sports Illustrated*, March 29, 2010, 21.

121. Sid Hartman with Joel Rippel, *Great Minnesota Sports Moments* (St. Paul: Voyageur Press, 2006), 87.

122. Bill Lester, Executive Director, Metropolitan Sports Facilities Commission, interview by author, June 15, 2010.

123. "10 Legislators Named to Area Stadium Study," *Minneapolis Star,* July 9, 1975.

124. House File 2281, *Minnesota House Journal,* 69th Leg., Reg. Sess., 3893 (1976).

125. Minutes of Local and Urban Affairs Committee, February 25 and March 8, 1976, Box 129.A.12.6, vol. 136, Minnesota State Archives; Sabo, interview, October 12, 2009.

126. Letter from Hubert H. Humphrey III to Metropolitan Sports Facilities Commission Chairman Wayne Terwilliger, September 28, 2009; copy in possession of author.

127. Minutes of Local and Urban Affairs Committee, March 1, 1976, Box 129.A.12.6, vol. 136, Minnesota State Archives.

128. 1976 Minnesota Laws 25. The amount of the appropriation was $500,000.

129. Eric Pianin and Betty Wilson, "Legislature Adjourns with No Stadium Bill," *Minneapolis Star,* April 7, 1976.

130. Steven Dornfeld, "House DFL Leaders Oppose Tax Rebate," *Minneapolis Tribune,* March 3, 1976.

131. Gary Dawson, "Legislative Residue—Bitterness," *St. Paul Pioneer Press,* April 11, 1976.

132. Dawson, "Legislative Residue"; Gary Dawson, "Closing Bell Signals Relief for Battered Coleman," *St. Paul Pioneer Press,* April 8, 1976.

133. Dawson, "Legislative Residue."

134. Pianin and Wilson, "Legislature Adjourns with No Stadium Bill."

135. Wilson, *Rudy!,* 58.

136. Dawson, "Legislative Residue."

137. Joe Graba, interview by author, October 20, 2009.

138. "Faricy Accuses Anderson Aides of Misleading Others, *Minneapolis Tribune,* April 16, 1975.

139. Faricy, interview.

140. *The First Branch of Government.*

141. "Adams Says He Won't Run in House Again," *Minneapolis Star,* December 3, 1975.

142. Rosalynn Carter, *First Lady from Plains* (Boston: Houghton Mifflin Co. 1984), 128.

143. Ibid., 136.

144. David Lebedoff, interview by author, August 20, 2010.

145. Pianin and Wilson, "Mondale: Political Futures on Line," *Minneapolis Star,* August 9, 1976.

146. Minnesota Statutes 202A.72 (1976).
147. Pianin and Wilson, "Mondale."
148. Wilson, *Rudy!*, 66.
149. *Time,* December 1, 1975. The name change lasted until 1995, when the party dropped "Independent" from its name.
150. Ibid.
151. Gary Dawson, "Optimism Dims for I-R Control in State Senate," *St. Paul Pioneer Press,* October 11, 1975.
152. "DFL Gains Firmer Hold on Legislature," *Minneapolis Tribune,* November 4, 1976.
153. David Roe, interview by author, May 26, 2010.
154. See http://www.washingtonpost.com/wp-srv/politics/campaigns/junkie/archive/junkie080699.htm, accessed August 2, 2012, for a listing of these races.
155. Roe, interview.
156. Andy Kozak, interview by author, July 8, 2010.
157. Wilson, *Rudy!*, 67.
158. Ibid., 70–72.
159. The fourth brother, Joe, became a psychiatrist and a leader in medical research in Washington, D.C; ibid., 22.

8. It's More Complicated Than It Looks

1. Harry Sieben and Bill Kelly, interviews by author, January 14, 2011; Bruce Nelson, "House Majority Leader Hangs onto His Post," *St. Paul Pioneer Press,* November 9, 1976; Savelkoul, interview; Rod Searle, *Minnesota Standoff: The Politics of Deadlock* (Waseca, Minn.: Alton Press, 1990).
2. "Savelkoul Names New I-R Leaders in House," *Austin Daily Herald,* December 13, 1976.
3. Governor's State of the State Message, January 5, 1977.
4. Steven Dornfeld, "A 'New Era' Is Foreseen by Perpich," *Minneapolis Tribune,* January 6, 1977.
5. Jack Coffman and Steven Dornfeld, "Perpich Slips Unescorted into Power-Line Area," *Minneapolis Tribune,* January 12, 1977.
6. Steve Brandt, "Republican Gagman Active on Slow Legislature Day," *Minneapolis Tribune,* January 13, 1977.
7. Ed Dirkswager, interview by author, February 28, 2011.
8. Governor's Budget Message, January 25, 1977. The power line was ultimately built, but the dispute continued with several years of litigation.
9. Steven Dornfeld, "State Budget Emphasizes Cutbacks," *Minneapolis Tribune,* January 26, 1977.
10. Steven Dornfeld and Steve Brandt, "Tight Money Will Limit Legislative . . . ," *Minneapolis Tribune,* January 2, 1977.

11. Gerry Nelson and Gene Lahammer, "No Urgency Compels '77 Legislature," *St. Paul Dispatch*, February 28, 1977.

12. Jack Coffman, "Temporary Halt in Road Debris Pickup Ordered," *Minneapolis Tribune*, February 27, 1977; Steven Dornfeld, "Oh Where, Oh Where Has Our Governor Gone?—Again," *Minneapolis Tribune*, March 1, 1977.

13. Al Hofstede, interview by author, December 30, 2010.

14. Martin Sabo, interview by author, December 30, 2010.

15. Ibid.

16. Linda Kohl, "Hofstede Wins over Stenvig by Big Margin," *St. Paul Dispatch*, November 9, 1977.

17. Hofstede, interview.

18. Ibid.

19. Minneapolis–St. Paul Study, Final Summary Report, State Planning Agency, June, 1978, Minnesota Legislative Reference Library; $270,700 was approved for the study. The Urban Institute in Washington, D.C., and the Center for Urban and Regional Affairs (CURA) at the University of Minnesota assisted the State Planning Agency on the study. Nick Coleman, Tom Berg, and a team of staff people including Eileen Baumgartner and Tom Todd from House Research helped Sabo monitor the two-year study.

20. Ibid.

21. Jay Kiedrowski, interview by author, January 6, 2011. Kiedrowski was appointed by Hofstede to be the budget director for Minneapolis in 1978. Kiedrowski later served as finance commissioner from 1983 to 1987 under Governor Perpich.

22. For a history of the pension issue and the continuing interplay between Minneapolis and the legislature, see Steve Brandt, "Minneapolis Pension Tension," *Star Tribune*, May 22, 2011; and Steve Brandt, "Legislature OKs Mpls. Police, Fire Pension Merger," *Star Tribune*, July 20, 2011.

23. Hofstede, interview.

24. Gary Currie, "Profile of Certain Elected Officials in Minnesota," January 1977, Minnesota Legislative Reference Library.

25. "Status of Women and Girls in Minnesota," Office on the Economic Status of Women, Minnesota Legislative Reference Library; Maricella Miranda, "Few Women's Voices on State's County Boards," *St. Paul Pioneer Press*, December 6, 2010.

26. Jack Coffman, "Revision of City Offices Is Urged," *Minneapolis Tribune*, March 4, 1977.

27. Martin Sabo, interview by author, December 7, 2010.

28. Ibid.

29. House File 1, *Minnesota House Journal*, 70th Leg., Reg. Sess., 33 (1977).

30. Steven Dornfeld, "State Bill Would Alter Way Social Services Are Financed," *Minneapolis Tribune*, April 3, 1977.

31. "House Panel Approves State Block Grant System," *Minneapolis Tri-*

bune, April 12, 1977; *Minnesota House Journal,* 70th Leg., Reg. Sess., 3721 (1977).

32. Paul McCarron, interview by author, December 28, 2010; 1979 Minnesota Laws 324.

33. 1969 Minnesota Laws 2284; Minnesota Poll, *Minneapolis Tribune,* July 26, 1970. The Metropolitan Council region was treated separately by the legislation.

34. Jack Coffman, "Regionalism, Rockefeller and Rebellion Rile Roberts," *Minneapolis Tribune,* May 9, 1976.

35. Don Spavin, "Misunderstanding Hampers Regional Planning Act," *St. Paul Pioneer Press,* September 13, 1970.

36. 1977 Index of *Minnesota House Journal,* 823; House File 545 (dissolution); House File 427 (withdraw); House File 269 (dissolution); House File 87 (termination).

37. Steve Brandt, "Regional Government Foes State Case," *Minneapolis Tribune,* August 22, 1976.

38. Jack Coffman, "State to Keep OSHA Control," *Minneapolis Tribune,* February 18, 1977.

39. Dirkswager, interview, February 28, 2011.

40. Ibid.

41. *Welsch v. Likins,* 373 F. Supp. 487 (D. Minn. 1974). For a more detailed discussion of the documents in this case, see the Minnesota Governor's Council on Developmental Disabilities, "With an Eye to the Past," www.mnddc.org/past/pdf/pdf-ndex_st-inst-welsch.html.

42. *Welch v. Likens,* 373 F. Supp. 487 (D. Minn.1974).

43. *Welsch v. Likins,* 550 F. 2d 1122, March 9, 1977.

44. *Welsch v. Likins,* Order of April 15, 1976, 21.

45. Rudy Perpich, letter to Judges Henley, Bright, and Harper, February 1, 1977; from the personal records of Luther Granquist.

46. Brief for the Senate and House of Representatives of the State of Minnesota and for the State of South Dakota as Amici Curiae supporting appellants, *Welsch v. Likins,* 550 F. 2d 1122 (1976).

47. *Welsch v. Likins,* 55 F. 2d 1122 (1976).

48. Budget Message of Governor Anderson, January 19, 1975; Budget Message of Governor Perpich, January 25, 1977.

49. Luther Granquist, interview by author, February 28, 2011.

50. Order by Judge Doty, *Welsch v. Schultz* (unreported), 1989.

51. Steven Dornfeld, "I've Got Bad News For You . . . I'm Pulling the Coffee Machine Plug," *Minneapolis Tribune,* March 13, 1977.

52. "Perpich to Donate Raise for Bocce Balls," *Minneapolis Tribune,* May 6, 1977.

53. Steven Dornfeld, "Perpich's Answers to Critics of His Style," *Minneapolis Tribune,* March 18, 1977.

54. Dornfeld, "I've Got Bad News For You."

55. Steven Dornfeld, "Perpich's Proposals Meeting Stiff Opposition in Legislature," *Minneapolis Tribune*, April 11, 1977.

56. Steve Brandt, "Spannaus to Begin Campaign to Tighten State Handgun Law," *Minneapolis Tribune*, March 14, 1977.

57. Steve Brandt, "Pistol Control Moves to Final Vote," *Minneapolis Tribune*, April 21, 1977.

58. Steve Brandt, "Gun Bill Clears House, Goes to Senate," *Minneapolis Tribune*, April 22, 1977.

59. Steve Brandt, "Senate Rejects Weakened Pistol Transfer Bill," *Minneapolis Tribune*, May 11, 1977; Steve Brandt, "Senate Passes Handgun Measure," *Minneapolis Tribune*, May 19, 1977; Blair Charnley, "House OK Sends Senate Gun Bill to Perpich," *Minneapolis Star*, May 21, 1977.

60. Steve Brandt, "House Votes Weakened Pistol Bill," *Minneapolis Tribune*, May 21, 1977.

61. Minnesota Constitution, art. IV § 9.

62. *Minnesota House Journal*, 70th Leg., Reg. Sess. (1977).

63. Jack Coffman, "Red-Hot Issue Bombs at the Capitol," *Minneapolis Tribune*, March 9, 1977.

64. Ibid.

65. *Minnesota Senate Journal*, 70th Leg., Reg. Sess., 1104 (1977).

66. "Pay-Raise Plan Fails in Minnesota House," *Minneapolis Tribune*, April 14, 1977.

67. Jack Coffman, "House Gives First Approval to Pay Bill," *Minneapolis Tribune*, April 15, 1977.

68. Steve Brandt, "Perpich Signs Pay Bill," *Minneapolis Tribune*, April 22, 1977.

69. 1978 Minnesota Laws 1224.

70. Allan Holbert, "Teams Win Stadium Game by Staying on Sidelines," *Minneapolis Tribune*, April 16, 1977.

71. Ibid.

72. *Minnesota House Journal*, 70th Leg., Reg. Sess., 395, 346, 440, 83 (1977).

73. Holbert, "Teams Win Stadium Game."

74. Allan Holbert, "No-Site Stadium Bill Gains in House," *Minneapolis Tribune*, April 6, 1977.

75. Allan Holbert, "House Approves No-Site Stadium Bill," *Minneapolis Tribune*, May 11, 1977; *Minnesota Senate Journal*, 70th Leg., Reg. Sess., 2071 (1977); 1977 Minnesota Laws 142.

76. 1977 Minnesota Laws 142.

77. Allan Holbert, "Stadium Site Panel Named," *Minneapolis Tribune*, May 13, 1977.

78. For a more detailed description of the building process and ongoing

legislative battles, see Amy Klobuchar, *Uncovering the Dome* (Prospect Heights, Ill.: Waveland Press, 1982). Klobuchar was elected to the U.S. Senate by voters in Minnesota in 2006.

79. Vance Opperman, "Hello Sun, Goodbye Dome," *Twin Cities Business,* December 2009, 87; Dee DePass, "Down It Came," *Star Tribune,* December 13, 2010. The game against the Giants was moved to Detroit's dome. The Vikings lost.

80. Ken Belson, "As Stadiums Vanish, Their Debt Lives On," *New York Times,* September 8, 2010.

81. Opperman, "Hello Sun, Goodbye Dome," 87.

82. 1977 Minnesota Laws 679. The legislation also changed the name of the Arts Council to the Board of the Arts.

83. Jimmy Carter, "The President's Proposed Energy Policy," April 18, 1977; Vital Speeches of the Day, vol. 43, no. 14, May 1, 1977, 418–20; At the Capitol, "Legislature Sets 4-Day Sessions for Energy Crisis," *Minneapolis Tribune,* January 25, 1977; Betty Wilson, "Legislature Passed 80% of What Perpich Wanted," *Minneapolis Star,* May 26, 1977.

84. *No Power Line Inc. v. Minnesota Environmental Quality Council,* 262 N.W.2d 312 (1977).

85. 1977 Minnesota Laws 1188; Wilson, "Legislature Passed 80% of What Perpich Wanted."

86. *U. S. v. Reserve Mining Company,* 543 F 2d 1210 (1976).

87. Peg Meier, "Area Elm Tree Loss Rises 176 Pct. in Year," *Minneapolis Tribune,* March 12, 1976.

88. *Minnesota Senate Journal,* 70th Leg., Reg. Sess., 3443 (1977).

89. 1977 Minnesota Laws 156.

90. Bill Kelly, interview by author, November 13, 2010; Rudy Perpich and Bill Kelly, "Do We Need a Tax Cut?" *Minneapolis Tribune,* November 5, 1977.

91. Steven Dornfeld, "Leaders Cool to Special Session," *Minneapolis Tribune,* May 25, 1977.

92. Kelly, interview, November 13, 2010.

93. 1977 Minnesota Laws 1018.

94. Martin Sabo, interview by author, December 12, 2010.

95. "'Something-For-All' Tax Bill Getting Final Legislative Touch," *Minneapolis Star,* May 20, 1977.

96. Steven Dornfeld, "Perpich Will Try for Lower Taxes Despite Questions," *Minneapolis Tribune,* October 14, 1977.

97. Robert J. O'Keefe, "$243 Million Tax Cut Proposed by State IR," *St. Paul Dispatch,* December 18, 1977.

98. Governor's Message to Minnesota Legislature, January 24, 1978.

99. Steve Brandt and Steven Dornfeld, "Governor Proposes $102-Million Tax Cut," *Minneapolis Tribune,* January 25, 1978.

100. Kelly, interview, November 13, 2010.

101. Steven Dornfeld, "Legislative Session Was Slowed by Trivia," *Minneapolis Tribune,* March 26, 1978; Patrick Marx, "Perpich Tax-Cut Plan Gets IR Praise," *Minneapolis Star,* January 25, 1978.

102. Dornfeld, "Legislative Session Was Slowed by Trivia"; Robert J. O'Keefe, "Perpich Comes Out a Winner on the Tax Front," *St. Paul Dispatch,* March 29, 1978.

103. O'Keefe, "Perpich Comes Out a Winner on the Tax Front."

104. Betty Wilson, "Legislators Cave In, Pass Tax Cuts," *Minneapolis Star,* March 24, 1978.

105. Dornfeld, "Legislative Session Was Slowed by Trivia."

106. Bill Marx, chief fiscal analyst, Minnesota House of Representatives, interview by author, January 31, 2011.

107. California Constitution, art. XIIIA, adopted June 6, 1978.

108. Daniel Mullins and Brown Wallin, "Tax and Expenditure Limitations: Introduction and Overview," *Public Budgeting and Finance,* Winter 2004.

109. "Democracy in California," *Economist,* April 23, 2011.

110. elections.nytimes.com/2010/results/california. California retained the provision requiring a two-thirds vote for tax increases.

111. 1973 Minnesota Laws 1081.

112. 1975 Minnesota Laws 604, sec. 91.

113. "Regulation and Control of Human Services Facilities," Legislative Audit Commission, February 17, 1977, Minnesota Legislative Reference Library; "Minnesota Housing Finance Agency," Legislative Audit Commission, April 19, 1977, Minnesota Legislative Reference Library; Reports of the Program Evaluation Division, Minnesota Office of the Legislative Auditor, www.auditor.Leg.state.mn.us/ped/stud-chr.htm.

114. "A Productive Legislature," editorial *Minneapolis Tribune,* May 25, 1977; Steven Dornfeld, "Senate, House Adjourn, Budget Hits $6.4 billion," *Minneapolis Tribune,* May 24, 1977.

115. Steven Dornfeld and Steve Brandt, "Legislative Reform Has Had a High Price Tag," *Minneapolis Tribune,* February 5–9, 1978.

116. Ibid.

9. The Minnesota Massacre, 1978 Version

1. Don Fraser, interview by author and project members, November 9, 2010.

2. Martin Sabo, interview with author, January 22, 2011.

3. "Great and Humble Pay Last Humphrey Tribute," *Daily Register* (Shrewsbury, N.J.), January 16, 1978.

4. Ibid.

5. Congressman Bob Berglund was named secretary of agriculture by

President Carter, and a Republican, Arlan Stangeland, then won the congressional seat in a special election. *Minnesota Legislative Manual, 1979–1980*.

6. Associated Press, "Perpich Signs Vacancies Bill," *Minneapolis Tribune,* January 29, 1978.

7. Steven Dornfeld, "Fraser Announces for Senate; Won't Run for House Regardless," *Minneapolis Tribune,* January 24, 1978.

8. Steve Brandt, "Sabo Announces for Fraser Seat; Others Bow Out," *Minneapolis Tribune,* January 26, 1978.

9. Steven Dornfeld, "Perpich Names Mrs. Humphrey to Senate Seat," *Minneapolis Tribune,* January 26, 1978.

10. Wilson, *Rudy!,* 96.

11. Steve Brandt and Al McMonagha, "Senate Contenders' Political Plans Unsettled," *Minneapolis Tribune,* January 26, 1978.

12. Ibid.

13. Steven Dornfeld, "Coleman Seeks U.S. Senate Backing in DFL," *Minneapolis Tribune,* February 4, 1978.

14. Steven Dornfeld, "Short Tells DFL He Wants Senate Job," *Minneapolis Tribune,* February 12, 1978. Menning dropped out of the race on April 20, 1978; "DFLer Menning Quits Race for U.S. Senate," *Minneapolis Tribune,* April 20, 1978; "HHH's Son to Seek Seat," *St. Paul Pioneer Press,* November 1, 1977.

15. Robert J. O'Keefe, "Durenberger Files for I-R Gubernatorial Nomination," *St. Paul Pioneer Press,* June 18, 1977; Steven Dornfeld, "Al Quie Confirms Bid for Governor," *Minneapolis Tribune,* September 1, 1977; for a biography of Quie, see Mitch Pearlstein, *Riding into the Sunrise: Al Quie: A Life of Faith, Service, and Civility* (Lakeville, Minn.: Pogo Press, 2008); Wilson, *Rudy!,* 99; "Rep. Arne Carlson Begins Drive for State Auditor," *St. Paul Dispatch,* August 29, 1977.

16. "Boschwitz Will Make IR Race for Senate," *Minneapolis Tribune,* October 14, 1977; Gary Dawson, "Knutson Denies Being a Stalking-Horse for Quie," *St. Paul Pioneer Press,* July 20, 1977.

17. "Enlarged Judiciary Bill Approved by House," *Minneapolis Tribune,* February 8, 1978; Robert J. O'Keefe, "Faricy Joins in Attorney General Race," *St. Paul Dispatch,* February 15, 1978; Robert J. O'Keefe, "Humphrey Will Seek Attorney General Post," *St. Paul Dispatch,* February 3, 1978; Associated Press, "Knutson Switches Race for Attorney General," *Minneapolis Tribune,* February 28, 1978.

18. Gerry Nelson, "Candidate-Lawmakers Stumping in Legislature," *Minneapolis Star,* February 7, 1978.

19. "What You Should Know to Take Part in Caucus," *Minneapolis Tribune,* February 26, 1978.

20. Steven Dornfeld, "Quie, Fraser Boosted in Voting," *Minneapolis Tribune,* March 2, 1978.

21. Sabo, interview, January 22, 2011.

22. "Humphrey Decides Not to Run for Senate Seat in November," *Minneapolis Tribune*, April 9, 1978; Fraser, interview.

23. Bill Salisbury, "Waiting Spannaus to Seek Re-election," *St. Paul Dispatch*, May 12, 1978.

24. Betty Wilson, "DFL's Berg Quits Legislature for Family, Law Practice," *Minneapolis Star*, May 24, 1978.

25. Savelkoul, interview; Bruce Nelson "I-R House Leaders to Leave Posts," *St. Paul Pioneer Press*, August 26, 1977.

26. "Sabo Adjourns His Last Session," *Minneapolis Tribune*, March 25, 1978.

27. Steven Dornfeld, "Durenberger Confirms He'll Run for Senate," *Minneapolis Tribune*, April 23, 1978.

28. Sabo, interview, January 22, 2011.

29. Robert J. O Keefe, "Al Quie Is Endorsed"; Gary Dawson, "I-R Party Endorses Boschwitz, *St. Paul Pioneer Press*, June 24, 1978.

30. Public Law 95-495 (1978).

31. Wilson, *Rudy!*, 100.

32. Robert J. O'Keefe, "Fraser–Short Contest Tops Primary," *St. Paul Pioneer Press*, September 10, 1978.

33. Walter Mondale, *The Good Fight: A Life in Liberal Politics* (New York: Scribner, 2010), 196.

34. Betty Wilson, "Primary Voting May Sway State's Politics for Years," *Minneapolis Star*, September 11, 1978.

35. O'Keefe, "Fraser–Short Contest Tops Primary."

36. Wilson, "Primary Voting May Sway State's Politics for Years."

37. Ibid.

38. "Moos Won't Seek Endorsement, May Run as Independent," *Minneapolis Tribune*, June 10, 1978; "Moos Is Hoping the Name's Familiar in Bid for Senate," *Minneapolis Tribune*, September 11, 1978.

39. *Minnesota Legislative Manual, 1979–1980*. In the Senate races, Wendell Anderson defeated John Connelly, a St. Paul lawyer, and Rudy Boschwitz defeated former Minnesota governor Harold Stassen.

40. The *St. Paul Pioneer Press* said Fraser had won, and the *Minneapolis Tribune* slightly hedged its bets with "Fraser Apparently Beats Short."

41. O'Keefe, " Fraser–Short Contest Tops Primary."

42. Wilson, *Rudy!*, 102.

43. Fraser, interview.

44. Bill Salisbury, "Incumbents Buck Taxpayers' Revolt," *St. Paul Pioneer Press*, September 14, 1978.

45. Sabo, interview, January 22, 2011.

46. Betty Wilson, "Back Roads Lead to Victory," *Minneapolis Star*, October 17, 1978.

47. "Carter to Join DFLers for $500-a-Head Benefit," *St. Paul Pioneer Press,* October 13, 1978.

48. Betty Wilson, "Gov. Quie? The Congressman Has Faith," *Minneapolis Star,* October 17, 1978; Robert J. O'Keefe, "Can Vote for Tax Trims on Nov. 7, Quie Declares," *St. Paul Dispatch,* September 23, 1978.

49. Minnesota Poll, *Minneapolis Tribune,* October 1, 1978.

50. Tom Matthews, "Quie Insisted on Being 'Mr. Nice Guy,'" *St. Paul Dispatch,* November 8, 1978; Lori Sturdevant, "Perpich Alleges 'Gutter Politics,'" *Minneapolis Tribune,* November 2, 1978.

51. Pearlstein, *Riding into the Sunrise,* 155.

52. Steven Dornfeld, "Short Says Durenberger to Blame for Calls, Threats," *Minneapolis Tribune,* November 2, 1978.

53. Steven Dornfeld and David Phelps, "Candidates Bank Heavily on Media to Reach Voters," *Minneapolis Tribune,* October 8, 1978; Steven Dornfeld and David Phelps, "Short, Boschwitz Big Spenders in Their Races for Senate Seats," *Minneapolis Tribune,* October 31, 1978.

54. Editorial, "Mountain or Volcano in Audit Papers?," *St. Paul Pioneer Press,* October 29, 1978; "Panel Rejects Perpich Plea for Audit Data, *Minneapolis Star,* September 1, 1978.

55. Editorial, "Mountain or Volcano in Audit Papers?"

56. Robert J. O'Keefe, "DFLers Release Working Papers," *St. Paul Pioneer Press,* October 29, 1978.

57. Pearlstein, *Riding into the Sunrise,* 154.

58. Linda Picone and Peg Meir, "Anderson Faces a Problem of Images; Boschwitz Carries a Surplus of Energy," *Minneapolis Tribune,* October 29, 1978.

59. Editorial, *Minneapolis Star,* October 19, 1978.

60. Picone and Meir, "Anderson Faces a Problem of Images."

61. Minnesota Poll, *Minneapolis Tribune,* November 6, 1978. The poll and the *Minneapolis Tribune* were severely criticized for using too small a sample in the poll; *Twin Cities Magazine,* December 1978.

62. Robert Whereatt, "IR Party Drooling over House Seats," *Minneapolis Star,* October 18, 1978.

63. Bill Kelly, interview by author, January 23, 2011.

64. *Minnesota Legislative Manual, 1979–1980.*

65. Wilson, *Rudy!,* 107.

66. *Minnesota Legislative Manual, 1979–1980.*

67. Ibid.

68. Ibid.

69. "Johnson Election Plan Worked," *Minneapolis Tribune,* November 9, 1978.

70. Savelkoul, interview.

71. Bill Salisbury, "I-R Gains Half of State House," *St. Paul Dispatch*, November 8, 1978. The even split caused an interesting period of negotiations, horse trading, and litigation that resulted in a bipartisan leadership team for the 1979 session. A special election was held in the interim between the 1979 and 1980 sessions, which the DFL won, giving them control for the 1980 session. The intrigue behind all this is well described in Searle, *Minnesota Standoff.*

72. Kelly, interview, January 23, 2011.

73. Ibid.

74. Mondale, *The Good Fight*, 197.

75. National Conference of State Legislatures, "Historic Partisan Control," www. ncsl.org (accessed March 20, 2011); United Press International, "GOP Hit Jackpot in State Legislatures," November 9, 1978.

76. Adam Clymer, "Democrats Dominate," *New York Times*, November 9, 1978; *Congressional Quarterly*, "Congressional Elections, 1946–1996," 172, 272, 275, 276.

77. Don Fraser, interview by author and project member, November 9, 2011; National Conference of State Legislatures, "2010 Election: Legislature Party Control Switch," www.ncsl.org (accessed March 20, 2011).

78. Wilson, *Rudy!,* 106.

79. Sabo, interview, January 22, 2011.

80. Gary Dawson, "Stung by Defeat, House DFLers Blame Perpich," *St. Paul Dispatch,* November 30, 1978.

81. Wilson, *Rudy!,* 101.

82. David Phelps, "Quie Declines Public Money," *Minneapolis Tribune,* March 1, 1978; Wilson, *Rudy!,* 106.

83. *Minnesota Legislative Manual, 1978–1979.*

84. Searle, *Minnesota Standoff,* 5.

85. Ibid., 16.

86. Ibid., 17.

87. Sabo, interview, January 22, 2011.

88. Savelkoul, interview.

89. Marx, interview.

90. Pearlstein, *Riding into the Sunrise,* 150.

91. Iric Nathanson, "Crossing the Partisan Divide: Minnesota Budgets and Politics in the 1980s," *MinnPost,* May 13, 2009, www.minnpost.com.

92. Ibid.

93. *Minnesota Legislative Manual, 1981–1982.*

10. Where Do We Go from Here?

1. Table B78, *Economic Report of the President* (Washington, D.C.: Government Printing Office, 2010).

2. *Minnesota Legislative Manual, 2011–2012*. In terms of the partisan split in state government, the 2010 election returned the state full circle to 1971: the DFL Party holding the governorship, and Republican Party legislators controlling the legislative branch.

3. Bill Marx, interview by author, November 8, 2011.

4. Carl Hulse, "In Leaving Congress, 3 Make Big Statement," *New York Times*, March 7, 2012.

5. Steven Thomma, "More Polarized Congress Emerges," *Star Tribune*, November 7, 2010.

6. David Brooks, "The Thing Itself," *New York Times*, October 13, 2011; Mondale, *The Good Fight*, 133; Matt Miller, "Why Are We Defining Democracy Down?," *Washington Post*, July 6, 2011.

7. Josh Goodman, "State Government Shutdowns: A Dangerous Game to Play," Stateline.org, http://www.stateline.org/live/details/story? contentID=578745 (accessed December 1, 2011).

8. "Harrisburg's Bankruptcy, Money Up in Smoke," *Economist*, October 29, 2011; Mark Curriden, "The Next Chapter," *ABA Journal*, October 2011. The cities filed under chapter 9 of the bankruptcy code. This is a unique law that was created in 1934, in the heart of the Great Depression, and is for certain municipalities.

9. Curriden, "The Next Chapter."

10. Arturo Perez, National Conference of State Legislatures, interview by author and project member, November 3, 2011.

11. Garrison Keillor, *Star Tribune*, January 26, 2010.

12. Lawrence E. Harrison, *The Central Liberal Truth* (New York: Oxford University Press, 2006), xvi.

13. Alexis de Tocqueville, *Democracy in America* (New York: Penguin Putnam, 2004), 106.

14. John F. Kennedy, National Governor's Conference, July 4, 1962.

15. Tip O'Neill with William Novak, *"Man of the House: The Life and Political Memoirs of Speaker Tip O'Neill"* (New York: Random House, 1987).

16. Virginia Metropolitan Area Study Commission Report 6 (1967). This report is also popularly known as the Hahn Commission Report.

17. Ibid.

18. Attributed to John W. Gardner (n.d.). in BrainyQuote.com; retrieved September 28, 2010, from http//www.brainyquote.com/quotes/quotes/j/ohnwgard105456.html.

19. Susan Ehrlich, "The Increasing Federalization of Crime," *Arizona State Law Journal* 32, 825 (2000).

20. Ibid.

21. James Madison, *The Federalist Papers* (New York: Signet Classic, Penguin Group, 2003), No. 10.

22. George Washington, Farewell Address, 1796.

23. Paul Quirk and Sarah Binder, eds., *The Legislative Branch* (New York: Oxford University Press, 2005), xvi-xvii.

24. Carl Hulse and David Herszenhorn, "Senate Debate on Health Care Exacerbates Partisanship," *New York Times,* December 21, 2009.

25. Quirk and Binder, eds., *The Legislative Branch.*

26. Savelkoul, interview.

27. Ibid.

28. Ibid.

29. Dan Rostenkowski, obituary, *Star Tribune,* August 12, 2010.

30. C. E. Steurle, "Why We Must Untie Our Fiscal Straitjacket: A Response to Henry J. Aaron," *Journal of Policy Analysis and Management* 29, 4 (2010): 891–93.

31. Walter W. Heller, *New Dimensions in a Political Economy* (Cambridge, Mass.: Harvard University Press, 1966), 127.

32. Sabo, interview, October 12, 2009.

33. Mondale, *The Good Fight,* 131.

34. Sabo, interview, October 12, 2009.

35. Mann and Ornstein, *The Broken Branch;* Mann and Ornstein, *It's Even Worse Than It Looks;* Quirk and Binder, eds., *The Legislative Branch.*

36. Minn. Stat. Ann. §245.4835; Minn. Stat. Ann. § 134.34.

37. Keith Carlson, executive director, Minnesota Inter-County Association, interview by author, August 20, 2010.

38. Will Rogers, Syndicated Newspaper Article, June 28, 1931.

39. *Citizens United v. Federal Election Commission,* 558 U.S. 50 (2010); *McComish v. Bennett,* 560 U.S. Order list (2010); editorial, "Keeping Politics Safe for the Rich," *New York Times,* June 9, 2010.

40. Brief for Senators Bill Bradley and Alan Simpson as Amici Curiae supporting Respondents, *Randall v. Sorrell,* 548 U.S. 230 (2006).

41. David Brooks, "A Case of Mental Courage," *New York Times,* August 23, 2010.

42. Report on retreat, 1973, personal records of author.

43. Kenneth Jost, "Redistricting Dispute," *CQ Researcher* 14, 10 (March 12, 2004).

44. Redistricting Reform Report, Center for the Study of Politics and Governance, Humphrey Institute, University of Minnesota; used in testimony at hearing of Minnesota Senate's Committee on State and Local Government Operations and Oversight, January 11, 2008; Norman Ornstein and Barry McMillion, "One Nation, Divisible," *New York Times,* January 24, 2005.

45. Lawrence Jacobs, "Redistricting Reform to Fix a Broken System and Restore Competition," Humphrey Institute, University of Minnesota, January 2008.

46. Ibid.

47. Ibid.

48. *Minnesota Legislative Manual, 1981–1982.*

49. Redistricting Reform Report, Center for the Study of Politics and Governance.

50. "Souter Urges ABA to Help Civic Education," *ABA Journal,* September 2009; Sandra Day O'Connor, as quoted in James Podgers, "Raise the Learning Curve," *ABA Journal,* August 2010.

51. Samuel P. Huntington, *Who Are We? The Challenge to America's National Identity* (New York: Simon and Schuster, 2004), 339.

52. "Lexington," *Economist,* September 25, 2010.

53. Stephen N. Zack, President's Page, *ABA Journal,* September 2010.

54. Robert Maynard Hutchins, as quoted in Terry Votel, President's Page, *Bench and Bar of Minnesota,* August 2010.

Selected Bibliography

Auerbach, Laura K. *Worthy to Be Remembered: A Political History of the Minnesota Democratic-Farmer-Labor Party*. Minneapolis: Democratic-Farmer-Labor Party of Minnesota, 1984.

Bowen, Catherine Drinker. *Miracle at Philadelphia: The Story of the Constitutional Convention, May to September, 1787*. Boston: Little Brown and Company, 1966.

Brandl, John E. *Money and Good Intentions Are Not Enough: Or, Why a Liberal Democrat Thinks States Need Both Competition and Community*. Washington, D.C.: Brookings Institution Press, 1998.

Burns, John. *The Sometime Governments: A Critical Study of the 50 American Legislatures*. New York: Bantam Books, 1971.

Carter, Rosalynn. *First Lady from Plains*. Boston: Houghton Mifflin Co., 1984.

Christenson, Gerald W. *A Minnesota Citizen: Stories from the Life and Times of Jerry Christenson*. Privately published, 2005.

Davies, Jack. *Legislative Law and Process*. St. Paul: West Publishing Co., 1986.

Elazar, Daniel J., Virginia Gray, and Wyman Spano. *Minnesota Politics and Government*. Lincoln: University of Nebraska Press, 1999.

Ellis, Joseph J. *American Creation: Triumphs and Tragedies at the Founding of the Republic*. New York: Alfred A. Knopf, 2007.

Fraser, Arvonne. *She's No Lady: Politics, Family, and International Feminism*. Minneapolis: Nodin Press, 2008.

Hanson, Royce, with the assistance of Charles Backstrom and Patrick McCormack. *Tribune of the People: The Minnesota Legislature and Its Leadership*. Minneapolis: University of Minnesota Press, 1989.

Harrison, Lawrence. *The Central Liberal Truth: How Politics Can Change a Culture and Save It from Itself*. New York: Oxford University Press, 2006.

Haynes, John Earl. *Dubious Alliance: The Making of Minnesota's DFL Party*. Minneapolis: University of Minnesota Press, 1984.

Heller, Walter. *New Dimensions in a Political Economy*. Cambridge, Mass.: Harvard University Press, 1966.

Huntington, Samuel P. *Who Are We? The Challenges to America's National Identity*. New York: Simon and Schuster, 2004.

Klobuchar, Amy. *Uncovering the Dome.* Prospect Heights, Ill.: Waveland Press, 1982.

Lebedoff, David. *The Twenty-First Ballot: A Political Party Struggle in Minnesota.* Minneapolis: University of Minnesota Press, 1969.

———. *Ward Number Six.* New York: Charles Scribner's Sons, 1971.

Lewis, Finley. *Mondale.* New York: Harper and Row, 1980.

Loewenberg, Gerhard. *On Legislatures: The Puzzle of Representation.* Boulder, Colo.: Paradigm Publishers, 2011.

Loftus, Tom. *The Art of Legislative Politics.* Washington, D.C.: CQ Press, 1994.

Mann, Thomas E., and Norman J. Ornstein. *The Broken Branch: How Congress Is Failing America and How to Get It Back on Track.* New York: Oxford University Press, 2006.

———. *It's Even Worse Than It Looks.* New York: Basic Books, 2012.

Mason, Alpheus Thomas. *Free Government in the Making: Readings in American Political Thought.* New York: Oxford University Press, 1956.

Milton, John Watson. *For the Good of the Order: Nick Coleman and the High Tide of Liberal Politics in Minnesota: 1971–1981.* St. Paul: Ramsey County Historical Society, 2012.

Mitau, G. Theodore. *Politics in Minnesota.* Rev. ed. Minneapolis: University of Minnesota Press, 1970.

Mondale, Walter F. *The Good Fight: A Life in Liberal Politics.* New York: Scribner, 2010.

Morrison, Samuel Elliot. *The Oxford History of the American People.* New York: Oxford University Press, 1965.

Munger, Mark. *Mr. Environment: The Willard Munger Story.* Duluth, Minn.: Cloquet River Press, 2009.

Nathanson, Iric. *Minneapolis in the Twentieth Century: The Growth of an American City.* St. Paul: Minnesota Historical Society Press, 2010.

O'Neill, Tip. *Man of the House: The Life and Political Memoirs of Speaker Tip O'Neill.* New York: Random House, 1987.

Pearlstein, Mitch, *Riding into the Sunrise: Al Quie: A Life of Faith, Service, and Civility.* Lakeville, Minn.: Pogo Press, 2008.

Quirk, Paul, and Sarah Binder, eds. *The Legislative Branch.* New York: Oxford University Press, 2005.

Reuss, Henry S. *Revenue Sharing: Crutch or Catalyst for State and Local Governments?* New York: Praeger Publishers, 1970.

Rosenthal, Alan. *Engines of Democracy: Politics and Policymaking in State Legislatures.* Washington, D.C.: CQ Press, 2009.

Rossiter, Clinton, ed. *The Federalist Papers.* New York: Signet Classic, Penguin Group, 2003.

Searle, Rod. *Minnesota Standoff: The Politics of Deadlock.* Waseca, Minn.: Alton Press, 1990.

Sibley, Joel H., ed. *Encyclopedia of the American Legislative System.* New York: Charles Scribner's Sons, 1994.

Spear, Allan H. *Crossing the Barriers: The Autobiography of Allan H. Spear.* Minneapolis: University of Minnesota Press, 2010.

Tocqueville, Alexis de. *Democracy in America.* New York: Penguin Putnam, 2004.

Weiner, Jay. *This Is Not Florida: How Al Franken Won the Minnesota Senate Recount.* Minneapolis: University of Minnesota Press, 2010.

White, Theodore H. *America in Search of Itself: The Making of the President, 1956–1980.* New York: Harper and Row, 1982.

Wilson, Betty. *Rudy! The People's Governor.* Minneapolis: Nodin Press, 2005.

Index

Page numbers in italics refer to photograph section.

Tom Berg is a Minneapolis attorney who was a member of the Minnesota state legislature from 1971 through 1978. He later served as the U.S. Attorney for the District of Minnesota.